The
HIDDEN INNS
of
EAST ANGLIA

Edited by
Peter Long

© Travel Publishing Ltd.

Published by:
Travel Publishing Ltd
7a Apollo House, Calleva Park
Aldermaston, Berks, RG7 8TN
ISBN 1-902-00785-9
© Travel Publishing Ltd

First Published: 2002

Regional Titles in the Hidden Inns Series:

East Anglia	Heart of England
Lancashire & Cheshire	North of England
Southeast England	South of England
Southern Scotland	Wales
Welsh Borders	West Country
Yorkshire	

Regional Titles in the Hidden Places Series:

Cambridgeshire & Lincolnshire	Chilterns
Cornwall	Derbyshire
Devon	Dorset, Hants & Isle of Wight
East Anglia	Gloucestershire , Wiltshire & Somerset
Heart of England	Hereford, Worcs & Shropshire
Highlands & Islands	Kent
Lake District & Cumbria	Lancashire and Cheshire
Lincolnshire and Nottinghamshire	Northumberland & Durham
Somerset	Sussex
Thames Valley	Yorkshire

National Titles in the Hidden Places Series:

England	Ireland
Scotland	Wales

Printing by: Ashford Colour Press, Gosport
Maps by: © MAPS IN MINUTES ™ 2002 © Crown Copyright, Ordnance Survey 2002
Line Drawings: Sarah Bird
Editor: Peter Long
Cover Design: Lines & Words, Aldermaston
Cover Photographs: The John Barleycorn, Duxford, Cambridgeshire;
                     The White Hart, Fulbourn, Cambridgeshire;
                     The Black Lion, High Roding, Essex

FOREWORD

The **Hidden Inns** series originates from the enthusiastic suggestions of readers of the popular **Hidden Places** guides. They want to be directed to traditional inns "off the beaten track" with atmosphere and character which are so much a part of our British heritage. But they also want information on the many places of interest and activities to be found in the vicinity of the inn.

The inns or pubs reviewed in the **Hidden Inns** may have been coaching inns but have invariably been a part of the history of the village or town in which they are located. All the inns included in this guide serve food and drink and many offer the visitor overnight accommodation. A full page is devoted to each inn which contains a line drawing of the inn, full name, address and telephone number, directions on how to get there, a full description of the inn and its facilities and a wide range of useful information such as opening hours, food served, accommodation provided, credit cards taken and details of entertainment. **Hidden Inns** guides however are not simply pub guides. They provide the reader with helpful information on the many places of interest to visit and activities to pursue in the area in which the inn is based. This ensures that your visit to the area will not only allow you to enjoy the atmosphere of the inn but also to take in the beautiful countryside which surrounds it.

The **Hidden Inns** guides have been expertly designed for ease of use. **The Hidden Inns of East Anglia** is divided into 4 regionally based chapters, each of which is laid out in the same way. To identify your preferred geographical region refer to the contents page overleaf. To find a pub or inn simply use the index and locator map at the beginning of each chapter which refers you, via a page number reference, to a full page dedicated to the specific establishment. To find a place of interest again use the index and locator map found at the beginning of each chapter which will guide you to a descriptive summary of the area followed by details of each place of interest.

We do hope that you will get plenty of enjoyment from visiting the inns and places of interest contained in this guide. We are always interested in what our readers think of the inns or places covered (or not covered) in our guides so please do not hesitate to write to us using the form at the back of the book. This is a vital way of helping us ensure that we maintain a high standard of entry and that we are providing the right sort of information for our readers. Finally if you are planning to visit any other corner of the British Isles we would like to refer you to the list of Hidden Inns and Hidden Places guides to be found at the rear of the book.

Travel Publishing

LOCATOR MAP

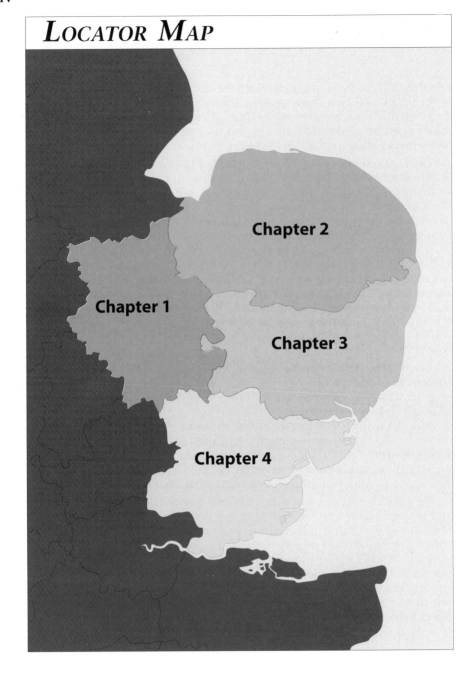

CONTENTS

1 Cambridgeshire

Places of Interest:

Pubs and Inns:

The Hidden Inns of East Anglia

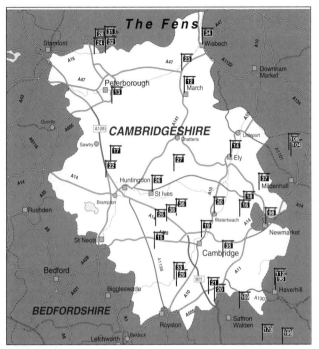

Please note all references refer to page numbers

Cambridgeshire

Cambridgeshire is a county with a rich rural heritage, with attractive village strung along the banks of the Great Ouse and the flat land of the Fens stretching north towards the Wash. Far removed from the hustle and bustle of modern life, the Fens contain some of the richest soil in England, but before they were a place of mist and marsh, of small islands whose inhabitants eked out a livelihood from fish and waterfowl. Today's landscape is the result of man's ingenuity down the centuries in creating productive farmland from a wilderness. The Romans were the first to construct embankments and drains, a process of reclamation that was continued through the Middle Ages and later by the Dutch, who made windmills a familiar sight in the region until the steam engine and electricity took over their pumping tasks.

Swaffham Prior Windmill

The Fens now offer unlimited opportunities for exploring on foot, by car, by bicycle or by boat. The jewel in the crown of the Fens is the city of Ely with its majestic Cathedral. A few miles south of Ely, the National Trust's Wicken Fen is the oldest nature reserve in the country, 600 acres of undrained fenland that is famous for its varied plant, insect and bird life. Southeastern Cambridgeshire covers the area around the city of Cambridge and is rich in history, with a host of archaeological sites, monuments and museums to visit. At the heart of it is Cambridge itself, one of the world's leading academic centres and a city that deserves plenty of time to explore.

The old county of Huntingdonshire is the heartland of the rural heritage of Cambridgeshire, and the home of Oliver Cromwell beckons with a wealth of history and pleasing landscapes. Many motorists follow the Cromwell Trail, which guides tourists around the places associated with the great man. The natural start of the trail is Huntingdon itself, where he was born the son of a country gentleman. The 26-mile Ouse Valley way follows the course of the Great Ouse, and a gentle cruise along this stretch of the river is a perfect way to spend a sunny summer's afternoon. Another watery attraction in the county is the Nene-Ouse Navigation Link, whose 28-mile length passes through several Fenland towns and a rich variety of wildlife habitats. For those looking for something a little more energetic on the water there are wide-ranging facilities at Grafham Water.

PLACES OF INTEREST

ARRINGTON

18th century **Wimpole Hall**, owned by the National Trust, is probably the most spectacular country mansion in the whole county. The lovely interiors are the work of several celebrated architects, and there's a fine collection of furniture and pictures. The magnificent formally laid-out grounds include a Victorian parterre, a rose garden and a walled garden. Landscaped

4

Wimpole Park, with hills, woodland, lakes and a Chinese bridge, provides miles of wonderful walking and is perfect for anything from a gentle stroll to a strenuous hike. A brilliant attraction for all

Chapel in the Hall, Wimpole

the family is **Wimpole Home Farm**, a working farm that is the largest rare breeds centre in East Anglia.

CAMBRIDGE

There are nearly 30 Cambridges spread around the globe, but this, the original, is the one that the whole world knows as one of the leading university cities - though it was an important town many centuries before the scholars arrived, standing at the point where forest met fen, at the lowest fording point of the river. The town flourished as a market and river trading centre, and in 1209 a group of students fleeing Oxford riots arrived. The first College was **Peterhouse**, founded by the Bishop of Ely in 1284, and in the next century Clare, Pembroke, Gonville & Caius, Trinity Hall and Corpus Christi followed. The total is now 31, the latest being **Robinson College**, the gift of self-made millionaire David Robinson. The Colleges are all well worth a visit, but places that simply must not be missed include **King's College Chapel** with its breathtaking fan vaulting, glorious stained glass and Rubens' *Adoration of the Magi*; **Pepys Library**, including his diaries, in Magdalene College; and Trinity's wonderful **Great Court**. A trip by punt along the 'Backs' of the Cam brings a unique view of many of the Colleges and passes under six bridges, including the **Bridge of Sighs** (St John's) and the extraordinary wooden

Mathematical Bridge at Queens'. Cambridge has nurtured more Nobel Prize winners than most countries and the list of celebrated alumni covers every sphere of human endeavour and achievement: Byron, Tennyson, Milton and Wordsworth; Marlowe and Bacon; Samuel Pepys; Charles Darwin; Charles Babbage; Bertrand Russell and Ludwig Wittgenstein; actors Sir Ian McKellen and Sir Derek Jacobi; Lord Burghley and Harold Abrahams who ran for England; Burgess, Maclean, Philby and Blunt who spied for Russia.

The Colleges apart, Cambridge is packed with interest for the visitor, with a wealth of grand buildings both religious and secular, and some of the country's leading museums, many of them run by the University. The **Fitzwilliam Museum** is renowned for its art collection, which includes works by Titian, Rembrandt, Gainsborough, Hogarth, Turner, Renoir, Picasso and Cezanne, and for its antiquities from Egypt, Greece and Rome. **Kettle's Yard** has a permanent display of 20th century art in a house maintained just as it was when the Ede family gave it, with the collection, to the University in 1967. The **Museum of Classical Archaeology** has 500 plaster casts of Greek and Roman statues, and the **University Museum of Archaeology and Anthropology** covers worldwide prehistoric archaeology with special displays relating to Oceania and to the Cambridge area. The **Museum of Technology**, housed in a Victorian sewage pumping station, features an impressive collection of steam, gas and electric pumping engines and examples great and small of local industrial technology. Anyone with an interest in fossils should make tracks for the **Sedgwick Museum of Geology**, while in the same street (Downing) the **Museum of Zoology** offers a

Bridge of Sighs, Cambridge

Trinity College, Great Court

over one over-arching structure. Before the draining of the Fens, this bridge crossed the point where the River Welland divided into two streams.

comprehensive and spectacular survey of the animal kingdom. The **Whipple Museum of the History of Science** tells about science through instruments; the **Scott Polar Research Institute** has fascinating, often poignant exhibits relating to Arctic and Antarctic exploration; and the **Botanic Gardens** boast a plant collection that rivals those of Kew Gardens and Edinburgh. The work and life of the people of Cambridge and the surrounding area are the subject of the **Cambridge and County Folk Museum**, housed in a 15th century building that for 300 years was the White Horse Inn. One of the city's greatest treasures is the **University Library**, one of the world's great research libraries with 6 million books, a million maps and 350,000 manuscripts.

Cambridge also has many fine churches, some of them used by the Colleges before they built their own chapels.

CROWLAND

It is hard to imagine that this whole area was once entirely wetland and marshland, dotted with inhospitable islands. Crowland was one such island, then known as Croyland, and on it was established a small church and hermitage back in the 7th century, which was later to become one of the nation's most important monasteries. The town's impressive parish church was just part of the great edifice which once stood on the site. A wonderful exhibition can be found in the Abbey at Crowland, open all year round. The remains cover a third of the Abbey's original extent.

Crowland's second gem is the unique Trinity Bridge - set in the centre of town on dry land! Built in the 14th century, it has three arches built

DUXFORD

Part of the Imperial War Museum, **Duxford Aviation Museum** is probably the leader in its field in Europe, with an outstanding collection of over 150 historic aircraft from biplanes through Spitfires to supersonic jets. The American Air Museum, where aircraft are suspended as if in flight, is part of this terrific place, which was built on a former RAF and US fighter base. Major air shows take place several times a year, and among the permanent features are a reconstructed wartime operations room, a hands-on exhibition for children and a dramatic land warfare hall with tanks, military vehicles and artillery.

ELY

Ely is the jewel in the crown of the Fens, in whose history the majestic **Cathedral** and the Fens themselves have played major roles. Ely owes its existence to St Etheldreda, Queen of Northumbria, who in 673AD founded a

Ely Cathedral

6

monastery on the 'Isle of Ely', where she remained as abbess until her death in 679. It was not until 1081 that work started on the present Cathedral, and in 1189 this remarkable example of Romanesque architecture was completed. The most outstanding feature in terms of both scale and beauty is the Octagon, built to replace the original Norman tower, which collapsed in 1322.

Alan of Walsingham was the inspired architect of this massive work, which took 30 years to complete and whose framework weighs an estimated 400 tons. Many other notable components include the 14th century Lady Chapel, the largest in England, the Prior's Door, the painted nave ceiling and St Ovin's cross, the only piece of Saxon stonework in the building. The Cathedral is set within the walls of the monastery, and many of the ancient buildings still stand as a tribute to the incredible skill and craftsmanship of their designers and builders. Particularly worth visiting among these are the monastic buildings in the College, the Great Hall and Queens Hall. Two other attractions which should not be missed are the **Brass Rubbing Centre**, where visitors can make their own rubbings from replica brasses, and the **Museum of Stained Glass**.

Ely's **Tourist Information Centre** is itself a tourist attraction, since it is housed in a pretty black and white timbered building that was once the home of Oliver Cromwell. Modern Ely bustles, and that bustle is at its most bustling on Thursday, when the largest general market in the area is held.

Five miles south of Ely off the A10/A1123, the **Stretham Old Engine**, a fine example of a land drainage steam engine, is housed in a restored, tall-chimneyed brick engine house. Dating from 1831, it is one of 90 steam pumping engines installed throughout the Fens to replace 800 windmills. At Wicken, 9 miles south of Ely, the National Trusts's **Wicken Fen** is the oldest nature reserve in the country, 600 acres of undrained fenland, famous for its rich plant, insect and bird life and a delight for both naturalists and ramblers. Features include boardwalk and nature trails, hides and watchtowers, a cottage with 1930s furnishings, a working windpump (the oldest in the country), a visitor centre and a shop. Open daily dawn to dusk. St Lawrence's Church is well worth a visit, small and secluded among trees. In the

churchyard are buried Oliver Cromwell and several members of his family.

GODMANCHESTER

Godmanchester is linked to Huntingdon by a 14th century bridge across the Ouse. It was a Roman settlement and one that continued in importance down the years, as the number of handsome buildings testifies. One such is **Island Hall**, a mid-18th century mansion built for John Jackson, the Receiver General for Huntingdon; it contains many interesting artefacts. This family home has lovely Georgian rooms, with fine period detail and fascinating possessions relating to the owners' ancestors since their first occupation of the house in 1800. The tranquil riverside setting and formal gardens add to the peace and splendour - the house takes its name from the ornamental island that forms part of the grounds.

Wood Green Animal Shelter at Kings Bush Farm, Godmanchester is a purpose-built, 50 acre centre open to the public all year round. Cats, dogs, horses, donkeys, farm animals, guinea pigs, rabbits, llamas, wildfowl and pot-bellied pigs are among the many animals for visitors to see, and there is a specially adapted nature trail and restaurant.

GRAFHAM

Created in the mid-1960s as a reservoir, **Grafham Water** offers a wide range of outdoor activities for visitors of all ages, with 1,500 acres of beautiful countryside, including the lake itself. A ten-mile perimeter track is great for jogging or cycling, and there's excellent sailing, windsurfing and fly fishing. The area is a Site of Special Scientific Interest, and an ample nature reserve at the western edge is run jointly by Anglian Water and the Wildlife Trust.

Grantchester

A pleasant walk by the Cam, or a punt on it, brings visitors from the bustle of Cambridge to the famous village of Grantchester, where Rupert Brooke lived and Byron swam. The walk passes through **Paradise Nature Reserve**.

"Stands the church clock at ten to three
And is there honey still for tea?"

The Orchard, with its Brooke connections, is known the world over. Brooke spent two happy years in Grantchester, and immortalised afternoon tea in The Orchard in a poem he wrote while homesick in Berlin. Time should also be allowed for a look at the Church of St Andrew and St Mary, in which the remains of a Norman church have been incorporated into the 1870s main structure.

HUNTINGDON

Oliver Cromwell was born in Huntingdon in 1599 and attended Huntingdon Grammar School. Samuel Pepys was also a pupil there. Cromwell was MP for Huntingdon in the Parliament of 1629, was made a JP in 1630 and moved to St Ives in the following year. Rising to power as an extremely able military commander in the Civil War, he raised troops from the region and made his headquarters in the Falcon Inn. Appointed Lord Protector in 1653, Cromwell was never proclaimed King, though he ran the country until his death in 1658. The school he attended is now the **Cromwell Museum**, located on Huntingdon High Street, housing the only public collection relating specifically to him, with exhibits that reflect many aspects of his political, social and religious life. **All Saints** Church, opposite the Cromwell Museum, displays many architectural styles, from medieval to Victorian. The Cromwell family burial vault is contained within the church, however, and it is here that Oliver's father Robert and his grandfather Sir Henry are buried. The church has a fine chancel roof, a very lovely

All Saints, Huntingdon

organ chamber and a truly impressive stained glass window.

Among Huntingdon's many fine former coaching inns is **The George Hotel**. Although badly damaged by fire in 1865, the north and west wings of the 17th century courtyard remain intact, as does its very rare wooden gallery. The inn was one of the most famous of all the posting houses on the old Great North Run. It is reputed that Dick Turpin used one of the rooms here. The medieval courtyard, gallery and open staircase are the scene of annual productions of Shakespeare.

About half a mile southwest of town stands **Hinchingbrooke House**, where visitors can see examples of every period of English architecture from the 12th to early 20th century. King James I was a regular visitor, and Oliver Cromwell spend part of his childhood here. The 1st Earl of Sandwich was a central figure in the Civil War and subsequent Restoration, while the 4th Earl (inventor of the snack named after him) was one of the most flamboyant politicians of the 18th century.

KEYSTON

A delightful village with a pedigree that can be traced back to the days of the Vikings. Major attractions both sacred and secular: the Church of St John the Baptist is impressive in its almost cathedral-like proportions, with one of the most magnificent spires in the whole county; the Pheasant is one of the country's best and best-known pub-restaurants.

KIMBOLTON

History aplenty here, and a lengthy pause is in order to look at all the interesting buildings. St Andrew's Church would head the list were it not for **Kimbolton Castle**, which along with its gatehouse dominates the village. Parts of the original Tudor building are still to be seen, but the appearance of the castle today owes much to the major remodelling carried out by Vanbrugh and Nicholas Hawksmoor in the first decade of the 18th century. The gatehouse was added by Robert Adam in 1764. Henry VIII's first wife Catherine of Aragon spent the last 18 months of her life imprisoned here, where she died in 1536. The castle is now a school, but can be visited on certain days in the summer (don't miss the Pellegrini murals).

LODE

Denny Abbey, easily accessible on the A10, is an English Heritage Grade l Abbey with ancient

8

earthworks. On the same site, and run as a joint attraction, is the **Farmland Museum**. The history of Denny runs from the 12th century, when it was a Benedictine monastery. It was later home to the Knights Templar, Franciscan nuns and the Countess of Pembroke, and from the 16th century was a farmhouse. The old farm buildings have been splendidly renovated and converted to tell the story of village life and Cambridgeshire farming up to modern times. **Anglesey Abbey** dates from 1600 and was built on the site of an Augustinian priory, but the house and the 100-acre garden came together as a unit thanks to the vision of the 1st Lord Fairhaven. The garden, created in its present form from the 1930s, is a wonderful place for a stroll, with wide grassy walks, open lawns, a riverside walk, a working water mill and one of the finest collections of garden statuary in the country. There's also a plant centre, shop and restaurant. In the house itself is Lord Fairhaven's magnificent collection of paintings, sumptuous furnishings, tapestries and clocks.

MADINGLEY

The **American Cemetery** is one of the loveliest, most peaceful and most moving places in the region, a place of pilgrimage for the families of the American servicemen who operated from the many wartime bases in the county. The cemetery commemorates 3,800 dead and 5,000 missing in action in the Second World War.

MARCH

March once occupied the second largest 'island' in the great level of Fens, and as the land was drained the town grew as a trading and religious centre, and in more recent times as a market town and major railway hub. **March and District Museum**, in the High Street, tells the story of the people and the history of March and the surrounding area, and includes a working forge and a reconstruction of a turn-of-the-century home. St Wendreda's uniquely dedicated church, at Town End, is notable for its magnificent timber roof, a double hammerbeam with 120 carved angels, a fine font and some impressive gargoyles. John Betjeman declared the church to be 'worth cycling 40 miles into a headwind to see'.

The **Nene-Ouse Navigation Link** runs through the town, affording many attractive riverside walks, and just outside the town, off the B1099, is **Dunhams Wood**, four acres of woodland set among the fens. The site contains an enormous variety of trees, along with sculptures and a miniature railway. Also on the outskirts, signposted from the A141 and B1101, is **Stagsholt Farm Park and Stud**, home to many horses (including the superb Suffolk Punch) and housing a fascinating array of farming and rural bygones.

PETERBOROUGH

The second city of Cambridgeshire has a long and interesting history that traces back to the Bronze Age, as can be seen in the archaeological site at Flag Fen. Although a cathedral city, it is also a New Town (designated in 1967), so modern development and expansion have vastly increased its facilities while retaining the quality of its historic heart. Its crowning glory is, of course, the Romanesque **Cathedral**, built in the 12th and 13th centuries on a site that had seen Christian worship since 655AD. Henry VIII made the church a cathedral, and his first queen, Catherine of Aragon, is buried here, as for a while was Mary Queen of Scots after her execution at Fotheringay. The **Peterborough Museum and Art Gallery** covers all aspects of the history of Peterborough from the Jurassic period to Victorian times.

Peterborough Cathedral

There are twin attractions for railway enthusiasts in the shape of **Railworld**, a hands-on exhibition dealing with modern rail travel, and the wonderful **Nene Valley Railway**, which operates 15-mile steam-hauled trips between Peterborough and its HQ and museum at Wansford. A feature on the main railway line at Peterborough is the historic Iron Bridge, part of the old Great Northern Railway and still virtually as built by Lewis Cubitt in 1852.

Just outside the city, by the river Nene, is **Thorpe Meadows Sculpture Park**, one of several open spaces in and around the city with absorbing collections of modern sculpture.

RAMSEY

A pleasant market town with a broad main street down which a river once ran. Ramsey Abbey became one of the most important in England in the 12th and 13th centuries, and as it prospered so did Ramsey, so that by the 13th century it had become a town with a weekly market and an annual three-day festival at the time of the feast of St Benedict. After the Dissolution of the Monasteries in 1539, the Abbey and its lands were sold to Sir Richard Williams, great-grandfather of Oliver Cromwell. Most of the buildings were then demolished, the stones being used to build Caius, Kings and Trinity Colleges at Cambridge, the towers of Ramsey, Godmanchester and Holywell churches, the gate at Hinchingbrooke House and several local properties. In 1938 the house was converted for use as a school, which it remains to this day.

The church of **St Thomas a Becket of Canterbury** forms an impressive vista at the end of the High Street. Dating back to about 1180, it is thought to have been built as a hospital or guesthouse for the Abbey. It was converted to a church to accommodate the many pilgrims who flocked to Ramsey in the 13th century. The church has what is reputed to be the finest nave in Huntingdonshire, dating back to the 12th century and consisting of seven bays. The church's other treasure is a 15th century carved oak lectern, thought to have come from the Abbey.

Most of **Ramsey Rural Museum** is housed in an 18th century farm building and several barns set in open countryside. Among the many fascinating things to see are a Victorian home and school; a village store; and restored farm equipment, machinery, carts and wagons. The wealth of traditional implements used by local craftsmen such as the farrier, wheelwright, thatcher, dairyman, animal husbandman and cobbler offer an insight into bygone days.

9

ST IVES

An ancient town on the banks of the Great Ouse which once held a huge annual fair and is named after St Ivo, said to be a Persian bishop who came here in the Dark Ages to spread a little light. In the Middle Ages, kings bought cloth for their households at great wool fairs and markets, and a market is still held every Monday. The Bank Holiday Monday markets are particularly lively affairs, and the Michaelmas fair fills the town centre for three days. Seagoing barges once navigated up to the famous six-arched bridge that was built in the 15th century and has a most unusual two-storey chapel in its middle. Oliver Cromwell lived in St Ives in the 1630s and the statue of him on Market Hill, with its splendid hat, is one of the most familiar landmarks. It was made in bronze, with a Portland stone base, and was erected in 1901. It was originally designed for Huntingdon, but they wouldn't accept it!

The beautiful parish church in its churchyard beside the river is well worth a visit. The quayside provides a tranquil mooring for holidaymakers and there are wonderful walks by the riverside.

Clive Sinclair developed his tiny TVs and pocket calculators in the town, and a famous son of St Ives was the great Victorian rower John Goldie, whose name is remembered each year by the second Cambridge boat in the Boat Race.

The **Norris Museum**, in a delightful setting by the river, tells the story of Huntingdonshire for the past 175 million years or so, with anything from fossils, mammoth tusks and models of the great historic reptiles through flint tools, Roman artefacts and Civil War armour to lace-making and ice-skating displays, and contemporary works of art.

"As I was going to St Ives I met a man with seven wives.

Each wife had seven sacks, each sack had seven cats, each cat had seven kits.

Kits, cats, sacks and wives, how many were going to St Ives?"

10

- Just one, of course, but today's visitors are certain to have a good time while they are here.

Just outside St Ives are **Wilthorn Meadow**, a Site of Natural History Interest where Canada geese are often to be seen, and Holt Island Nature Reserve, where high-quality willow is being grown to re-introduce the traditional craft of basket-making. Spot the butterflies, dragonflies and kingfishers.

St Neots

St Neots dates back to the founding of a Saxon Priory, built on the outskirts of Eynesbury, in 974. Partially destroyed by the Danes in 1010, it was re-established as a Benedictine Priory in about 1081 by St Anselm, Abbot of Bec and later Archbishop of Canterbury. For the next two centuries the Priory flourished. Charters were granted by Henry I to hold fairs and markets. The first bridge over the Great Ouse, comprising 73 timber arches, was built in 1180. The name of the town comes from the Cornish saint whose

Riverside Walk, St Neots

remains were interred in the Priory some time before the Norman Conquest. With the Dissolution of the Monasteries, the Priory was demolished. In the early 17th century the old bridge was replaced by a stone one.

St Neots repays a visit on foot, since there are many interesting sites and old buildings tucked away. The magnificent parish church of St Mary the Virgin is a very fine edifice, known locally as the Cathedral of Huntingdonshire. It is an outstanding example of Late Medieval Architecture. The gracious interior complements the 130 foot Somerset-style tower, with a finely carved oak alter, excellent Victorian stained glass and a Holdich organ, built in 1855.

St Neots Museum - opened in 1995 - tells the story of the town and the surrounding area. Housed in the former magistrates court and police station, it still has the original cells. Eye-catching displays trace local history from prehistoric times to the present day. Open Wednesday to Saturday.

Less than three miles north of St Neots at **Little Paxton** is **Paxton Nature Reserve**. Created alongside gravel workings, the Reserve attracts thousands of water birds for visitors to observe from hides.

Thorney

Thorney Abbey, the church of St Mary and St Botolph, is the dominating presence even though what now stands is but a small part of what was once one of the greatest of the Benedictine Abbeys. Gravestones in the churchyard are evidence of a Huguenot colony settling here after fleeing from France in the wake of the St Bartholomew's Day massacre of 1572. The **Thorney Heritage Museum** is a small, independently run museum of great fascination, describing the development of the village from a Saxon monastery, via Benedictine Abbey to a model village built in the 19th century by the Dukes of Bedford. The main innovation was a 10,000 gallon water tank that supplied the whole village; other villages had to use unfiltered river water.

Wisbech

One of the largest of the Fenland towns, a port in medieval times and still enjoying shipping trade with Europe. The finest of many fine properties is undoubtedly **Peckover House**, built in 1722 and bought at the end of the 18th century by Jonathan Peckover, a member of the Quaker banking family. The family gave the building to the National Trust in 1948. Behind its elegant facade are splendid panelled rooms, Georgian fireplaces with richly carved overmantels, and ornate plaster decorations. At the back of the house is a beautiful walled garden with summerhouses and an orangery.

No 1 South Brink is the birthplace of Octavia Hill (1838-1912), co-founder of the National Trust and a tireless worker for the cause of the

Museum Square, Wisbech

poor, particularly in the sphere of housing. The house is now the **Octavia Hill Museum** with displays and exhibits commemorating her work. The **Wisbech and Fenland Museum** is one of the oldest purpose-built museums in the country, and in charming Victorian surroundings visitors can view displays of porcelain, coins, rare rocks, Egyptian tomb treasures and several items of national importance, including the manuscript of Charles Dickens' *Great Expectations*, Napoleon's Sèvres breakfast set captured at Waterloo, and an ivory chess set that belonged to Louis XIV.

12

The Acre

9 Acre Road, March,
Cambridgeshire
PE15 9JD
Tel/Fax:
  01354 657116

Directions:

The inn is in the centre
of March by the river,
the park and the library.

The Acre - originally a grain store for the mill - is a handsome and substantial brick building standing alongside the River Nene in the centre of town. Space is in generous supply here, both in the comfortable L-shaped bar and outside, where there are benches on front and rear patios and a lawned garden. The Acre has very experienced tenants in Mike and Trish Smith, who make sure that no visitor to the inn ever goes thirsty or hungry. Both are members of the British Institute of Innkeepers, and their pub was a runner-up for the Greene King Pub of the Year award in 2001. Greene King IPA is always on tap, and several guest ales are rotated regularly.

Food is available from noon to 10 o'clock at night seven days a week, and the printed menu and specials board offer plenty of choice. Sandwiches and ploughman's platters make excellent quick snacks, and jacket potatoes and giant Yorkshire puddings come with a selection of really tasty fillings. Other choices include a jug of prawns with a marie rose dip, spicy chicken wings, meat or vegetarian lasagne, grills, burgers, and the very popular home-cooked pies - chicken, ham & leek or steak & ale. The Sunday roasts served with all the trimmings are a 'must have' weekly treat for many of the regulars. Major sports events are shown on tv, and the decor includes sports memorabilia, notably a signed Liverpool shirt in a frame on the ceiling. On Wednesday the Acre hosts a popular quiz. A riverside walk is a good prelude to tucking in at the Acre, and March has a number of places to interest the visitor, including the museum in the High Street and the fine Church of St Wendreda, which John Betjeman declared was 'worth cycling 40 miles into a headwind to see'.

Opening Hours: 11-11, Wed & Sat 10-11, Sun 12-10.30

Food: A la carte bar menu

Credit Cards: Diners, Mastercard, Visa

Accommodation: None

Facilities: Car park, disabled facilities

Entertainment: Quiz Wednesday

Local Places of Interest/Activities:
March Museum, Church of St Wendreda

The Black Swan

13

Main Street,
Farcet,
Nr Peterborough,
Cambridgeshire
PE7 3DF
Tel: 01733 240387

Directions:
Farcet is on B1091 2
miles south of
Peterborough.

Off the A15 south of Peterborough, the **Black Swan** presents a smart, freshly painted frontage and a brand new pub sign on the main street at the lower end of the village of Farcet. Go-ahead tenants John and Jean Hollings have made a great impact since their arrival in the spring of 2002, with a wider range of food and drink and a regular programme of events and entertainment. The Fenman is an excellent locals bar serving a wide selection of beers and other drinks, and food is served in the cosy lounge bar. Jacket potatoes and made-to-order sandwiches provide satisfying lunchtime snacks, and the main choice includes stalwarts such as fish & chips, lasagne, sausages, grills and the 'best ever' cottage pie - the meat comes from a very good butcher in Chatteris. Pensioners enjoy special lunch deals on Thursday and Friday, and curries, Italian and Mexican are among the themes for the popular theme food nights.

There's a separate room for the pool table, darts have been re-introduced, and the local clay pigeon shooting club meets here (but not for shooting!). Not all the entertainment is inside - a new petanque pitch has been laid in the attractive rear garden. The Black Swan has no guest bedrooms, but is registered with the Touring Caravan Club and has some spaces for caravans. Farcet is the home of Colman's mustard (or at least of the plantbeds that provide the seeds used in the mustard-making process) and every May the Black Swan leads the village in a rhubarb festival. Walking and cycling are popular activities hereabouts, and the 850-year-old village church is well worth taking time to visit, as is the Church of St Peter at nearby Yaxley, with one of the most outstanding of all Fenland towers.

Opening Hours: 12-2 & 5-11, all day Fri, Sat & Sun

Food: Bar meals

Credit Cards: Mastercard, Visa.

Accommodation: None (caravan spaces available)

Facilities: Car park

Entertainment: Occasional live music, karaoke, quiz and race nights.

Local Places of Interest/Activities:
Peterborough 2 miles, Yaxley 2 miles, Stilton 5 miles, Whittlesey 5 miles, Flag Fen Bronze Age Excavations 7 miles

Internet/Website:
website: www.blackswan.netfirms.com

14

Castle Lodge

New Barns Road, Ely,
Cambridgeshire
CB7 4PW
Tel: 01353 662276
Fax: 01353 666606

Directions:

The hotel is five
minutes walk from the
Cathedral, just north
of the B1382
Prickwillow Road.

Five minutes' walk from Ely's magnificent Cathedral, **Castle Lodge Hotel** dates back in part to 1848, with an extension added in 1928. Part of it has indeed the look of a little castle, complete with crenellations. Small and intimate, the hotel is a very pleasant base for individuals, families and small groups. It is owned and run by the Stevenson family, who came here in early August 2002; Mr Stevenson is the general manager, his wife and daughter run front of house and the two sons are the chefs. A full English breakfast is served in the dining room, where the main menu offers a good selection of dishes to suit most tastes and appetites; for residents planning trips around the area, packed lunches can be provided. Liquid refreshment includes cask ales and a selection of wines. The 14 guest bedrooms are all en suite, with central heating, tv and tea-making facilities.

The owners welcome children, and a cot and high chair can be made available. Facilities for disabled guests are among the Stevenson family's plans. A function room with its own bar can be booked for weddings, parties and other special occasions. Neat and bright throughout, and with the enthusiastic Stevensons at the helm, the Castle Lodge is a good base for discovering Ely, which is often referred to as the jewel in the crown of the Fens. The splendid Cathedral, completed in the 12th century, is top of any visitor's list, but there are other attractions, too, including the Museum, once the town jail, and Oliver Cromwell's House.

Opening Hours: 12-11

Food: A la carte

Credit Cards: Mastercard, Visa.

Accommodation: 14 en suite rooms.

Facilities: Car park, function room

Entertainment: None

Local Places of Interest/Activities: Ely Cathedral, Brass Rubbing Centre and Museums, Newmarket 12 miles

The Duke Of Wellington — 15

Alms Hill, Bourn,
Cambridgeshire
CB3 7SH
Tel/Fax:
   01954 719364

Directions:

From Cambridge
A1303 then A428;
turn left after about 3
miles onto minor
road signposted
Bourn; or take A603
then B1046.

The Duke of Wellington is a smartly renovated Georgian house in the charming village of Bourn. The Duke is in the safe hands of Alex and Lynn Williams, who are both experienced and accomplished chefs. In the spacious non-smoking dining area à la carte and fixed-price menus provide a really mouthwatering choice of dishes, some traditional pub classics, others more exotic and adventurous, but all skilfully prepared and thoroughly enjoyable. Heading the 'old brigade' are smoked salmon, scampi, game sausages and sirloin or rump steaks, while flying the flag of modern British cuisine are such delights as pan-fried sea bass fillets on chive mash with a lobster-infused fish velouté, or escalope of veal stuffed with blue cheese on a fondant potato with café au lait sauce.

Vegetarians are very well catered for (three main courses on the carte), and Sunday lunch brings a choice of three prime roasts and chicken, fish and vegetarian alternatives. Yet another option is the 2- or 3-course Great British Grub menu of familiar favourites like tomato soup, bangers & mash, fish & chips and apple pie & custard. Fine wines, personally chosen by Alex, accompany this superb food, and beer-drinkers have a choice of real ales. Bourn has a delightful high street and a triangular green. The Church of St Helen and St Mary is well worth a visit, and outside the village on the road to Caxton is the famous Bourn Mill of 1636, said to be the oldest post mill in Britain. Cambridge, with more places of interest per acre than almost anywhere in the land, is an easy eight-mile drive away.

Opening Hours: 11.30-2.30 & 6-11 (Closed Sun eve & all Mon)

Food: A la carte

Credit Cards: Amex, Mastercard, Visa.

Accommodation: None

Facilities: Car park

Entertainment: Occasional live music

Local Places of Interest/Activities: Caxton (2 old mills) 3 miles, Hilton Turf Maze 8 miles, Madingley (American Cemetery) 6 miles, Cambridge 8 miles

Internet/Website:
website: www.duke-of-wellington.net/

16

The Dyke's End

8 Fair Green, Reach,
Nr Cambridge,
Cambridgeshire
CB5 0JD
Tel: 01638 743816

Directions:

Reach is located off the B1102 8 miles northeast of Cambridge. The pub overlooks the village green.

The Dyke's End is a delightful free house owned collectively by residents of the village and run by tenants Phil and Tessa Vincent. The Dyke in the pub's name is the imposing Devil's Dyke, built around AD 370, and the pub attracts visitors from the Dyke as well as from Cambridge and Newmarket, both eight miles away. But the pub is a destination in its own right, combining a friendly, relaxed ambience with charming hosts, well-kept ales and excellent food. Real ales on tap include several local brews, and the annual beer festival in August features no fewer than 40 ales. The food, prepared from the pick of the local produce by Phil and Tessa, has won wide acclaim, and it's always a good idea to book, especially on Friday, Saturday and lunch on Sunday (no food Sunday evening or Monday). Fresh fish is delivered daily for seafood specials that could by anything from mussels to turbot and sea bass, and for meat-eaters the steaks are great favourites. Seasonal game includes hare, partridge and venison, and there's always a good choice for vegetarians. Portions are very generous, but room should definitely be left for one of the scrumptious home-made puddings.

A very good wine list accompanies the food, prompting a local wine expert to declare that this is the best pub in Cambridgeshire. The interior of the pub is very cosy and comfortable, with an open plan bar that has three distinct areas, including a non-smoking section for diners; there's also a fine restaurant area upstairs. The white-painted front of the pub is adorned with colourful window boxes and hanging baskets, and there's a pleasant little grassed area set with picnic benches. At the back is a lovely garden that comes into its own in fine weather; there's also a car park at the back. The village of Reach hosts what is thought to be the oldest fair in England, dating back more than 800 years.

Opening Hours: 12-2 & 7-9

Food: Extensive à la carte menu

Credit Cards: All the major cards

Accommodation: None

Facilities: Car park at rear

Entertainment: Annual beer festival

Local Places of Interest/Activities: Reach Fair, Cambridge 8 miles, Newmarket 8 miles, Burwell Museum 2 miles

Internet/Website:
e-mail: phil@the-dykesend.pub.com
website: www.the-dykesend.pub.com

The Elephant & Castle   17

The Green,
Wood Walton,
Nr Huntingdon,
Cambridgeshire
PE28 5YN
Tel/Fax:
   01487 773337

Directions:

Wood Walton is 7 miles north of Huntingdon and 12 miles south of Peterborough . A14, then A1(M) J14, then B1090.

The Elephant & Castle is a pleasant, characterful establishment set in tranquil surroundings yet very accessible to motorists. The original building is a 200-year-old white-painted house with a couple of picnic benches set out on a tiny lawned area at the front. Opposite the house is a charming cluster of horse chestnuts. There's a lovely cosy feel in the black-beamed bar, where a good choice of drinks includes resident and guest real ales. There are darts and tv in the bar whilst a separate room has pool. Owner Valerie Kelly offers a varied selection of food, from bar snacks to full meals. Among the favourites dishes are steak & kidney and chicken & mushroom pies, lasagne, burgers and excellent steaks from a local butcher; T-bone steaks are the inn's speciality. This is very much a place of two parts, as the overnight accommodation is as modern as the free house is traditional.

There are eight motel rooms, all with shower en suite, smart, practical furniture, electric heater, tv, radio-alarm and tea/coffee making facilities. All the rooms are on the ground floor, making them accessible to less mobile guests. Interconnecting suites are available for larger families, and there's ample parking for everyone, with a large garden area. A full English breakfast is served in the pub part. The Elephant & Castle is situated in a conservation area among nature reserves and sanctuaries (Woodwalton Fen, Monkswood, Aversley Wood). This is also excellent walking country, both in open countryside and woodland, and history abounds in nearby Huntingdon, Ramsey and St Ives. Pets welcome.

Opening Hours: 12-3 (weekends) & 7-11

Food: Pub food

Credit Cards: All the major cards

Accommodation: 8 en suite motel rooms

Facilities: Car park.

Entertainment: Occasional bands and karaoke

Local Places of Interest/Activities:
Woodwalton Fen, Huntingdon 7 miles, Ramsey 8 miles, St Ives 10 miles

Internet/Website:
e-mail: pubwoodwalton@aol.co.uk
website: www.pub-woodwalton.co.uk

18

The Five Bells

High Street, Burwell,
Cambridgeshire
CB5 0HD
Tel: 01638 741404

Directions:

From Newmarket, take the B1103 to Burwell (about 5 miles). From Cambridge, take the A1303 then the B1102 (about 10 miles).

Burwell is a village of many attractions, which much to detain the visitor, and near the top of the list is the **Five Bells** on the main street. Behind its handsome cream-painted frontage there's a popular public bar, a tasteful lounge and an excellent new non-smoking dining room with a wood-burning stove in an inglenook fireplace. The hosts are Kevin George and Kate North, who have enhanced the pub's good name since taking the reins in 2001. There are plenty of real ales, beers and lagers on hand to quench thirsts, and a good choice of food is served from 12 to 2 and from 6 to 9 every day except Sunday evening. Filled baguettes, jacket potatoes and omelettes are favourite lunchtime fare, and the à la carte selection includes pasta, seafood (moules marinière, tuna steaks), beef steaks, gammon and chicken.

Wines from Greene King, including good house wines, complement the food perfectly. When the weather is kind, a garden menu comes into play, offering such things as Cumberland sausage with fries, breaded scampi and ribs with a barbecue sauce. There are plenty of picnic benches in the garden, which has a splendid new children's play area devised and largely constructed by Kevin. This is a very sociable pub, with the classic pub games like darts, dominoes, cribbage and shove ha'penny all having their fans. Musical duos perform on occasions. The sights of Burwell include a fascinating museum, a restored windmill, and a very fine church with superb Perpendicular features and roof carvings of animals.

Opening Hours: 12-3 & 5-10.30

Food: Snack and à la carte menus

Credit Cards: All the major cards

Accommodation: None (B&B nearby)

Facilities: Car park, children's play area

Entertainment: Dominoes Monday, occasional live music

Local Places of Interest/Activities: Burwell Museum and Church of St Mary, Swaffham Prior (2 churches, 2 windmills) 2 miles, Lode (Anglesey Abbey) 4 miles, Denny Abbey and Farmland Museum 4 miles, Newmarket 5 miles, Cambridge 10 miles

Haymakers   **19**

High Street,
Chesterton,
Cambridgeshire
CB4 1NG
Tel:
  01223 367417

Directions:

Off the ring road north of Cambridge. After the A10 Milton turn-off, third set of traffic lights, left into Union Lane then into High Street.

In the High Street of Chesterton, **Haymakers** is one of the most conivivial and lively pubs in the Cambridge region. Performers and public alike rate this the best music pub in the area, and four nights a week there are live performances from soloists, groups and bands that cover a wide spectrum of styles. Music isn't the only entertainment at this most sociable of pubs: darts and pool teams play in the local leagues, and the darts team were winners of the 2002 summer league. The interior offers a choice of ambience - cheerful, with the games and Sky Sports in the public bar, or quieter, in the little snug.

Andy and Wendy Smith, here since the summer of 2001, keep their customers happy and well nourished with a good choice of drinks and home cooking. The latter offers the best choice at lunchtime, when the options run from toasted sandwiches to burgers, bangers & mash, pies and the trio of Sunday roasts. And every day the chef produces four specials, which could include filled Yorkshire puddings, pasta, chicken curry, beef & onion pie, cold meats and salads and honey roast ham with eggs and chips. Music lovers are in their element here, while lovers of almost anything else are well catered for in the vicinity: the beauty of the countryside to the north, Denny Abbey and Anglesey Abbey a few miles away, the marvellous windmill at Swaffham Prior, the colleges, museums, churches and all-embracing culture of Cambridge, just minutes down the road.

Opening Hours: 11-11, Sun 12-3 & 7-10.30

Food: Bar meals

Credit Cards: Mastercard, Visa.

Accommodation: None

Facilities: Car park

Entertainment: Live music four nights a week

Local Places of Interest/Activities: Cambridge (colleges, museums, libraries, bridges, churches, punting) 1 mile, Denny Abbey 5 miles, Anglesey Abbey 5 miles

20   The Ickleton Lion

9 Abbey Street,
Ickleton,
Nr Saffron Walden,
Cambridgeshire
CB10 1SS
Tel: 01799 530269
Fax: 01799 531764

Directions:

Ickleton is 8 miles
south of Cambridge
off the A1301. Close
to the M11, J10 or 9.

Food is a major attraction at the **Ickleton Lion,** where Doug and Paula Bollen are the excellent hosts (they also have the John Barleycorn at nearby Duxford). The building is thought to date back to the 1700s, and its grounds include an enclosed lawned garden, children's play area and a barbecue/picnic area. The interior has carpeted pine floors and beamed supports; pictures of local places of interest hang on the walls, and there's a handsome inglenook fireplace in the cosy snug bar. Four real ales, including a regularly changing guest, are always on tap, and food is served throughout the pub and throughout its opening hours, seven days a week. Everything is prepared and cooked on the premises, and Doug, who trained as a master chef in his native North Yorkshire, sees that quality and value for money are present in every dish.

The choice is long and varied, featuring British classics such as steak & ale pie, beef Wellington, roast chicken or poached smoked haddock. For quicker or lighter meals, the snack menu offers baguettes, omelettes, jacket potatoes, salads and pizza. Monday is curry night, steaks have their own menu on Wednesday and on Friday it's fish & chips. The wine list includes four house wines available by the glass. On Tuesday evening, the weekly quiz provides food for thought. The wartime fighter pilot ace Douglas Bader was a regular here when he was stationed at nearby Duxford aerodrome. The Aviation Museum at Duxford is one of the biggest attractions in the area, with frequent air shows through the year. In Ickleton itself, the Church of St Mary has some wonderful 12th century wall paintings.

Opening Hours: 12-10

Food: A la carte and snacks

Credit Cards: All the major cards

Accommodation: None

Facilities: Car park, play area

Entertainment: Quiz Tuesday

Local Places of Interest/Activities: Duxford Aviation Museum 1 mile, Saffron Walden (Audley End House) 4 miles, Great Chesterford (Roman remains) 3 miles, Cambridge 8 miles

Internet/Website:
website: themothergoosepub.co.uk

The John Barleycorn | **21**

3 Moorfields Road,
Duxford,
Cambridgeshire
CB2 4PP
Tel/Fax:
  01223 832699

Directions:

Duxford is located 8 miles south of Cambridge off the A505, very close to Junction 10 of the M11.

Named after the legendary figure who travelled round the country sowing seeds, the **John Barleycorn** is a wonderful thatched pub dating back to 1660. Hanging baskets and flower tubs enhance the already beautiful exterior, and the inside fully lives up to expectations, with low beamed ceilings, pew benches and refectory tables with brass nameplates such as 'Poachers Corner' or 'Smugglers Retreat'. Old proverbs are painted on the exposed beams, and on one wall is a list of all the landlords from 1720 to the present day. The current incumbents are Doug and Paula Bollen. Doug has been in the licensed trade for most of his working life and has been voted Licensee of the Year for the Anglia region. The pub has also received many awards, including National Pub of the Year 2002, earned for its excellent atmosphere and hospitality, for its real ales and for its outstanding food. The daytime menu is served from noon to 5pm, when the supper menu takes over until last orders at 10 o'clock.

The super menu provides a terrific choice running to a dozen starters and about 30 main courses; these could include a classic Irish stew with dumplings, sizzling spicy or sweet & sour chicken, minty lamb steaks and paupiettes of trout with tarragon and white wine, stuffed with leek, carrot and fennel. A splendid meal could end with luxury ice cream or a classic dessert such as bread & butter pudding or spotted dick served with custard or cream. The wine list does full credit to the fine food. The pub has an attractive garden with a safe play area for children. Newly on stream for 2002 are four pleasant timber-framed guest bedrooms in chalet style. The Ickleton Lion, at Ickleton near Saffron Walden, is in the same ownership as the John Barleycorn.

Opening Hours: 11-11

Food: A la carte menu

Credit Cards: All the major cards

Accommodation: 4 en suite rooms

Facilities: Car park

Entertainment: None

Local Places of Interest/Activities: Duxford Aviation Museum, Hinxton water mill 1 mile, Cambridge 8 miles

Internet/Website:
websites: www.themothergoosepub.co.uk
    and www.etccountrypubs.co.uk

22 The Manor House Hotel

Chapel Street,
Alconbury,
Nr Huntingdon,
Cambridgeshire
PE28 4DY
Tel: 01480 890423
Fax: 01480 891663

Directions:
Alconbury lies just off
the A14/A1 5 miles
northwest of
Huntingdon.

In a pretty village just off the A1/A14 north of Huntingdon, the **Manor House Hotel** is a 16th century building with an immaculate white-painted facade, steeply raked tiled roof and windows with tiny criss-cross panes. Day rooms in traditional style include a non-smoking area in the comfortable lounge bar and a 45-seat dining room that is also a popular venue for functions and special occasions. The Manor House is owned by Karen Kingswell, who was a nurse in Florida for 20 years before returning to this venture, which she runs with Kevin, an accomplished chef of many years' standing. From his kitchen comes a wide variety of dishes to appeal to all tastes and appetites. The bar menu offers sandwiches, baguettes and jacket potatoes with a choice of fillings, plus dishes such as creamy garlic mushrooms, pasta, ploughman's and chicken, bacon and mushroom pie. The main menu starts with the likes of brie wedges with cranberry sauce or hot buffalo wings and progresses to a long list of fish dishes (breaded plaice, chargrilled tuna, Thai cod & prawn fishcakes), pork ribs, steak pies, chicken Kiev, steaks from 8 oz to 32 oz and a mighty mixed grill of pork chop, lamb chop, gammon, rump steak, sausages, eggs, tomato, mushrooms, onion rings, chips and peas that's strictly for trenchermen.

The Manor House also offers excellent guest accommodation in 8 well-appointed en suite bedrooms with large-screen tv, telephone, tea-makers and points for internet access. Rooms include singles, doubles, twins and a spacious family room. In the hotel's large car park is a rare Californian oak tree that is at least 300 years old. Attractions in this Fenland village include a 15th century bridge and the interesting church of St Peter and St Paul, mostly 13th century, with a rare early Gothic chancel.

Opening Hours: Mon 6-11, Tues-Fri 12-2.30 & 6-11, Sat & Sun 12-11

Food: A la carte and snacks

Credit Cards: All the major cards

Accommodation: 9 rooms, 4 en suite

Facilities: Car park

Entertainment: Live music monthly

Local Places of Interest/Activities: Fenland walks, Hamerton Wildlife Park 5 miles, Huntingdon 5 miles, Grafham Water 6 miles, Woodwalton Fen nature reserve 5 miles

Internet/Website:
website: www.manorhousealconbury.com
e-mail: stayatmanorhouse@aol.com

Oliver Twist Free House 23

High Road,
Guyhirn,
Nr Wisbech,
Cambridgeshire
PE13 4EA
Tel: 01945 450523

Directions:

Guyhirn is located 6 miles south of Wisbech on the A47; 4 miles north of March on the A141. The pub is signposted from the Guyhirn roundabout.

The Oliver Twist is a smart redbrick, tile-roofed pub rebuilt to replace a much older pub. Signposted from the A47/A141 Guyhirn roundabout, it nestles below the bank on the Peterborough side of the River Nene. The interior is in unpretentious mock-Tudor style, and in winter real fires keep things snug. Mick and Jacqui Thornton have been here six years, and since Mick is a champion cellarman, it is only to be expected that the real ales and other beers are kept in the best condition. Filled rolls and baguettes and ploughman's platters make excellent quick snacks, and in the spacious restaurant a full à la carte menu is served. Typical main courses on the regularly changing list could include salmon en croûte, pork stroganoff, rack of lamb and chicken with mushrooms, white wine, cream and parsley. A carefully selected range of sweets or cheese and biscuits round off a very enjoyable meal complemented by well-chosen wines.

The owners plan to bring on stream six en suite guest bedrooms for 2003. Walking, cycling and boating are popular pastimes in this Fenland region, and fishing can be arranged on the River Nene. Wisbech and March are within an easy drive, and six miles to the west is the model village of Thorney with its abbey and church. An ideal base for exploring the North Norfolk coast, Lincolnshire fens or even the East Midlands

Food available: Mon-Sat 11.30-2 & 6-10; Sun 12-2 & 6-9

Food: A la carte and bar snacks

Credit Cards: Mastercard, Visa

Accommodation: 6 en suite rooms planned for 2003

Facilities: Car park

Entertainment: Monthly quiz

Local Places of Interest/Activities: Thorney Abbey 6 miles, Wisbech 6 miles, Peterborough 14 miles

Internet/Website:
e-mail: mickthornton@the-oliver-twist.co.uk
website: www.the-oliver-twist.co.uk

24   The Packhorse

4 Lincoln Road,
Northborough,
Nr Peterborough,
Cambridgeshire
PE6 9BL
Tel: 01733 252300

Directions:

Northborough is 6 miles north of Peterborough off the A15 and B1166.

Opposite the gatehouse of the 14th century Northborough Manor, the **Packhorse** is a delightful hostelry built of dressed stone, with tall brick chimneys and a steeply raked slate-tiled roof. At the front of the inn, surrounded by a small wooden fence, is a little grassed area with a couple of picnic benches. Inside, the bar, lounge and games room are small, intimate and very inviting, and the inn has long been a popular place for the villagers to meet over a pint. John Smith's Cask, Old Speckled Hen and two guest ales are always on tap, and a selection of straightforward snacks and bistro-style meals is served lunchtime and evening.

Darts is the favourite pub game, and other entertainment is provided by quiz nights and occasional live music sessions. A separate room is available as a meeting place for local clubs and societies. A road running from the inn and the manor leads to the Norman Church of St Andrew, while a few miles to the east is the village of Crowland with its twin attractions of the Abbey and the unique Trinity Bridge. The Packhorse has the same owners as Todd's in Market Deeping and the Walnut Tree in Deeping St James.

Opening Hours: 11-11, Sun 12-10.30

Food: Bistro menu

Credit Cards: None

Accommodation: None

Facilities: Car park, meeting room

Entertainment: Quiz nights, live music nights

Local Places of Interest/Activities: Northborough Manor opposite the inn, Peterborough 6 miles

The Poacher At Elsworth | 25

Brockley Road,
Elsworth,
Nr Cambridge,
Cambridgeshire
CB3 8JS
Tel: 01954 267219
Fax: 01954 267942

Directions:

From Cambridge take
the A14 for about 4
miles; turn left at sign
to Boxworth and
Elsworth.

The Poacher at Elsworth is an outstanding country inn with a pinkwashed facade topped by immaculate thatching. Inside, all is equally spick and span, with raspberry-pink walls and old beams - an ideal setting for relaxing with a glass of real ale. The choice of ales changes all the time, with as many as 50 different varieties appearing in a six month period, and there's also an excellent, eclectic choice of wines served by the glass or bottle. Host Andrew Banham is a wine buff, and everything on the list is worth trying. His wife Sue is also an expert, and her culinary skills are attracting an ever growing clientele, who come from a wide catchment area to enjoy her dishes.

The menus change daily, and typical items on the evening menu run from a superb chicken liver paté and spicy Oriental crabcake among the starters to salmon pasta florentine, casseroled lamb with stilton dumplings and pork hock with sage and onion served with an apple and sage jus. There are always main course options for vegetarians, and excellent English cheeses are an alternative to the mouthwatering desserts. The Poacher has a very pleasant garden with plenty of comfortable seats. Elsworth is a pretty, peaceful village with a lovely church where the Reverend Awdry of Thomas the Tank Engine fame was once the incumbent. Cambridge, St Ives and Huntingdon are easy drives away, and other accessible places of interest include the National Trust's imposing Wimpole Hall and the Wood Green animal shelter.

Opening Hours: 12-2.30 & 5.30-11

Food: A la carte menu

Credit Cards: Mastercard, Visa

Accommodation: None

Facilities: Car park, beer garden

Entertainment: Background music

Local Places of Interest/Activities:
Cambridge 8 miles, St Ives 10 miles,
Huntingdon 12 miles

Internet/Website:
website: www.ukcountrypubs.com

26 The Robin Hood Tavern

Market Hill,
St Ives,
Cambridgeshire
PE17 4AL
Tel: 07929 414910

Directions:

The tavern is in the centre of St Ives beside the market square.

The ancient town of St Ives is full of interesting places to see and things to do, and on a tour round the town visitors should allow time to drop in at the **Robin Hood Tavern**. Beside the market square in the centre of town, this atmospheric Scottish & Newcastle tavern sports not only a sign of Robin Hood but also a life-size figure of the outlaw perched in an alcove above the door. Behind the green and white painted frontage with its tiled roof and small paned windows, the tavern has been stylishly updated to create a light, inviting ambience in which to enjoy a glass of real ale, one of the several excellent lagers or something from the well-chosen wine list. The menu has been updated as well as the decor, and offers an extensive menu that runs from tapas-style light bites and home-made burgers to lasagne and Aberdeen Angus steaks. Diners order at the bar, and a buzzer at their table tells them when the food is ready to be collected from the bar counter.

Tenant Jemma Buckingham not only sees that her customers are well fed and watered, she keeps them entertained with a variety of diversions, including live music on Thursday, Friday and Saturday nights, quiz nights and karaoke. All this should still leave time for looking at the sights of St Ives, notable among which are the fascinating Norris Museum, the bridge over the Ouse with a two-storey chapel in the middle, the parish church with its dark, theatrically elaborate interior, and - in the same street as the Robin Hood - the statue of Oliver Cromwell which was designed for Huntingdon but came here instead because Huntingdon didn't want it.

Opening Hours: 11-11.

Food: A la carte and snacks

Credit Cards: Mastercard, Visa.

Accommodation: None

Facilities: Parking at rear or in market square

Entertainment: Quiz, karaoke, weekend live music

Local Places of Interest/Activities:
Norris Museum, Wilthorn Meadow 1 mile

The Rose & Crown 　　　　　27

High Street,
Somersham,
Cambridgeshire
PE28 3EE
Tel: 01487 840228

Directions:

On the main street of Somersham, 4 miles northeast of St Ives at the junction of the B1050 and B1086.

On a corner site in the middle of Somersham, the **Rose & Crown** is a 250-year-old listed building with go-ahead tenants in Mick and Jane Vilic. They moved here from Peterborough in March 2002 and are breathing new life into the place. The public bar is once again the favourite place in town for socialising over a glass or two from the wide selection of draught and bottled beers on sale. Pool and darts are the preferred bar games, and once a month a quiz takes place. Live groups perform on Saturday, and Sunday is karaoke night and once in a while, visitors can see Harry the labrador do his tricks. Mick and Jane initially served only bar snacks, but with the creation of an excellent new kitchen the pub will now be serving full meals in the smartly refurbished 30-cover restaurant. Sunday lunches are sure to bring in the crowds, so too the regular food theme nights based round, for example, chilli or curries.

Other improvements made by the new tenants include the toilets, including one that is wheelchair accessible. The agreeable Fenland village of Somersham, home to artists, potters and classic car owners, has a lovely square where a brass band plays on special occasions. Nearby is the Raptor Foundation, where owls and other birds of prey find refuge and give flying displays. Birds in their natural habitat can be seen at the Ouse Washes, which start at Earith, two miles from Somersham.

Opening Hours: 11-11.

Food: Good pub food and bar snacks

Credit Cards: All the major cards

Accommodation: None

Facilities: Restaurants can be used as function rooms

Entertainment: Live music or disco Fri, live music Sat, karaoke Sun, monthly quiz

Local Places of Interest/Activities: Raptor Foundation 1 mile, Earith 2 miles, St Ives 4 miles, Huntingdon 6 miles

28 The Rose Inn

Frognall,
Deeping St James,
Peterborough,
Cambridgeshire
PE6 8RR
Tel: 01778 344150

Directions:

Frognall is on the B1525 1 mile east of Market Deeping, 5 miles north of Peterborough.

Arriving in early 2002 for their first venture into the licensed trade, Steve and Jane Osborn have already made a big hit at the **Rose Inn** with the local community. But 'local' is spreading out in all directions as news gets around of the welcome and the hospitality, and above all the excellent home-cooked food served every lunchtime and evening. Steve is an experienced and accomplished chef, and in the Rose Inn's bar or comfortable 70-cover restaurant there's always a good choice of dishes to suit all tastes, from bar lunches with a glass of cask ale to full evening meals with wine from a list selected by Steve. In addition to the standard sessions, Steve holds special theme nights on a regular basis, centred round curries, perhaps, or Italian gourmet dishes, and in the summer the barbecues are always popular occasions. Booking is advisable for meals at the weekend. Children are welcome.

Inside the inn, flagstone floors, low beamed ceilings and comfortable settees provide an inviting, relaxed ambience for enjoying a chat and a drink - the beer choice includes Old Speckled Hen, Greene King IPA and regularly changing guest ales. Outside, there are seats for 60 in a spacious, pretty garden featuring a pagoda. Among the many visitor attractions within easy reach of the Rose are Peterborough Cathedral, the Nene Valley Railway and the bulbfields of south Lincolnshire. Also nearby is the charming little village of Peakirk, with it's Norman Church of St Pega.

Opening Hours: All day from 12 noon; Sat breakfast from 10am

Food: A la carte, barbecue

Credit Cards: All the major cards

Accommodation: None

Facilities: Car park

Entertainment: None

Local Places of Interest/Activities: Peterborough 5 miles, Crowland Abbey 4 miles.

Internet/Website:
e-mail: theroseinn@btopenworld.com
website: www.therose-inn.co.uk

The Royal Oak 29

West Green,
Barrington,
Nr Cambridge,
Cambridgeshire
CB2 5RZ
Tel: 01223 870791

Directions:

Barrington lies off
the A10 six miles
southwest of
Cambridge.

The village of Barrington is one of the most attractive spots in the area, with a large village green on either side of the road fronting rows of delightful cottages. One of the very prettiest sights in the village is the **Royal Oak**, a glorious black-and-white timbered building with an immaculate thatched roof. The picture inside is just as appealing, with low ceilings, beams, traditional furnishings, horse brasses, gleaming copper pans and rustic bric-a-brac in the bars. To the rear is a conservatory restaurant, while out at the front is a lawned area with benches and parasols. In this most atmospheric and inviting of settings Chef-patron David Tumber and manager Morag Tumber regale their customers with a splendid selection of beers headed by a choice of cask ales and a distinguished wine list to accompany David's outstanding cooking. He spent some time learning his trade in Tuscany, so it is not surprising that his menus are influenced by Mediterranean cuisine.

Typical of the fine, fresh dishes on the regularly changing list might include white risotto with lemon thyme, mascarpone and pecorino; buffalo mozzarella with ripped basil, purple figs, Parma Ham and honey dressing; pan-fried scallops with roasted aubergine, pousse, sweet chilli dressing and crème fraiche; and fillet of beef with roasted red onions, chips, portobello mushrooms and vine tomatoes. Food is served from 12 to 2 and from 7 to 9 every day. A walk round this delightful village will prepare visitors for the culinary treats in store at the Royal Oak, and while in the area the Aviation Museum at Duxford, the wildlife sanctuary at Shepreth, Fowlmere nature reserve and the National Trust's magnificent Wimpole Hall are all well worth a visit.

Opening Hours: 11.30-3 & 6-11

Food: A la carte

Credit Cards: Mastercard, Visa.

Accommodation: None

Facilities: Car park

Local Places of Interest/Activities:
Wimpole Hall and Home Farm 4 miles,
Shepreth Wildlife Sanctuary 4 miles, Duxford
5 miles, Cambridge 6 miles

Internet/Website:
website: www.theroyaloak.biz

30

The Slap Up

Waterbeach,
Nr Cambridge,
Cambridgeshire
CB5 9NN
Tel/Fax:
01223 860174

Directions:

On the A10 4 miles north of Cambridge, 11 miles south of Ely.

Slap bang on the A10, with Cambridge to the south and Ely to the north, the **Slap Up** sounds as though it should be a good place to stop for a meal. And the name dose not misleading, as this cheerful roadside pub has built up a good reputation with its wide-ranging choice of home prepared and home cooked dishes. Partners Kevin and Carol Flitton, Christine and Alan make an excellent team, dispensing hospitality, good beers and good food in generous measures. Snack food includes baguettes and sandwiches, jacket potatoes and big burgers, and there are special £5 meal deals with popular classics such as fish & chips, scampi, steak & kidney pie or toad in the hole.

Typical dishes on the main menu include chicken Madras, liver with bacon and onions, pork loin with a rich apricot and brandy cream sauce, and steaks served plain or with peppercorn or diane sauce. Vegetarians have an exceptionally good choice, while fish-lovers will relish the likes of haddock mornay, Thai-style salmon or Mediterranean sea bass. The enjoyment level stays high to the end with a choice of up to a dozen desserts, and the food is complemented by an interesting selection of wines chosen personally by Kevin. The Sunday carvery brings in the crowds, so booking is definitely advised. The Slap Up has live music once a month. It's an easy drive up or down the A10 to Ely or Cambridge, and among other accessible places of interest are Anglesey Abbey, Denny Abbey and Swaffham Prior with its windmills and churches.

Opening Hours: 12-2 (Sunday to 3) & 6-9

Food: Snack and à la carte menus

Credit Cards: All the major cards

Accommodation: None

Facilities: Car park

Entertainment: Live music once a month

Local Places of Interest/Activities: Denny Abbey 2 miles, Cambridge 4 miles, Anglesey Abbey 6 miles, Ely 11 miles

Internet/Website:
website: www.theslapup.co.uk

Todd's

13 Market Place,
Market Deeping,
Cambridgeshire PE6 8EA

Directions:
In the town centre next door but one to the Town Hall.

Built in 1788 for one of the traders who developed Market Deeping's town centre, **Todd's** has recently undergone a change of ownership and a change of role. After extensive renovations, the distinguished three-storey stone building has emerged to serve the needs of the local community in a variety of capacities: as a traditional free house and a meeting place with a convivial, sociable ambience, as an eating place, and as a venue for small conferences, receptions and special occasions. In the two bars, which feature trussed oak-beamed ceilings and a fine original oak staircase, real ale fans have a wide, constantly changing choice, which at any one time might include some or all of Varsity Ale, Pendle Witches Brew, Broadside, Speckled Hen and Timothy Taylor's Landlord.

In the bars and dining areas an extensive menu runs from bar snacks to a full à la carte selection. Everything is prepared on the premises using local suppliers, and among the main courses are minted lamb pie, monster rack of lamb and the wonderfully named grunt, gobble, zoom and coo pie. All the best known traditional pub games are played here - darts, cribbage, dominoes - and there are regular quizzes and a weekly live music session. Todd's is in the same ownership as the Packhorse in Northborough and the Walnut Tree in Deeping St James. Market Deeping stands on the A15/A16 a short drive north of Peterborough. Stamford lies to the west, Spalding to the northeast, and among the attractions close to the town is Crowland Abbey.

Opening Hours: Mon-Wed 9am-midnight, Thurs-Sat 9am-1am, Sun 12-11.30

Food: A la carte + bar snacks

Credit Cards: All the major cards + cash machine

Accommodation: None

Facilities: Function and conference centre

Entertainment: Live music weekly

Local Places of Interest/Activities: Peterborough 4 miles

32   The Walnut Tree

32 Horsegate,
Deeping St James,
Nr Peterborough,
Cambridgeshire
PE6 8EW
Tel: 01778 342467
Fax: 01778 380102

Directions:

The inn is situated 1 mile from the centre of Market Deeping on the B1525 Spalding road.

The Walnut Tree is a neatly kept roadside pub located in the village of Deeping St James, about a mile from the centre of Market Deeping on the B1525 Spalding road. Dating from 1756 and until recently called the Horsegate Tavern, it has family owners and a very warm and friendly atmosphere. Much of its original decor and many of its old fittings have been retained, including the red tiled floor, wood features and pew seating. The pub's long opening hours are appreciated by the locals, and it has long been famous for the excellent English breakfast served from opening time (10am) until 3 o'clock.

Food is an important part of the business here, and the choice covers many tastes and appetites, ranging from bar snacks to a full bistro menu and succulent steaks. There's also an excellent selection of real ales, with London Pride, Broadside and Summer Lightning among the residents, and guest ales that change regularly. As well as classic food and drink, the Walnut Tree also offers classic pub entertainment, from darts, dominoes and cribbage to live music, quiz nights and bonus ball bingo. The Walnut Tree does not take credit cards, but it has the useful facility of a cash machine. In the same ownership as the Packhorse in Northborough and Todd's in Market Deeping.

Opening Hours: 10am-11pm, Sun 12-10.30

Food: Bar snacks, bistro menu, breakfast 10-3

Credit Cards: None, but cash machine

Accommodation: None

Facilities: Car park

Entertainment: Quiz nights, live music nights, bonus ball bingo nights

Local Places of Interest/Activities:
Market Deeping 1 mile, Peterborough 4 miles, Spalding 8 miles

Internet/Website:
e-mail: riggersmailbox@aol.com

The Wheatsheaf 33

Cambridge Road,
Harlton,
Cambridgeshire
CB3 7HA
Tel:
  01223 262298

Directions:

The inn is on the A603 5 miles southwest of Cambridge.

Out of Cambridge on the A603 towards Sandy, the **Wheatsheaf** is the first pub on the left. A pub since the 1700s, it has established a fine reputation as a very friendly local that also has a warm welcome for visitors from outside the area. The landlord is Jamie Edmunds, who at 20 became the youngest Greene King licence holder when he took over in August 2002. He runs the inn with his father Gary, and this sociable team make the inn a very happy and convivial place, a real pleasure to visit. The L-shaped bar is bright and airy, with a piano and dartboard; a separate room has a pool table. Real ales include an excellent Greene King IPA, and in the 20-cover dining area traditional bar food is served all day, every day, with steaks a speciality.

The inn has a family-size guest bedroom with a private bathroom, and on secure ground at the back is a half-acre caravan site. In the large lawned garden with willow tress and picnic benches outdoor events are organised in the summer, and in the bar there's lively entertainment throughout the year: occasional karaoke, live music every Friday, and on Saturday something a little out of the ordinary - an old-time singalong with a free buffet. The inn has ample parking space and access for wheelchairs. Cambridge is a short drive up the A603, and in the other direction, at Arrington, the National Trust's Wimpole Hall is probably the most spectacular country mansion in the whole county. The hall and the landscaped grounds are well worth a visit, as is Wimpole Home Farm, the hall's model farm with a range of rare breed farm animals and a collection of historic farm machinery.

Opening Hours: 11-11

Food: A la carte bar menu

Credit Cards: All the major cards

Accommodation: 1 family room + caravan site

Facilities: Car park, disabled access

Entertainment: Live music Friday, old time music singalong + free buffet Saturday

Local Places of Interest/Activities:
Cambridge 5 miles, Grantchester 3 miles

34 The Wheel Inn

High Road,
Wisbech St Mary,
Cambridgeshire
PE13 4RH
Tel: 01945 410504

Directions:

3 miles southwest of
Wisbech off the A47
or B1166

A gleaming white facade by the roadside invites motorists to pause awhile at the **Wheel Inn**, a family-friendly hostelry with an inviting, traditional interior. This is an Elgoods pub, and the excellent products of that notable Wisbech brewery can be enjoyed in the bar. Tenants Andrew and Belinda Trotman, who took over early in 2002, woo the whole family with a friendly greeting, a relaxed, unpretentious ambience and a selection of good-value dishes to suit all appetites. Omelettes and filled baguettes make excellent lunchtime snacks, and other options run from giant Yorkshire puddings to fish specials, prime steaks and vegetarian dishes. The traditional Sunday roast is a surefire winner, and lasagne and curries could appear on the Friday and Saturday specials board. Children can choose from their own menu then romp in the safe playing area in the very pleasant enclosed garden.

Next to this area is a family room, and the dining area is separate from the bar, so there are plenty of options for parents and their offspring. One of the attractions in nearby Wisbech is definitely for grown-ups. This is the famous Elgoods Brewery, which organises conducted tours. Also here are the splendid Church of St Peter and St Paul, the Octavia Hill Museum and the National Trust's Peckover House.

Opening Hours: 12-3 & 7-11

Food: A la carte and snacks

Credit Cards: None

Accommodation: None

Facilities: Car park, children's play area

Entertainment: Occasional live music

Local Places of Interest/Activities: Wisbech (Elgoods Brewery, Peckover House, Octavia Hill Museum) 3 miles, Parson Drove 2 miles, Peterborough 10 miles, Kings Lynn 15 miles

The White Hart | **35**

Balsham Road, Fulbourn,
Nr Cambridge, Cambridgeshire CB1 5BZ
Tel: 01223 880264
Fax: 01223 880330

Directions:

Fulbourn is situated 4 miles east of Cambridge. From Cambridge, take the Cambridge Road off the A1307 through Cherry Hinton to Fulbourn. In Fulbourn, follow the main road through towards the A11, the pub is on a bend on the left hand side. From the A11, turn left about 3 miles north of junction A1307 on to a minor road signposted Fulbourn.

Customers come from Cambridge and a wide catchment area to the **White Hart**, where Adrian Browne and his hard-working team dispense hospitality and good cheer in generous measure. The substantial premises date from 1869, and the bar is warm and inviting, with real fires and decor that includes old farm implements hanging on an exposed brick wall. The scene can shift outside at almost any time of the year, as the paved beer garden is kept warm by heaters on podiums. Greene King IPA, Abbot Ale and regularly changing guests head the beer list, and the pub has earned the Cask Marque, awarded by an independent organisation formed to raise the standard of cask ales served to the customer. An alternative to the perfect pint is a list of wines that can be ordered by bottle, glass or large glass.

Food is taken every bit as seriously as drink here, and the menu covers a good range of traditional and European dishes. Meals are enjoyable throughout and end on a particularly high note with a selection of speciality home-made desserts such as blackcurrant cheesecake, bread & butter pudding and treacle sponge. There are plenty of dishes for vegetarians and a special children's menu. Friday evenings and Sunday lunch bring a carvery with a choice of four roasts. Fresh fish is served daily, there are BBQ's in the summer months and there are also monthly speciality evenings such as Greek, Mexican or French. This is a very popular spot, particularly at the weekend, and it's always best to book to be sure of a table. For tourists or those with business to attend to in nearby Cambridge, the White Hart makes an excellent base away from the city's rush. Of the nine letting bedrooms, seven are en suite and all have multi-channel tv and tea/coffee making facilities.

Opening Hours: 11-11, Sun 12-10.30

Food: English & European cuisine.

Credit Cards: All the major cards

Accommodation: 9 rooms (7 en suite)

Facilities: Disabled access & toilet, heated beer garden, no smoking area, car park.

Entertainment: Occasional

Local Places of Interest/Activities: Fulbourn Nature Reserve, Wandlebury Nature Reserve 2 miles, Cambridge 4 miles, golf.

36 The White Horse Inn

1 Market Street,
Swavesey,
Cambridgeshire
CB4 5QG
Tel: 01954 232470
Fax: 01954 206188

Directions:

From Huntingdon, take the A14 for about 5 miles; turn left at Fen Stanton on road signposted Fen Drayton and Swavesey.

On a prominent corner site in the village of Swavesey, the **White Horse Inn** has a history going back more than 480 years. In its time is has been an auction house, a public health office and a meeting place for numerous societies, and today it still fulfils the last role as well as its major role as a friendly village pub. When the popular and personable landlord took over, he was returning to the village where three generations of his family had lived. Before that he travelled widely in the music business, being a professional drummer and sometime sound engineer to the band Slade. Up to five real ales are always on tap, along with a staggering selection of about 50 malt whiskies. Food is served from 12 to 2 every day and from 6 to 9 Monday to Saturday. The choice is excellent, from lunchtime snacks to curries, scampi, cod, chicken dishes, minted lamb chops, grills and steaks aplenty. Spicy stuffed aubergines are a very popular order.

The bars are warm and welcoming, with open log fires and exposed oak beams. Old photographs of the village share wall space with prints and drawings of Cambridge colleges. Outside, there's a patio garden and children's play area. Cribbage, darts, pool and bar billiards are the favourite pub games, but the sporting connection goes much further: the pub supports 13 local football teams, a golfing society organises regular outings, and fishing permits for fishing on the Ouse can be obtained next door. The White Horse is also the regular meeting place of many clubs and societies, including the MG owners club. Various charities benefit from events organised here, the most notable event being the annual barrel-rolling contest.

Opening Hours: Mon-Fri 12-2.30 & 6-11; all day Sat and Sun.

Food: Snacks and à la carte menu

Credit Cards: All major cards except Amex and Diners.

Accommodation: None

Facilities: Children's play area, beer garden, pool room, function room.

Entertainment: Occasional

Local Places of Interest/Activities: St Ives 6 miles, Fenstanton (grave of Capability Brown) 8 miles, Houghton Mill 8 miles, Huntingdon 10 miles, Cambridge 7 miles

The White Pheasant　　37

Market Street,
Fordham,
Nr Ely,
Cambridgeshire
CB7 5LQ
Tel:
　01638 720414
Fax:
　01638 720447

Directions:

Fordham is on the
A142 about 8 miles
southeast of Ely.

New owners Liz and Stuart are enhancing the already considerable appeal of the **White Pheasant** with subtle improvements that preserve all the period charm. The original building dates from the 1600s and is little changed down the years, and inside, wooden floors, pine furniture and pastel shades create an attractive, stylish ambience. The inn is to a large extent food driven, and Stuart at the stoves produces 'traditional British food with a fusion'; he uses top local suppliers for the very best ingredients, including super seafood and rare breeds beef, to regale his customers with dishes of a sophistication not often seen in a country inn. His influences are global, and the wine list also tours the world.

There are seats for 50+ diners, and food is served every lunchtime and evening. The inn stands on the A142, with quick and easy access to Newmarket in one direction and Ely in the other. The Cathedral is just one of numerous attractions in Ely - there are also two fascinating museums - and Newmarket is known far and wide as the racing capital of the world. Even closer to the White Pheasant are Downfield Windmill at Soham and the National Trust's Wicken Fen, Britain's oldest nature reserve, whose 600 acres of undrained fenland are famous for its rich plant, insect and birdlife, a delight for both naturalists and walkers.

Opening Hours: 12-3 & 6-11 (Sun to 10.30)

Food: A la carte

Credit Cards: Amex, Mastercard, Visa.

Accommodation: None

Facilities: Car park

Entertainment: None

Local Places of Interest/Activities: Ely 8 miles, Wicken Fen 4 miles, Mildenhall 5 miles

38   The White Swan

Elsworth Road,
Conington,
Nr Fenstanton,
Cambridgeshire
CB3 8LN
Tel/Fax:
  01954 267251

Directions:

Conington is
located off the A14
between Cambridge
and Huntingdon.
Signposted at
Fenstanton.

The White Swan is a handsome redbrick building on the edge of the village of Conington, which is signposted on the A14 at Fenstanton or the next turning south. The short detour off that busy road will be rewarded with a friendly welcome from Kevin and Teresa Parfett and a comfortable, civilised ambience for enjoying a chat, a drink and something to eat. Greene King head the list of real ales, and there's a good selection of wines to enjoy by the glass on their own or to accompany Teresa's food. Her repertoire, based as far as possible on locally sourced produce, covers all the traditional pub classics and much more besides: lunchtime baguettes, ploughman's, jacket potatoes and excellent omelettes; salads; scampi; steaks; gammon; the tastiest pies - cottage, steak & kidney, chicken & mushroom; Sunday roasts; apple pie and fruit crumbles.

    The bar-lounge and non-smoking restaurant are pleasant, comfortable rooms, and when the weather is kind the paved patio comes into its own. Adjacent to it is an area where children can play and be watched. Every Tuesday, the White Swan hosts a meeting of local BSA owners, attracting 30, sometimes as many as 40 riders and their venerable mounts. The manifold attractions of Cambridge are an easy drive along the A14, and in the churchyard of St Peter and St Paul at Fenstanton the noted landscape gardener Lancelot 'Capability' Brown is buried with his wife and son. This is also a good area for walking, and Kevin and Teresa will point visitors in the right direction for walks through the pleasant local countryside.

Opening Hours: 12-11

Food: A la carte

Credit Cards: Diners, Mastercard, Visa

Accommodation: None

Facilities: Car park, children's play/activity centre

Entertainment: None

Local Places of Interest/Activities:
Fenstanton 2 miles, Cambridge 6 miles, Huntingdon 7 miles

2 Norfolk

PLACES OF INTEREST:

PUBS AND INNS:

The Hidden Inns of East Anglia

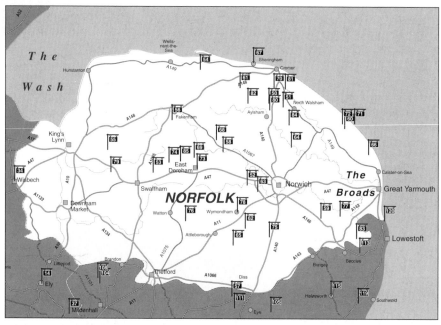

Please note all references refer to page numbers

Norfolk

In South Norfolk, the area between the border with Suffolk and the county capital of Norwich is mainly flat farmland, with quiet villages, handsome old farmhouses and the charming spires and towers of churches. The major centres of population include Diss, an old market town with a mix of Tudor, Georgian and Victorian houses, and Wymondham, with timber-framed houses, a picturesque market place and an Abbey church that bears comparison even with the majestic Norwich Cathedral. Norwich, once an important centre of the worsted trade, retains many medieval buildings, some of which now serve as museums. The area to the east contains the unique Norfolk Broads, beautiful stretches of shallow water, most of them linked by navigable rivers and canals. This is Britain's finest wetland area, a National Park in all but name, with three main rivers, the Ant, the Thurne and the Bure, threading their way through the marshes.

Norwich Cathedral

The Broads, long popular for relaxing holidays, are also a refuge for many species of endangered birds and plants. On the coast due east of Norwich is the old port and modern holiday resort of Great Yarmouth, where the visitor will find miles of sandy beaches, a breezy promenade, two traditional piers and a rich maritime tradition that lives on to this day. A journey along the North Norfolk coast rewards the visitor with spectacular sea views, an abundance of fresh air and miles of quiet, sandy beaches. Substantial stretches are in the hands of the National Trust, and the North Norfolk coast is of major importance for its birdlife. Cromer is a charming resort with a pier and a long fishing tradition: Cromer crabs are renowned far and wide.

Cley Mill

The most important town on the northwest coast is the busy seaside resort of Hunstanton, whose cliffs are made of layers of red, white and brown. On the Great Ouse three miles inland from The Wash, King's Lynn was one of Britain's most important ports in medieval times. To the northeast is the prosperous market town of Fakenham, while to the north, in the valley of the River Stiffkey, the Shrine of Our Lady of Walsingham was in medieval times second only to Thomas à Becket's shrine at Canterbury as a place of pilgrimage. The area stretching down from Fakenham towards Thetford and into Suffolk is known as Breckland, a region of ancient heathland with old pine forests and traces of 4,000-year-old mines. Breckland has five market towns - Dereham, Swaffham, Watton, Attleborough and Thetford - each with its own distinct character, as well as 100 villages scattered through the quiet countryside.

AYLSHAM

Aylsham, set beside the River Bure, is the northern terminus of the **Bure Valley Railway**. It has an unspoilt **Market Place**, surrounded by late 17th and early 18th century houses, reflecting the prosperity the town enjoyed in those years from the cloth trade, and a 14th/15th century church, St Michael's, said to have been built by John O'Gaunt. In the churchyard is the tomb of one of the greatest of the 18th century landscape gardeners, Humphrey Repton, the creator of some 200 parks and gardens around the country.

May Day at Blickling Hall

One of Repton's many commissions was to landscape the grounds of **Blickling Hall**, a 'dream of architectural beauty' which stands a mile or so outside Aylsham.

BLAKENEY

One of the most enchanting of the North Norfolk coastal villages, Blakeney was a commercial port until the beginning of the 20th century when silting up of the estuary prevented all but pleasure craft from gaining access. The

Seals at Blakeney Point

silting has left a fascinating landscape of serpentine creeks and channels twisting their way through mud banks and sand hills. In a side street off the quay is the 14th century **Guildhall** (English Heritage), which was probably a private house and contains little of interest apart from the undercroft, or cellar, which is notable as an early example of a brick-built vaulted ceiling. The beautifully restored Church of St Nicholas, set on a hill overlooking village and marshland, offers much more to the visitor. The chancel, built in 1220, is lovely Early English work, and the magnificent west tower, 100 feet high, is a landmark for miles around. In a small turret on the northeast corner of the chancel a light would once burn as a beacon to guide ships safely into Blakeney Harbour.

BRESSINGHAM

The **Bressingham Steam Museum** boasts one of the world's finest collections of British and Continental locomotives, amongst them the famous *Royal Scot*. The sheds also contain many steam-driven industrial engines, traction engines, and **The Fire Museum** whose collection

Bressingham Steam Museum

of fire engines and fire-fighting equipment could form a complete museum in its own right. Visitors can view the interior of the Royal Coach and ride along five miles of track through the woods and gardens. The six acres of landscaped grounds are notable in themselves since they are planted with more than 5,000 alpine and other types of plant. A two-acre plant centre adjoins the gardens and here there are thousands of plant specimens, many of them rare, available for purchase. Bressingham is renowned for its special Steam Days, when the engines can be seen in full steam on the three narrow gauge lines, and talks and footplate rides are given on the standard gauge locomotives.

BURNHAM MARKET

There are seven Burnhams in all, strung along the valley of the little River Burn. Burnham Market is the largest of them, its past importance reflected in the wealth of Georgian buildings surrounding the green, and the two churches that lie at each end of its broad main street, just 600 yards apart. In the opinion of many, Burnham Market has the best collection of small Georgian houses in Norfolk and it's a delight to wander through the yards and alleys that link the town's three east-west streets.

BURNHAM THORPE

From the tower of All Saints' Church, the White Ensign flaps in the breeze; the only pub in the village is the *Lord Nelson*; and the shop next door to it is called the Trafalgar Stores. No prizes for deducing that Burnham Thorpe was the birthplace of Horatio Nelson. His father, the Revd Edmund Nelson was the Rector here for 46 years and Horatio was the sixth of his eleven children.

There's more Nelson memorabilia in the church, among them a crucifix and lectern made with wood from *HMS Victory*; a great chest from the pulpit used by his father; and two flags from *HMS Nelson*.

CAISTER-ON-SEA

In Boadicea's time, this modern holiday resort with its stretch of fine sands, was an important fishing port for her people, the Iceni. After the Romans had vanquished her unruly tribe, they settled here sometime in the 2nd century and built a 'castra', or castle, or Caister, of which only a few foundations and remains have yet been found. **Caister Castle**, which stands in a picturesque setting about a mile to the west of the town, is a much later construction, built in 1432-5. Caister Castle was the first in England to be built of brick and is in fact one of the earliest brick buildings in the county. The 90 foot tower remains, together with much of the moated wall and gatehouse, now lapped by still waters and with ivy relentlessly encroaching. The castle is open daily from May to September and, as an additional attraction, there is a Motor Museum in the grounds which houses an impressive collection of veteran, Edwardian, and vintage cars, an antique fire engine, and the original car used in the film of Ian Fleming's *Chitty Chitty Bang Bang*.

CROMER

As you enter a seaside town, what more reassuring sight could there be than to see the pier still standing? **Cromer Pier** is the genuine article, complete with Lifeboat Station and the Pavilion Theatre which still stages traditional end-of-the-pier shows. The Pier's survival is all the more impressive since it was badly damaged in 1953 and 1989, and in 1993 sliced in two by a drilling rig which had broken adrift in a storm.

Cromer Crabs are reckoned to be the most succulent in England. During the season, between April and September, crab-boats are launched from the shore (there's no harbour here), sail out to the crab banks about 3 miles offshore, and there the two-man teams on each boat deal with some 200 pots.

The **Lifeboat Museum** is housed in the former Lifeboat Station, it tells the dramatic story of the courageous men who manned the town's rescue service. Also well worth visiting is the **Cromer Museum**, housed in a row of restored fishermen's cottages near the church.

DISS

The late Poet Laureate, John Betjeman, voted Diss his favourite Norfolk town, and it's easy to understand his enthusiasm. The River Waveney running alongside forms the boundary between Norfolk and Suffolk, but this attractive old market town keeps itself firmly on the northern bank of the river. The town is a pleasing mixture of Tudor, Georgian and Victorian houses grouped around **The Mere**, a six-acre stretch of standing water.

FAKENHAM

Fakenham is a busy and prosperous-looking market town, famous for its National Hunt Racecourse, antique & bric-a-brac markets and auctions, and as a major agricultural centre for the region. Straddling the River Wensum, this attractive country town has a number of fine

44

late-18th and early-19th century brick buildings in and around the Market Place. And it must surely be one of the few towns in England where the former gasworks (still intact) have been turned into a **Museum of Gas & Local History**, housing an impressive historical display of domestic gas appliances of every kind. Southeast of Fakenham, **Pensthorpe Waterfowl Park** is home to Europe's best collection of endangered and exotic waterbirds.

GREAT YARMOUTH

Great Yarmouth has a 5-mile stretch of sandy beaches and countless amusements, with a breezy promenade from which one can watch the constant traffic of ships in Yarmouth Roads, and two fine old traditional piers, the Britannia (810 feet long) and the Wellington (600 feet). Of the host of entertainments on offer, the **Sea Life Centre**, **Amazonia** and the **Merrivale Model Village** are all top family attractions. Also on the sea front are the **Maritime Museum of East Anglia**, housed in what was formerly the Shipwrecked Sailors' Home; the **Elizabethan House** (National Trust), a merchant's house of 1596, now a museum of domestic life with 16th century panelled rooms and a functional Victorian kitchen; and, behind South Beach, the 144 foot high **Nelson's Monument** crowned by a statue, not of Norfolk's most famous son, but of Britannia. A sinew-stretching climb up the 217 steps to the viewing platform is rewarded by some striking views.

HOLKHAM

If the concept of the Grand Tour ever needed any justification, **Holkham Hall** amply provides it. For six years, from 1712 to 1718, young Thomas Coke (pronounced Cook) travelled extensively in Italy, France and Germany, studying and absorbing at first hand the glories of European civilisation. And, wherever possible, buying them. When he returned to England, Coke realised that his family's modest Elizabethan manor could not possibly house the collection of treasures he had amassed. His new building, its classical balance and restraint emphasised by the pale honey local brick used throughout, has been described as "the ultimate achievement of the English Palladian movement"

HUNSTANTON

The busy seaside resort of Hunstanton can boast two unique features: one, it has the only cliffs in England made up of colourful levels of red, white and brown strata, and two, it is the only east coast resort that faces west, looking across The Wash to the Lincolnshire coast and the unmistakable tower of the 272 foot high Boston Stump (more properly described as the Church of St Botolph).

Hunstanton's social standing was assured after the Prince of Wales, later Edward VII, came here to recover from typhoid fever. He stayed at the Sandringham Hotel which, sadly, has since been demolished, along with the grand Victorian pier, and the railway. But Hunston, as locals call the town, still has a distinct 19th century charm about it and plenty to entertain visitors.

The huge stretches of sandy beach, framed by those multi-coloured cliffs, are just heaven for children who will also be fascinated by the **Kingdom of the Sea**, on the South Promenade, where an underwater glass tunnel provides a fascinating opportunity to watch the varied and often weird forms of marine life that inhabit Britain's waters. A popular excursion from Hunstanton is the boat trip to Seal Island, a sandbank in The Wash where seals can indeed often be seen sunbathing at low tide.

KING'S LYNN

In the opinion of James Lee-Milne, the National Trust's architectural authority, "The finest old streets anywhere in England" are to be found at King's Lynn. Tudor, Jacobean and Flemish houses mingle harmoniously with grand medieval churches and stately civic buildings. The best place to start an exploration of the town is at the beautiful Church of **St Margaret**, founded in 1101 and with a remarkable leaning arch of that original building still intact.

Alongside the north wall of St Margaret's is the **Saturday Market Place**, one of the town's two market places, and a few steps further is one of the most striking sights in the town, the **Guildhall of the Holy Trinity** with a distinctive chequerboard design of black flint and white stone. The Guildhall was built in 1421, extended in Elizabethan times, and its Great Hall is still used today for wedding ceremonies and various civic events.

1549, the leader of the rebellion against land enclosures, Robert Kett, was hung in chains and left to starve to death. The Castle is now a lively **Museum** where the old dungeons house a forbidding display of instruments of torture, along with the death masks of some of the prisoners who were executed here.

Among the countless other fascinating exhibits are the **Bulwer and Miller** collection of more than 2,600 English china teapots; the Langton collection of around 100 cats, fashioned

Custom House

Norwich Castle

The Town Hall houses the **Museum of Lynn Life** where the greatest treasure in the municipal regalia collection is King John's Cup, a dazzling piece of medieval workmanship with coloured enamel scenes set in gold. The Cup was supposed to be part of King John's treasure which had been lost in 1215 when his overburdened baggage train was crossing the Nene Estuary and sank into the treacherous quicksands.

NORWICH

"Norwich has the most Dickensian atmosphere of any city I know" declared J.B. Priestley in his *English Journey of 1933*. "What a grand, higgledy-piggledy, sensible old place Norwich is!"

The first **Norwich Castle**, a wooden structure, was replaced in the late 1100s by a mighty fortress in stone which, unlike most blank-walled castles of the period, is decorated with a rich facade of blind arcades and ornamental pilasters. The great fort never saw any military action and as early as the 13th century it was being used as the county gaol, a role it continued to fill until 1889. From its walls, in December

in porcelain, ivory, bronze, glass, and wood, and originating from anywhere between Derbyshire and China; and Margaret Elizabeth Fountaine's mind-boggling accumulation of 22,000 butterflies which she had personally netted during her travels around the world. Pride of place must go however to the Museum's incomparable collection of paintings by the group of artists known as the Norwich School. The Castle's function has changed over the years, but the **Cathedral** is still the focus of ecclesiastical life in the county. It's even older than the castle, its service of consecration taking place 900 years ago, in 1101. This peerless building, its flint walls clad in creamy-white stone from Caen is, after Durham, the most completely Norman cathedral in England, its appeal enhanced by later Gothic features such as the flying buttresses.

Outside, beneath the slender 315 foot high spire soaring heavenwards, the **Cathedral Close** is timeless in its sense of peace. There are some 80 houses inside the Close, some medieval, many Georgian, their residents enjoying an idyllic refuge free from cars.

Dominating the western side of the market square is **City Hall**, modelled on Stockholm City Hall and opened by King George VI in 1938.

Around the corner from London Street, in Bridewell Alley, is the **Bridewell Museum**, a late 14th century merchant's house now dedicated to Norfolk's crafts and industries. And right next door another museum/shop celebrates the county's great contribution to world cuisine, mustard. Back in the early 1800s, Jeremiah Colman perfected his blend of mustard flours and spice to produce a condiment that was smooth in texture and tart in flavour. Together with his nephew James he founded J & J Colman in 1823 and, a century and a half later, **The Mustard Shop** was established to commemorate the company's history. It also serves as a showcase for the range of Colman products which nowadays includes a variety of drinks and foods. On the western edge of the city stands the **University of East Anglia**, where the

Museum of the Broads

Sainsbury Centre for Visual Arts contains the eclectic collection of a 'passionate acquirer' of art, Sir Robert Sainsbury. To the south of Norwich are the remains of **Venta Icenorum**, the Roman town established here after Boadicea's rebellion in AD 61. Unusually, this extensive site has not been disturbed by later developments, so archaeologists have been able to identify the full scale of the original settlement. Sadly, very little remains above ground, although in dry summers the grid pattern of the streets show up as brown lines in the grass. Most of the finds discovered during excavations in 1920s and 1930s are now in **Norwich Castle Museum**, but the riverside site is still worth visiting, especially if you have a vivid imagination.

POTTER HEIGHAM

Modern Potter Heigham, one of the liveliest of the Broadland boating centres, sprang up around the medieval bridge over the River Thurne, a low-arched structure with a clearance of only 7 foot at its highest, a notorious test for novice sailors. A pleasant excursion from Potter Heigham is a visit to **Horsey Mere**, about six miles to the east, and **Horsey Windpump** (both National Trust). From this early 20th century drainage mill, now restored and fully working, there are lovely views across the Mere. A circular walk follows the north side of Horsey Mere, passes another windmill, and returns through the village.

SANDRINGHAM

Sandringham House is the royal family's country retreat. Unlike the State Rooms at Windsor Castle and Buckingham Palace, where visitors marvel at the awesome trappings of majesty, at Sandringham they can savour the atmosphere of a family home. The rooms the visitor sees at Sandringham are those used by the royal family when in residence, complete with family portraits and photographs, and comfortable armchairs. Successive royal owners have furnished the house with an intriguing medley of the grand, the domestic and the unusual. Just across from the house, the old coach-houses and stables have been converted into a fascinating museum. There are some truly splendid royal vehicles here, including the first car bought by a member of the royal family - a 1900 Daimler - and an evocative series of old photographs depicting the life of the royal

Sandringham House

family at Sandringham from 1862 until Christmas 1951.

SHERINGHAM

Like so many other former fishing villages in England, Sheringham owes its transformation into a resort to the arrival of the railway. During the Edwardian peak years of rail travel, some 64 trains a day steamed into the station but the line became yet another victim of the Beeching closures of the 1960s. Devotees of steam trains joined together and by dint of great effort and enthusiasm managed to re-open the line in 1975 as the **North Norfolk Railway**, better known as **The Poppy Line**.

Just to the west of the town, at Upper Sheringham, footpaths lead to the lovely grounds of **Sheringham Park** (National Trust).

SNETTISHAM

Snettisham is best known nowadays for its spacious, sandy beaches and the **RSPB Bird Sanctuary**, both about two miles west of the village itself. But for centuries Snettisham was much more famous as a prime quarry for carrstone, an attractive soft-white building-block that provided the "light relief" for the walls of thousands of Georgian houses around the country, and for nearby Sandringham House.

SWAFFHAM

Swaffham's one-time claim to be the 'Montpellier of England' was justified by the abundance of handsome Georgian houses that used to surround the large, wedge-shaped market place. A good number still survive, along with the **Assembly Room** of 1817 where the quality would foregather for concerts, balls and soirees. The central focus of the market square is the elegant **Butter Cross** presented to the town by the Earl of Orford in 1783. It's not a cross at all but a classical lead-covered dome standing on eight columns and surmounted by a life-size statue of Ceres, the Roman goddess of agriculture, an appropriate symbol for this busy market town from which ten roads radiate out across the county. From the market place an avenue of limes leads to the quite outstanding Church of **St Peter & St Paul**, a 15th century masterpiece with one of the very best double hammerbeam roofs in the county, strikingly embellished with a host of angels, their wings widespread.

Market Cross, Swaffham

48

THETFORD

Some 2,000 years ago, Thetford may well have been the site of **Boadicea's Palace**. In the 1980s excavations for building development at Gallows Hill, north of the town, revealed an Iron Age enclosure. It is so extensive it may well have been the capital of the Iceni tribe which gave the Romans so much trouble. Certainly, the town's strategic location at the meeting of the Rivers Thet and Little Ouse made it an important settlement for centuries. At the time of the Domesday Book, 1086, Thetford was the sixth largest town in the country and the seat of the Bishop of East Anglia, with its own castle, mint and pottery.

Of the **Castle**, only the 80 foot motte remains, but it's worth climbing to the top of this mighty mound for the views across the town. Perhaps the most striking of the town's many fine old buildings is the **Ancient House** Museum in White Hart Street, a magnificent 15th century timber-framed house with superb carved oak ceilings. It houses the Tourist Information Centre and a museum where some of the most interesting exhibits are replicas of the Thetford Treasure, a 4th century hoard of gold and silver jewellery discovered as recently as 1979 by an amateur archaeologist with a metal detector.

Even older than the Ancient House is the 12th century **Cluniac Priory** (English Heritage), now mostly in ruins but with an impressive 14th century gatehouse still standing. Thetford's industrial heritage is vividly displayed in the **Burrell Steam Museum**, in Minstergate, which has full-size steam engines regularly in steam, re-created workshops and many examples of vintage agricultural machinery. The Museum tells the story of the Burrell Steam Company which formed the backbone of the town's industry from the late 18th to the early 20th centuries, their sturdy machines famous around the world.

To the west of the town stretch the 90 square miles of **Thetford Forest**, the most extensive lowland forest in Britain. The Forestry Commission began planting in 1922, and although the woodland is largely given over to conifers, with Scots and Corsican Pine and Douglas Fir predominating, oak, sycamore and beech can also be seen throughout. There is a particularly varied trail leading from the Forestry Commission Information Centre which has detailed information about this and other walks through the area.

On the edge of the forest, about two miles west of Thetford, are the ruins of **Thetford Warren Lodge**, built around 1400. At that time a huge area here was preserved for farming rabbits, a major element of the medieval diet. The vast warren was owned by the Abbot of Thetford Priory and it was he who built the Lodge for his gamekeeper. Still in the forest, reached by a footpath from the village of Santon Downham, are **Grimes Graves** (English Heritage), the earliest major industrial site to be discovered in Europe. At these unique Neolithic flint mines, Stone Age labourers extracted the materials for their sharp-edged axes and knives. It's a strange experience entering these 4,000 year old shafts which descend some 30 feet to an underground chamber. (The experience is even better if you bring your own high-powered torch.)

WEST RUNTON

West Runton's major tourist attraction is undoubtedly the **Norfolk Shire Horse Centre** where twice a day, during the season, these noble beasts are harnessed up and give a half-hour demonstration of the important role they played in agricultural life right up until the 1930s. They are the largest (19 hands/6 feet 4 inches high) and heaviest horses in the world, weighing more than a ton, and for generations were highly valued both as war-horses and draught animals. Several other heavy breeds, such as the Suffolk Punch, Clydesdale and Percheron, also have their home here, along with no fewer than nine different breeds of pony.

A couple of miles south of West Runton is one of Norfolk's grandest houses, **Felbrigg Hall** (National Trust).

WYMONDHAM

The exterior of **Wymondham Abbey** presents one of the oddest ecclesiastical buildings in the county, while the interior reveals one of the most glorious. The Abbey was founded in 1107 by the Benedictines, or Black Monks, as they were known from the colour of their habits. The superb hammerbeam roof is supported by 76 beautifully carved angels; there's an interesting 16th century tomb, of the last Abbot, in delicate terracotta work; and a striking modern memorial, a gilded and coloured reredos and tester, commemorating the local men who lost their lives in the First World War.

Railway buffs will want to visit Wymondham's historic **Railway Station**, built in 1845 on the Great Eastern's Norwich-Ely line. At its peak, the station and its section employed over 100 people. Still providing a rail link to Norwich, London and the Midlands, the station has been restored, and its buildings house a railway museum, restaurant and tea room, and a piano showroom.

50   Alby Horse Shoes

Cromer Road,
Erpingham, Norfolk
NR11 7QE
Tel: 01263 761378

Directions:

The inn is situated
next to Alby Crafts
on the A140
Norwich-Cromer
road, halfway
between Aylsham
and Cromer.

Alby Horse Shoes started life as a turnpike inn and maintains its tradition of hospitality in the enthusiastic and dedicated care of owners Richard and Margaret Rushmer, who have made many improvements to its decor and facilities. It's an excellent place to pause for a drink and a snack, to linger over a leisurely meal or to spend the night while touring this delightful part of the world. Four real ales are always on draught, including Admiral's Reserve from the local brewer Woodforde and Adnams Bitter, and an excellent range of food, much of it sourced from local suppliers, is served lunchtime and evening in the non-smoking dining room. The room is named after the painter Sir Alfred Munnings P.R.A., who stayed here in 1908 and painted local scenes. All appetites are catered for on menus that run from sandwiches and light bar snacks to burgers, Cromer crab and lobster, grills, chilli, the day's roast, vegetarian dishes and a wide variety of fish dishes served battered and deep-fried, poached or grilled.

The public bar has a pool table and dartboard, but in the lounge bar the locals also play two much more unusual games in twister and ring the bull. Twister is an early form of roulette, and only one other board is known to survive in the country; in ringing the bull, the players aim a bull's nose ring attached to a string to hook over a bull's horn set in the wall. Richard and Margaret are both keen classic car enthusiasts, and the pub hosts a very popular classic car rally complete with food and music. Bed and Breakfast accommodation is available in two double rooms, one with en suite bathroom, the other with private bathroom. The Alby Horseshoes has a lovely garden and ample car parking space at the side and rear.

Opening Hours: 11.30-2.30 & 6-11, Sat 11.30-11, Sun 12-10.30

Food: A la carte

Credit Cards: Mastercard, Visa

Accommodation: 2 double rooms (+1 for 2003). 1 en-suite and 2 with private bathrooms.

Facilities: Car park, garden

Entertainment: Traditional pub games

Local Places of Interest/Activities:
Alby Crafts, Aylsham (Blickling Hall, Bure Valley Railway) 5 miles, Cromer 7 miles

Internet/Website:
e-mail: info@albyhorseshoes.co.uk
website: www.albyhorseshoes.co.uk

The Banningham Crown   51

Church Road,
Banningham,
Nr Aylsham,
Norfolk
NR11 7DY
Tel: 01263 733534
Fax: 01263 733677

Directions:

Banningham lies
just off the B1145 3
miles northeast of
Aylsham (A140 then
B1145).

The Banningham Crown is an immaculate old country inn opposite the village green. Run since the early 1990s by the tireless Jeanette Feneron, it is everything a village local should be, serving the community as a social hub as well as a place to come for good food and drink, also as a Post Office - that's located at the far end of the bar and is open for business from 9 to 1 on Monday, Tuesday, Thursday and Friday. Open every lunchtime and every evening is the restaurant, where the chef insists on the freshest local ingredients for dishes that include oysters, lobsters and crab as well as excellent pasta dishes, curries and their infamous steak and kidney puddings. Sunday lunch is a popular occasion for all the family.

The Crown's private function room, with seats for up to 30, can cater for parties, birthdays, anniversaries and all sorts of special occasions, and menus can be tailored to suit individual requirements. The inn's owner is very active in raising funds for local good causes with various events including darts matches, football breakfasts and a Christmas draw. 2002 saw the tenth annual trad jazz festival, with several bands, a barbecue, a raffle and a church service. This is a great part of the world for walking, and the staff at the Crown have details of a number of attractive walks in the neighbourhood including Weavers Way. The towns of Aylsham and North Walsham are very close by, and Cromer is easily reached up the A140.

Opening Hours: 12-2.30 (Sun to 3.30) & 7-11 (Sat from 6.30, Sun to 10.30)

Food: A la carte & Bar snacks

Credit Cards: Mastercard, Visa, Switch.

Accommodation: None

Facilities: Car park, Post Office, function room for up to 30, Patio and gardens

Entertainment: Annual trad jazz festival in August

Local Places of Interest/Activities:
Aylsham 3 miles, North Walsham 3 miles, Weavers Way 1 mile, Craft centre 1 mile

52

The Bell

Bawburgh Road,
Marlingford,
Nr Norwich,
Norfolk NR9 5HX
Tel: 01603 880263
Fax: 01603 881313

Directions:

From the A47
Norwich-Dereham
road, turn left 2 miles
west of Norwich on
to the B1108. After
about 1½ miles turn
right on to minor
road signposted

Much altered and extended since being built 100 years ago, **The Bell** stands on a bend in the road in the village of Marlingford. The inn is run by John Lockett and Colleen Thomas, who provide visitors with a civilised, relaxed ambience for enjoying good food and drink. A large wood-burning stove in a brick alcove keeps the cold at bay in the L-shaped bar, where Adnams Best and Greene King Abbot are among the real ales on offer. The bar is a smoking alternative to the delightful, newly built non-smoking restaurant with seats for 50 and its own bar.

Food is a serious business here; the choice is unusually wide and interesting, and everything on the frequently changing menus is prepared to a commendably high standard. From a typical lunch menu come open sandwiches, game pie, Thai fish cakes and salads of shredded chicken and orange, or tofu and wild mushrooms. The main à la carte selection includes an equally varied and tempting choice, with many dishes unique to the Bell, and the vegetarian menu is one of the very best. The enjoyment level stays high to the end with desserts like chilled mango and passion fruit soufflé or steamed apricot and orange nutty pudding served with crème anglaise or vanilla mascarpone. Booking is definitely recommended for Sunday lunch, which features three roasts. The inn has ample parking and tables and chairs out in the garden; the bars and toilets are wheelchair accessible. Marlingford can be reached by a number of little roads running off the A47 between Norwich and Dereham.

Opening Hours: Mon-Thurs 5-11, Fri 4-11,
Sat 12-3 & 6-11, Sun 12-10.30

Food: A la carte

Credit Cards: All the major cards

Accommodation: None

Facilities: Car park, disabled access and
toilets

Entertainment: None

Local Places of Interest/Activities:
Norwich 5 miles

The Black Swan 53

The Street,
Little Dunham,
Nr Swaffham,
Norfolk
PE32 2DG
Tel: 01760 722200

Directions:
Little Dunham lies
5 miles northeast of
Swaffham off the
A47.

Christine Bowen and Paul Tucker are maintaining a long tradition of hospitality at the **Black Swan**, which stands in the centre of a pleasant little village near Swaffham. Flower tubs stand in a colourful row outside the front of the pub, which retains much of the period character of its 17th century origins. The bar is a favourite local meeting place, where the regulars gather for a chat and a glass or two of one of the several real ales that are always on tap. The choice includes Greene King IPA and Abbot Ale and frequently changing guests, and there's also a good range of other draught and bottle beers, lagers, cider, wines and spirits.

The original barns and stables have been sensitively converted into a comfortable and charming restaurant, where the menu offers a good variety of wholesome, freshly prepared dishes. Fish and chips is the Friday speciality, and there's always a good selection of vegetarian dishes. Food is served Tuesday to Friday lunchtime and evening and all day Saturday and Sunday. The bar only is open from 7.00pm on Mondays. Pool darts and cribbage are played in the bar, and there are occasional live music evenings. For outdoor types, good walks, a nine-hole golf course and excellent trout fishing are available nearby, and among the places of interest to the visitor in the vicinity are the evocative ruins of Castle Acre Priory, the Village Museum at Litcham and the museums and marvellous 15th century Church of St Peter and St Paul at Swaffham.

Opening Hours: 7-11 Mon, 12-3 & 6.30-11 Tue-Fri, all day Sat & Sun

Food: Traditional home cooked cuisine

Credit Cards: All the major cards

Accommodation: None

Facilities: Car park, patio with tables in summer.

Entertainment: Occasional Live music

Local Places of Interest/Activities: Fishing, golf

Internet/Website:
e-mail: chris-paul@supanet.com

54

The Bluebell

Holt Road, Langham,
Norfolk NR25 7BX
Tel: 01328 830502

Directions:

The Bluebell is in the centre of Langham, on the B1158 2 miles inland from the A149 at Blakeney.

In the centre of a small village two miles inland from the A149 at Blakeney, the **Bluebell** has a long tradition of hospitality. Continuity is a strong point here, and the inn has had only three families holding the licence in its 400-year history. The current incumbents are Pat and Bridget Newman and their son Shaun. In the comfortable and inviting ambience of the bar, the decor features RAF memorabilia, recalling the time when Langham was a wartime air base. Shaun is the experienced and talented chef, and his menu of freshly prepared food is served in a non-smoking dining area. The choice caters for all appetites, from sandwiches, jacket potatoes and light snacks to battered cod, salmon steak, Yorkshire pud filled with chilli or curry, roast duck, steak, kidney & Guinness pie and grilled steaks, gammon and pork chop. There's a choice of vegetarian main courses, a separate dessert menu and a takeaway menu that includes pizzas (lunchtime and evening) and fish & chips (all day Friday).

Meals on the premises are complemented by a good selection of keg and cask ales, including Greene King IPA, and a variety of old and new world wines. Facilities include a toilet with disabled access, a baby changing area and an ATM cash machine. Pub games, both traditional (darts, pool, crib, dominoes, shove ha'penny) and modern (fruit and quiz machines), are played at this lively pub, which has a great fund-raising record - the East Anglian Air Ambulance is among the major beneficiaries. This part of Norfolk is classified as an Area of Outstanding Natural Beauty, and apart from the scenery the local attractions include the shrines at Walsingham; the bird sanctuary at Blakeney Point; the horse-drawn bus at Holt; and the steam-hauled Poppy Line that runs from Holt to Sheringham.

Opening Hours: 11-3 & 7-11, Fri 11-11, Sat 11-4 & 7-11, Sun 12-4.30 & 7-10.30

Food: A la carte + takeaway

Credit Cards: Amex, Mastercard, Visa

Accommodation: None

Facilities: Car park

Entertainment: Traditional pub games and varied live music evenings

Local Places of Interest/Activities:
Blakeney 2 miles

Internet/Website:
e-mail: newmanp@btconnect.com

The Crown

55

Lynn Road, Gayton,
Nr King's Lynn,
Norfolk PE32 1PA
Tel/Fax:
   01553 636252

Directions:

Gayton is on the
B1145 4 miles east of
King's Lynn.

After a long association with **The Crown**, including many years as a customer, Felicity Atherton took over the reins in March 1999. The building dates from the 13th century and first served as a home for stonemasons working on the village church; it later became a stopping place on the King's Lynn-Norwich coaching run, and remains today a great place to pause for hospitality and refreshment, as well as a popular destination for food. Set back from the road, its cheerful green and white frontage adorned with flowers, the inn is immensely appealing even from the outside, and the bars and restaurant have the traditional look and charm of the classic English inn, with beams, open fires, candle light, old photographs and a collection of china plates.

The bar snack menu, available every lunchtime and evening, offers soup, sandwiches made with freshly baked bloomer bread, and all-time favourites like burgers, scampi, ham & eggs and home-made steak & kidney pie. The evening menu is served from 7 to 9 Sunday to Thursday and from 6.30 to 9.30 on Friday and Saturday and provides a mouthwatering choice that changes with the seasons and the availability of the best produce. Some dishes are familiar - garlic mushrooms, chicken provençale, steaks - while others are more unusual, such as bacon-topped halloumi or Mongolian lamb. And Christmas pudding is usually available all year! As well as a mecca for food-lovers, the Crown is a magnet for real ale fans, with a wide choice of well-kept ales including Greene King XX Mild and IPA, Ruddles County, Abbot and Old Speckled Hen. The Crown provides diverse regular entertainment, including jazz and folk music evenings and quizzes. Children are very welcome, and there's good access (including toilets) for visitors in wheelchairs. There's also a large garden where you can enjoy a drink in the summer months.

Opening Hours: 11.30-2.30 (Sat 11-3) & 6-11 (from 5.30 Fri), Sun 12-3 & 7-10.30. Open all day Sat & Sun in July & August

Food: A la carte; buffet lunch hot in winter, cold in summer

Credit Cards: All the major cards

Accommodation: None

Facilities: Car park, disabled facilities incl toilet

Entertainment: Regular quizzes, folk music 1st Sun of month, jazz 3rd Sun of month

Local Places of Interest/Activities: King's Lynn

Internet/Website:
e-mail: crownath2wf@supanet.com

56 The Crown At Colkirk

Crown Road, Colkirk,
Nr Fakenham,
Norfolk NR21 7AA
Tel: 01328 862172
Fax: 01328 863196

Directions:
Colkirk is located 1½
miles south of
Fakenham off the
B1146.

Right at the centre of the delightful, peaceful village of Colkirk, the **Crown** is a comfortable, traditional country pub with a history going back 300 years. Behind the redbrick facade, the two bars are bright, convivial spots where locals and visitors from further afield meet for a chat and a drink, perhaps a glass of Greene King's IPA or Abbot Ale or one of the frequently changing guest ales, or one of the many wines that are available by the glass. Proprietors Roger and Bridget Savell, here since October 2001, run the place with friendly efficiency, and their golden retriever Morse is always there with a welcoming wag. The Lions Club meets here on the first evening of each month, and the next day brings a gathering of classic MGs and their owners.

Food is served every day in the bars and restaurant, with a wide choice of home-cooked dishes from the standard menu and the specials board. Food orders are taken between 12 and 1.30 and from 7 to 9, and bookings are accepted for Sunday lunch. The weekday light lunch menu offers baguettes, ploughman's, paté, scampi, garlic mushrooms and salads, while main courses on the standard menu and specials board might include grilled skate wing, plaice with prawns, chicken fillet in ginger sauce, fruity pork curry and minute, fillet or sirloin steaks. There are always vegetarian main courses, and the meal ends with home-made puddings and a range of coffees. Children are welcome, and dogs are allowed in the bar area; there's a patio area, and a lawned garden and car park at the rear. Nearby Fakenham stages competitive National Hunt racing, and other attractions in the area include Pensthorpe Waterfowl Park.

Opening Hours: 11-2.30 & 6-11, Sun 12-3 & 7-10.30

Food: A la carte

Credit Cards: Diners, Mastercard, Visa

Accommodation: None

Facilities: Car park

Entertainment: Occasional live music (jazz, R&B)

Local Places of Interest/Activities:
Fakenham 1½ miles, Raynham Hall 2 miles, Pensthorpe Waterfowl Park 5 miles

Internet/Website:
e-mail: thecrown@paston.co.uk

The Dolphin Inn   57

Bury Road,
Wortham,
Nr Diss, Norfolk
IP22 1PX
Tel: 01379 898401
Fax: 01379 898412

Directions:
Wortham is located
4 miles west of Diss
just off the A143.

On the village green at Wortham, the **Dolphin Inn** has been dispensing hospitality since the early years of the 19th century. For the past six years it has been in the care of Cheryl and Peter Woods, who are triumphantly maintaining its position as the social hub of the village. Visitors can be sure of a particularly friendly and genuine welcome, and the spacious flagstoned bar is a great spot to relax with good conversation and a glass of well-kept real ale. The walls of the bar are hung with photographs of the village in days gone by and the pub's sports teams. There are separate pool and children's rooms, an area set for dining and a 25-cover restaurant that overlooks the garden.

Peter is one of the chefs who provide an exceptional choice of home-cooked dishes from both the traditional and the modern British repertoires. Scampi with chips and salad, steak and ale pie and lasagne are enduring pub classics, while representing the contemporary cuisine are Thai tempura prawns with a sweet and sour sauce, or chicken breast stir-fry with black bean sauce served on a bed of egg noodles. There are always several vegetarian main courses and a children's menu, and sandwiches and jacket potatoes cater for quicker, snackier lunches. Special diets can usually be accommodated with a little notice. The fine food is complemented by an excellent cellar. But the Dolphin's appeal doesn't end with food and drink, as it has a strong sporting connection. The village football, tennis, cricket and bowls teams use the pub as a regular meeting place and there are four resident pool teams. Friday brings live music performances (normally R&B), and in winter there's a quiz on the first Tuesday of every month.

Opening Hours: 11-3 & 6-11, Sat all day, Sun 12-3 & 7-11

Food: A la carte

Credit Cards: Diners, Mastercard, Visa

Accommodation: None

Facilities: Car park, cashback service

Entertainment: Live music Friday, quiz 1st Tuesday in the month in winter

Local Places of Interest/Activities:
Bressingham Steam Museum and Gardens 3 miles, Diss 4 miles

58 The Fox & Hounds

The Street, Lyng, Norfolk NR9 5AL
Tel: 01603 872316
Fax: 01603 879030

Directions:

Lyng is about 10 miles northwest of Norwich signposted off the A1067.

On the main street of the charming village of Lyng, the **Fox & Hounds** dates back almost 300 years. It was taken over in June 2002 by local couple Adam and Amanda Quinton, who generate a very warm and pleasant atmosphere in the beamed, tile-floored bar, where horse brasses and photographs of the pub contribute to the traditional look and feel of the place. Real ales on tap include Adnams Best Bitter, Woodfordes Wherry and both IPA and Abbot from Greene King. In the bar or in the separate restaurants (smoking and non-smoking available) freshly prepared dishes make up a very appealing and wide-ranging menu, supplemented by daily specials. Steaks are top of the list of favourites and the house specialities include various fish and vegetarian options. The children's menu treats children as budding adults rather than babies - a rare and welcome change. On Thursdays Senior Citizens, as well as every-body else, get a special lunchtime deal, whilst on Mondays you can get a half price 16oz steak with all the trimmings. Wednesday sees a Chinese style menu and Pizzas can be cooked to eat in or take-away until closing time any day of the week.

Pool, darts and board games are played in the bar, and lone visitors will find either someone to chat to or plenty of things to read, so they won't even be tempted to use their mobile phones - something that will definitely please the landlords! A separate games room is available for the under-14s, so Mum and Dad can share a quiet drink in the children free bar area. A quiz is held on the first Thursday of every month and a local Folk club meet in the bar on the first Wednesday. The Wensum Valley is a lovely part of the county, very popular with walkers and anglers, and for a break from the outdoor action, there's nowhere more agreeable than the Fox & Hounds, where even the ghost (of an old-time landlady) is friendly.

Opening Hours: 12-3 & 5-11 Mon-Fri; Sat all day; Sun 12-4 & 7-10.30

Food: A la carte + snack menu, served 12-2 and 6-9.30

Credit Cards: Diners, Mastercard, Visa

Accommodation: None

Facilities: Car park, pool room, large beer garden

Entertainment: Quiz night, Folk night, live music

Local Places of Interest/Activities: Walking, fishing, golf, Wild-life Park and Dinosaur Park, Dereham 7 miles, Norwich 10 miles

The George & Dragon   59

2 The Street,
Thurton,
Nr Norwich,
Norfolk
NR14 6AL
Tel/Fax:
*   01508 480242*

Directions:

The inn is
situated on the
A146 8 miles
from Norwich.

Deep in the Norfolk countryside, the **George & Dragon** enjoys the best of both worlds - a peaceful, picturesque location combined with easy access on the main A146 north to Norwich and south to Beccles and Lowestoft. The black and white frontage is topped by roofs tiled in red or slate grey, and the inside is pleasingly traditional, with lots of black beams and a wood-panelled bar counter. Open lunchtime and evening, and all day at the weekend, the inn has excellent hosts in Bob and Mary Shaw, who since 1995 have been welcoming their loyal regular customers, motorists taking a break from their journey and tourists visiting the nearby Norfolk Broads.

There are always at least two real ales and plenty of lagers for quenching thirsts generated by walks in country lanes, and from the kitchen comes a full range of home-cooked food, with salads and vegetarian dishes as well as daily changing fish and meat specials and traditional Sunday roasts. The inn has a beer garden, and overnight parking for caravans is available. Strolling in the country lanes is a popular pastime hereabouts, and the numerous little villages in the area include Poringland, which is surrounded by mustard fields whose summer glow is said in local folklore to shine all the way up to the Moon. Colmans Mustard Shop is one of the many places to be visited on a trip to Norwich, an easy drive up the A146.

Opening Hours: 11-2.30 & 6-11, Sat 11-11, Sun 12-10.30

Food: A la carte

Credit Cards: None

Accommodation: None

Facilities: Caravan park

Entertainment: None

Local Places of Interest/Activities: Norfolk Broads 3 miles, Norwich 8 miles

60   The Greyhound

The Green,
Hickling,
Norfolk
NR12 0YA
Tel: 01692 598306

Directions:

Hickling is about
10 miles north of
Great Yarmouth,
signposted off the
A149 just beyond
Potter Heigham.

The Greyhound dates back at least as far as 1735, and hosts Tony and Debi have worked hard over the past eight years to see that none of the inn's old world charm is lost. Visitors to the inn enjoy the very best of hospitality combined with excellent food and drink and very comfortable accommodation. Chef Anthony Escot Francklin and his brigade produce food for every occasion and every appetite, from bar snacks to a full à la carte menu featuring the best seafood and prime locally sourced meat and poultry. Theme nights are a regular attraction, and the team can cater admirably for private dinner parties and special occasions.

    The inn's resident grey hound is a delightful miniature schnauzer called Bertie, and Bertie's Place immediately behind the inn can accommodate up to six guests in four rooms with tv, trouser press, hairdryer and tea/coffee making facilities. Breakfast is served at a very civilised hour, and in the summer months it can be taken on the patio overlooking the award-winning gardens. The inn is in one of Norfolk's most popular tourist spots, but although the little lanes get very crowded in high season, it's also easy to escape the throngs and enjoy the delights of the waterways and the countryside. Hickling Broad, right on the doorstep, is the largest and wildest of the Broads, and has 1,200 acres of nature reserve where visitors can enjoy the scenery and the rich abundance of wildlife; the keen eyed might spot the bittern, the swallowtail butterfly and the rare Norfolk hawker dragonfly. Fishing is another popular activity hereabouts, and the Greyhound's bar is a favourite spot to talk about the day's sport over a glass of Adnams or Greene King IPA.

Opening Hours: 12-11, Sun to 10.30

Food: A la carte + bar snacks

Credit Cards: Mastercard, Visa.

Accommodation: 4 rooms (1 en suite)

Facilities: Car park

Entertainment: None

Local Places of Interest/Activities:
Hickling Broad and Nature Reserve, Horsey Mere and Wind Pump 4 miles, Potter Heigham 4 miles

The Hare & Hounds 61

Hempstead Road,
Hempstead,
Nr Holt,
Norfolk NR25 6LD
Tel: 01263 712329
Fax: 01263 711962

Directions:

From Holt follow signs for Hempstead Industrial Estate for 3 miles into village. 1st right, then 1st right again.

When Norwich native Jonathan Bruton bought the **Hare & Hounds** at the end of 2000 it has been closed for 18 months, and it re-opened in May 2001 after he had overseen a total refurbishment programme. The brick-and-flint pub was built in 1640 as an ale house on the Blickling Estate and underwent many alterations down the years. Inside, the scene is one of classic old-world charm, with beams, inglenooks, a wood-burning stove and upholstered milk churns as bar stools. Outside is a beer garden with a children's play area. The Hare & Hounds is a free house, and regularly changing guest ales provide alternatives to the resident Adnams and Woodforde's brews.

There are seats for 40 + in the two non-smoking dining areas, where the daily changing blackboard menus feature home-cooked dishes based on fresh fish (sardines, plaice, cod, trout, salmon and red mullet all make regular appearances) and locally supplied meat, game and poultry. Traditional desserts round off a meal in style. The pub is well worth seeking out for its food, but it also an excellent base for touring this very pleasant part of the county. Guest accommodation comprises three en suite rooms - a double, a twin and a generously sized family room - and a converted barn providing self-catering facilities for up to 6. The nearby town of Holt will reward an hour or two's stroll, and other places of interest in the locality include the East Anglian Falconry Centre at Bodham and the evocative ruins of Baconsthorpe Castle.

Opening Hours: 11-4 & 6-11, Sun 12-4 & 6.30-10.30

Food: A la carte

Credit Cards: Diners, Mastercard, Visa.

Accommodation: 3 en suite rooms + self-catering in former barn

Facilities: Car park, children's play area

Entertainment: None

Local Places of Interest/Activities:
Holt 3 miles, Baconsthorpe Hall 2 miles, North Norfolk Railway 2 miles, Blickling Hall 6 miles, Baconsthorpe Castle

62   The Kings Head

The Turnpike,
Norwich Road,
Ashwellthorne,
Norfolk
NR16 1EL
Tel: 01508 489419

Directions:

The inn is situated
off the B1113 about
8 miles south of
Norwich.

A pair of cottages built in the 1600s later became a turnpike where horses on the Norwich coaching run were changed and rested. For the past nine years of its long history the **Kings Head** has been run by a Norfolk family, Ian Robinson, his mother Pat and his sister Elaine. Baskets and pots of flowers adorn the smart cream-painted frontage, where picnic benches are set out in the summer and inside, the long beamed bar is roomy and comfortable. There's an area for playing pool and darts, and two separate non-smoking dining areas. The family have a friendly greeting for visitors, a greeting that is also offered, perhaps a little more cautiously, by Henry, a 50-year-old green parrot with a serious outlook and a fairly fruity vocabulary.

The choice of real ales served in the bar is varied and interesting, with frequently changing guests accompanying the Woodforde's resident, and the girls prepare a good range of traditional pub food. Daily chalkboard specials add to the choice, and among the most popular orders are an all-day breakfast and a very tasty, very hearty steamed beef pudding. Sandwiches and bar snacks are available for quicker or lighter bites. The family propose to add guest accommodation in the shape of a family room with a shower and full facilities; this is due to come on stream early in 2003, and when it does the Kings Head will become an excellent base for touring this pleasant part of Norfolk. Norwich is easily reached up the B1113, but even closer to the pub are Attleborough, where the Church of St Mary is one of the finest in the county, and Wymondham, with its splendid twin-towered abbey, heritage museum and historic railway station.

Opening Hours: 11-11, Sun 12-3 & 7-10.30

Food: A la carte and snacks

Credit Cards: Mastercard, Visa, Electron

Accommodation: Family room planned for early 2003

Facilities: Car park

Entertainment: None

Local Places of Interest/Activities:
Wymondham 4 miles, Norwich 8 miles

The Kings Head 63

Harts Lane, Bawburgh,
Nr Norwich,
Norfolk NR9 3LS
Tel: 01603 744977
Fax: 01603 744990

Directions:

Bawburgh lies about 4 miles west of Norwich. From the A47 Norwich southern by-pass turn left on to the B1108 and almost immediately take minor road on the right marked Bawburgh.

Since arriving at the **Kings Head** in 1984, Anton Wimmer has made this grand old coaching inn one of the leading food pubs in the region, attracting a broad cross-section of the local and not-so-local populace. The front part of the inn is a solid red-painted building, while behind it is a larger and very handsome extension painted immaculate white, with a steeply raked tiled roof. Inside, solid pine floors and doors underline the quality of the place, and the bars, which have lots of intimate little corners, boast three huge feature fireplaces which burn logs throughout the winter; in the summer the large garden and patio come into their own.

Michael Hunt's (head chef) menus offer a wide range of dishes classic and less familiar, and his steak & kidney pudding is just one of many which have earned him his lofty reputation and a number of prestigious awards. Other choices might include Duo of duck, spring rolls, prawn corn cakes, mango salsa, chilli dipping sauce, Stilton & pickled pear cheesecake, lime and wholegrain mustard dressing, organic Salmon, courgette and leek linguine, orange fish cream sauce, crab ravioli, flash fried calves liver, creamed leeks, bacon and black pudding potato cake, red wine sauce, saffron and white wine poached pears, hazelnut shortbread and blackcurrant mousse.Lunchers with no time to spare can phone, fax or e-mail their order by 10am and the food will be ready at the table as soon as they arrive. Anton and his staff keep the Kings Head in tip-top condition, and there are plans to widen its appeal still further by creating overnight guest accommodation. When these rooms come on stream, the inn will become a super base not only for enjoying more of Michael's splendid cooking but also for touring the area. Norwich is only a few minutes' drive away, and all around the inn are delightful little villages to explore and some excellent country walks. The inn, which hosts a live music evening every other Monday, has a most unusual amenity in the shape of four squash courts.

Opening Hours: 11-11.

Food: A la carte

Credit Cards: Mastercard, Visa.

Accommodation: Planned

Facilities: Car park

Entertainment: Live music every other Monday

Local Places of Interest/Activities: Norwich 4 miles

Internet/Website:
e-mail: anton@kingshead-bawburgh.co.uk
website: www.kingshead-bawburgh.co.uk

64 The Kings Head

Wroxham Road,
Coltishall, Norfolk
Tel: 01603 737426

Directions:

Coltishall is about 7 miles north of Norwich. Take the A1151 from Norwich and turn left on to the B1354 towards Coltishall.

Built in the 17th century and much extended down the years, the **Kings Head** enjoys a splendid setting beside the River Bure, with the houseboats and river craft passing by at the end of the garden. The pub is run by Kevin and Sue Gardner, who have made it one of the most popular eating places in the area. Kevin is passionate about food - he writes a foodie column in the local paper - and food-lovers arriving hungry at the Kings Head can be sure that they will leave well-fed and contented. Freshness and quality are evident throughout Kevin's repertoire, and the choice changes regularly to reflect the pick of the season's produce. Seafood and steaks are always in demand, and particular favourites include herring roes, lemon sole, duck and venison.

The 70-seat restaurant is open lunchtime and evening seven days a week except for Sunday nights from January to March with further space available upstairs at weekends. The bar has plenty of well placed seats and a fisherman's theme - in a glass case is one of the biggest pikes you'll ever see, a monster weighing in at more than 50 pounds. The inn has outside tables and an enormous car park, and for visitors staying overnight there are four letting bedrooms, two of them with en suite facilities. Coltishall is a charming place of leafy lanes, a village green, elegant Dutch-gabled houses and a thatched church - and, of course, the river. One of its more unusual attractions is the Ancient Lime Kiln, a protected building of finely finished brickwork, constructed in a style unique to Norfolk.

Opening Hours: 11-3 & 6-11, Sun 12-3 & 6-10.30

Food: A la carte

Credit Cards: Mastercard, Visa.

Accommodation: 4 rooms (2 en suite)

Facilities: Car park

Entertainment: None

Local Places of Interest/Activities:
Redwings Horse Sanctuary 2 miles, Bure Valley Railway 2 miles, Wroxham 2 miles, Norwich 7 miles

The Kings Head

Market Place,
New Buckenham,
Nr Norwich,
Norfolk
NR16 2AN
Tel: 01953 860487

Directions:

New Buckenham is
on the B1113 about
15 miles south of
Norwich. From Diss
(7 miles) take the
A1066, then right
on to B1077 to
junction with
B1113

The Kings Head is a cosy country pub with a history going back at least as far as 1645. The oldest records in the village show it as a stopover on the popular London-Norwich coaching run, and today it remains a haven of hospitality and a delightful place to take a break on a journey. Real ales at this free house include Adnams, Bass and a frequently changing guest, and landlady Jackie Watts keeps her customers happy and well fed with her excellent home cooking. Traditional favourites are the backbone of the menu, with a splendid steak & kidney pudding among the most popular dishes.

Some of the regulars here are ace cribbage players, and the pub's team has carried off many prizes in local competitions. Jackie is soon to add another string to her bow with the coming on stream of guest Bed & Breakfast accommodation. Two doubles and a single are due to be available from the spring of 2003, at which time the Kings Head will become a very agreeable base for exploring the local sights. The Buckenhams, Old and New, have some very attractive cottages and houses, and the Church of St Mary in nearby Attleborough is one of the very finest in the county, with some beautiful vaulting and paintings of saints. Diss, about eight miles away, is a particularly attractive old market town, and the village of Bressingham has triple magnets in the form of superb gardens, a steam railway and the Dad's Army National Collection.

Opening Hours: 12-2.30 (Sat & Sun to 3) and 7-11

Food: A la carte

Credit Cards: None

Accommodation: 3 rooms planned for spring 2003

Facilities: Patio garden

Entertainment: Award winning crib team

Local Places of Interest/Activities:
Attleborough 6 miles, Bressingham 6 miles, Diss 8 miles

66

The Lacon Arms

Beach Road,
Hemsby,
Nr Great Yarmouth,
Norfolk NR29 4HS
Tel: 01493 730806
Fax: 01493 733930

Directions:

Hemsby is a small
coastal resort about
8 miles north of
Great Yarmouth.
A149 then B1159.

1934 saw the opening of the **Lacon Arms**, a classic redbrick inn with of considerable size and character. Inside and out, the place is kept in immaculate order by Steve and Beryl Norris, who have worked tirelessly since arriving in the summer of 2001 to enhance the appeal of the inn to both local residents and occasional visitors. Hemsby is an agreeable little family holiday resort with all the usual seaside attractions, and the Lacon Arms provides an excellent place to escape from the fun of the fair and relax. The big open-plan interior, with a comfortable ambience of carpets, curtains and fine dark oak, also has plenty of space for diners. The menus offer a well-balanced, well-priced selection of dishes served lunchtime and evening seven days a week.

Competition is fierce for custom, and with its welcoming atmosphere and its good food and drink, the Lacon Arms is well able to hold its own. With the traditional seaside attractions close at hand, the pub needs no diversions beyond its good hospitality, but the winter quizzes keep local wits sharp, and the cashback service is very handy for families planning to splash out in the funfairs. Hemsby, which straddles the B1159, is right on the coast, but for those who prefer their amusement inland, the Village Experience at Burgh St Margaret has a wealth of attractions for all the family. Even closer is one of the deep broads, Ormesby Broad, with its diverse flora and fauna. In 2003 the Lacon Arms will be closed from January 1st to February 10th.

Opening Hours: 11-11, Sun 12-10.30

Food: A la carte and Home cooked style menu

Credit Cards: Mastercard, Visa

Accommodation: None

Facilities: Car park, cashback service

Entertainment: Quiz nights in winter

Local Places of Interest/Activities:
Caister 5 miles, Great Yarmouth 8 miles

Internet/Website:
e-mail: steve1n@hotmail.com
website: www.laconarms.co.uk

The Lobster 67

*13 High Street,
Sheringham,
Norfolk NR26 8JP
Tel: 01263 822716
Fax: 01263 824560*

Directions:
The inn is in the
centre of
Sheringham, 5 miles
west of Cromer on
the A148.

Fifty yards from the beach in the centre of Sheringham, the **Lobster** has a long history as the social hub of the town. Built as a coaching inn in the 1800s, it remains a busy, lively place that appeals both to the local residents and holidaymakers. It's a home from home for the lifeboat crew, and the walls in the bar are adorned with photographs of the lifeboat and Air Sea Rescue, along with ship's lanterns, lobster pots and other nautical paraphernalia. The inn has a comfortable beamed lounge area and public bar with a pool table and darts. The non-smoking room is accessible to wheelchairs. Proprietor Alistair Deans, an accomplished and experienced chef, has taken the food at the Lobster to new heights; he specialises in traditional English cuisine, and as far as possible the ingredients are sourced from the region.

That naturally features the renowned local lobster and crab and also includes organic free-range eggs and the best of beef, lamb, poultry and vegetables. An all-day menu runs from sandwiches and ploughman's lunches to crab (baked or in a salad), chilli and smoked salmon tortilla, and in the evening the full menu covers a good selection of fish, meat and vegetarian dishes that includes excellent steaks. There's a special children's menu, too, and a Sunday carvery. To complement the fine food are cask conditioned ales (CAMRA member) and well-chosen, well-priced wines from old and new worlds. The patio and garden are ablaze with flowers in the summer, when Sunday hog roast barbecues take place by a large tented canopy. Pool and darts are played in the bar, and Sunday afternoon brings on the live folk or country music at this most cheerful and sociable of pubs.

Opening Hours: 11.30-11, Sat 11-11, Sun 12-10.30

Food: A la carte & bar snacks

Credit Cards: None

Accommodation: None

Facilities: Car park adjacent

Entertainment: Live music Sun pm

Local Places of Interst/Activities:
Beach 50 yards, North Norfolk Railway (Poppy Line), Sheringham Park (NT), Cromer 5 miles

68

The Natterjack

Chapel Road, Foxley West,
Nr Dereham,
Norfolk NR20 4AH
Tel: 01362 688304

Directions:
Foxley lies just off the A1067 about 8 miles north of Dereham, 12 miles northwest of Norwich. From Dereham, B1147 to Bawdeswell, left on to A1067, first right to Foxley.

Ex-Cunard Line man David Marshall knows all there is to know about customer service, and the **Natterjack**, which he runs with his wife Denise, has earned a great reputation for its hospitality and the best of pub dining. Dating from the 1960s, but blending well into the quaint village scene, the pub is kept in immaculate order, and the carpeted bar with its solid oak counter is a perfect place to unwind with a drink before settling down to enjoy Denise's high-class cuisine. Devilled whitebait, Thai-style prawns or Camembert fritters with a cranberry compote could start the meal, followed perhaps by ham 'n' eggs, lasagne, a steak or a seafood platter.

Among the all-time favourites are the super, flavoured-packed pies - steak & kidney or chicken, ham and mushroom. Vegetarians are not forgotten, and the enjoyment level stays high to the end with desserts such as jam sponge pudding, tira mi su or lemon meringue ice box gateau. The Sunday carvery is always guaranteed to bring a good crowd. Food for thought is provided every other Thursday in winter, when the Natterjack hosts a quiz evening. The pub, which is closed all day Monday, lies in a small community just a few yards off the A1067 Norwich-Fakenham road. Close by is a great attraction for lovers of nature and the open air: the Norfolk Wildlife Trust's Foxley Wood is the county's largest ancient woodland, thought to be 6,000 years old and noted for its majestic oaks and a wide variety of flora and fauna.

Opening Hours: 12-2 (Fri, Sat & Sun to 3) & 6-11. Closed Monday

Food: A la carte

Credit Cards: Mastercard, Visa.

Accommodation: None

Facilities: Car park

Entertainment: None

Local Places of Interest/Activities:
Foxley Wood 2 miles, Dereham 8 miles, Fakenham 10 miles

The New Inn · 69

Fakenham Road,
Beetley,
Nr Dereham,
Norfolk NR20 4BT
Tel: 01362 860392
Fax: 01362 869133

Directions:

Beetley is located left off the B1110 4 miles north of Dereham.

Built in the early 19th century and later extended, the **New Inn** is located in the little village of Beetley, a short drive north of Dereham. Since early 2001 the inn has been in the capable hands of Paul and Jane Painter; they enjoy running the place and intend to be here for many years, which is good news not just for the regular customers but for anyone dropping in for a drink or a meal. (Paul is also the lead assessor in a firm of quality assurance consultants.) The inn has a very pleasant and welcoming home-from-home feel, making it an excellent place to relax and unwind. Adjoining the main lounge is a neat non-smoking restaurant where food is served every lunchtime and every evening. The full-time chef cooks a good variety of mainly traditional English dishes and takes great pride in the presentation as well as the preparation of the food.

The inn has ample off-road parking and a garden with a children's play area. Once a month it hosts an evening of live music. Beetley is a small community lying north of Dereham between the B1110 and B1146. It's a great area for country walks, and there's also excellent fishing nearby. A mile or so south of the inn is one of the region's major attractions, the Norfolk Rural Life Museum. Besides the many exhibits of Norfolk life over the past 150 years, the site has 50 acres of countryside run as a 1920s farm. A little further south is Dereham, whose sights include the imposing Church of St Nicholas and the neighbouring St Withburga's Well.

Opening Hours: 12-3 & 6-11, Sun 12-3 & 7-10.30

Food: A la carte

Credit Cards: None

Accommodation: None

Facilities: Car park

Entertainment: Live music once a month

Local Places of Interest/Activities:
Gressenhall 1½ miles, Dereham 4 miles

70   The New Inn

Norwich Road,
Roughton,
Norfolk
Tel:
  01263 761389
Fax:
  01263 768868

Directions:

The inn is on
the A140 4 miles
south of Cromer.

The New Inn is a big bold pub dating from the late 1800s. Easy to find on the A140 Norwich Road south of Cromer, it offers a very agreeable, traditional ambience in which to unwind with a glass of beer in the public bar or enjoy a leisurely meal in the comfortable dining area. The well-established hosts are Sean and Tina Crampsie, both excellent cooks, whose respective Irish and Eastern origins enable the inn to offer a particularly interesting choice of dishes. Simple pub grub will please traditionalists, while the more adventurous will look for something more exotic from the Far East. Typical of Tina's interesting, often innovative dishes is Serhaban, pan-fried duck with redcurrants and kiwi fruit.

   Food is served lunchtime and evening seven days a week, and the 48 seats include 16 in a non-smoking section. This is the sort of food which can easily become addictive, and for those who need a really good fix, the best solution is to take one of the two guest bedrooms and take the chance to explore the region between meals. And there's no shortage of things to do and places to see. Cromer, a short drive up the A140, is a charming fishing port turned holiday resort, and south of Cromer, in a designated Area of Outstanding Natural Beauty, is the National Trust's splendid Felbrigg Hall with its art treasures and wonderful gardens.

Opening Hours: 12-11, Sun to 10.30

Food: A la carte (traditional + oriental)

Credit Cards: Amex, Mastercard, Visa

Accommodation: 2 rooms sharing facilities

Facilities: Car park

Entertainment: Karaoke nights in winter

Local Places of Interest/Activities:
Cromer 4 miles, Fellbrigg Hall 4 miles.

The Old Hall Inn　　71

Coast Road,
Sea Palling,
Norfolk
NR12 0TZ
Tel: 01692 598323
Fax: 01692598822

Directions:

Sea Palling lies on
the Norfolk coast.
From Norwich, take
the A1151 through
Wroxham and
Hoveton to Stalham;
turn left on to B
road to Sea Palling.

The Old Hall Inn is a substantial building just minutes from the shore in the tiny coastal village of Sea Palling. Dating back to the middle of the 17th century, the inn has a solidly, reassuringly traditional look both from the outside and within. The bar and lounge provide plenty of uncluttered space for enjoying a drink and something from the menu of home-cooked dishes; these could be anything from a light lunchtime snack to a full meal centred round one of the favourites, perhaps liver & bacon or a hearty steak & ale pie. A couple of tables and chairs are set out under a canopy at the front, while at the back of the pub is a delightful beer garden; there's also ample car parking space behind the pub.

The Old Hall Inn is run by Tony Etheridge and Liza Hall, who fear for the future of the English country pub and are very determined that their splendid old inn should survive. With six bright, comfortable guest bedrooms, four of them with en suite facilities, the Inn is a good base for exploring the many aspects of a part of Norfolk that is popular with cyclists and ramblers as well as motorists and sailors. Sea Palling is very close to the North Sea, as are two villages to its south, Waxham and Horsey, where the Mere, a wildfowl refuge, and the National Trust's restored drainage windmill are visitor attractions. A short distance inland from Sea Palling is the largest of the Broads, Hickling, with its National Nature Reserve.

Opening Hours: 11-11, Sun 12-10.30

Food: A la carte

Credit Cards: Mastercard, Visa.

Accommodation: 6 rooms (4 en suite)

Facilities: Car park

Entertainment: None

Local Places of Interest/Activities:
Hickling Broad 2 miles, Horsey Windpump
and Mere 4 miles, Happisburgh 5 miles

72   The Pleasure Boat

Staithe Road,
Hickling,
Norfolk
NR12 0YW
Tel: 01692 598211

Directions:

From Great
Yarmouth, take the
A149 for about 10
miles to Potter
Heigham, then turn
right on to a minor
road marked
Hickling Green and
Hickling.

The name could not be more appropriate, as the **Pleasure Boat Inn** is situated right next to a point on the northern edge of Hickling Broad where the boats of holidaymakers tie up. The main part of the inn dates back to the 17th century, and the later additions are in happy harmony. The inn presents a cheerful, flower-decked face in the spring and summer, and the bar and lounge are delightful places to relax with a drink while enjoying the river view. There are also plenty of seats outside to take even better advantage of the splendid setting. The pub offers several real ales, both resident and guests from smaller local breweries. The restaurant is located in the recent extension and its more modern look blends well with the rural feel in the lounge. Food is served every session, and the chef changes the menu frequently to make use of the best local, seasonal ingredients he can find. Fish & chips is a great favourite, but everything's good, and the theme nights are becoming well entered in local diaries.

Next to the pub is a shop that sells coffee and snacks and also hires out bicycles. The inn's enthusiastic, hands-on leaseholders, Paul and Penny Layburn, are both passionate about this part of Norfolk and are also devotees of blues music; live performers, mainly duos, entertain most Saturdays, and on August Bank Holiday the pub hosts a blues and rock festival. Brown tourist signs guide motorists or walkers Hickling Broad National Nature Reserve, where visitors can follow nature trails and spot the wide variety of resident flora and fauna. The nearest accessible seaside villages are Sea Palling, Waxham and Horsey, all a short drive away, while inland attractions include the Museum of the Broads by the quayside at Stalham.

Opening Hours: 11-11, Sun 12-10.30

Food: A la carte (also coffee & snacks next door)

Credit Cards: Mastercard, Visa.

Accommodation: None

Facilities: Car park

Entertainment: Live music + annual festival

Local Places of Interest/Activities:
National Nature Reserve 1 mile, Stalham 2 miles, Horsey Windpump and Mere 4 miles

The Plough & Furrow

73

Quebec Street, Dereham,
Norfolk NR19 2DJ
Tel: 01362 692076

Directions:

In the centre of Dereham, which
is located on the A47 14 miles
west of Norwich.

Proprietor Joanne Cross is the
lifeblood of the **Plough & Furrow**,
an imposing public house in the
centre of Dereham. The extensive
bar areas are full of character, with
beams everywhere, intimate low
lighting and wall-length mirrors
that make the place look even more
spacious than it is. In this inviting
setting Joanne, here since the early
1990s, looks after her customers in
fine style, providing a good range
of liquid refreshment and generous
portions of well-priced bar food
Monday to Friday lunchtimes. Very much a hub of Dereham life, the Plough & Furrow has
a late night club licence at the weekend, and on the first Thursday of every month there's an
evening of live music.

The Plough & Furrow's history is definitely more unusual than most! It was built in 1857
as the Corn Hall, a grand structure that was a symbol of the town's agricultural prosperity
until it became a cinema in 1925. A statue of Thomas Coke, the great agricultural improver,
once topped its facade, but it was struck by lightning in 1950. Dereham is one of the most
ancient towns in the county, with a history that goes back at least to 654 AD. The Church of
St Nicholas, the second largest in Norfolk, should not be missed on a visit to the town, and
just by the church is St Withburga's Well, whose waters were said to have miraculous healing
properties. Some pilgrims still come, but nowadays anyone feeling a little under the weather
would be better advised to head for the Plough & Furrow, where Joanne and her staff will
soon make things better.

Opening Hours: 11-11, till 12 at the weekend

Food: A la carte (no food at the weekend)

Credit Cards: None

Accommodation: None

Facilities: None

Entertainment: Night club at the weekend

Local Places of Interest/Activities:
Dereham Church and St Withburga's Well,
Norfolk Rural Life Museum at Gressenhall 3
miles

74   The Ploughshare

The Street,
Beeston,
Nr King's Lynn,
Norfolk PE32 2NF
Tel: 01328 701845

Directions:

Beeston is located
1½ miles north of
the A47 between
Dereham and
Swaffham.

Behind the classic brick and tile-roofed frontage, the **Ploughshare**, owned and run by Julie Howard and her husband Rob Mullenger, has an equally traditional and appealing interior, with beams, bench seating and a wood-burning stove in an inglenook fireplace. The bar contains photographs and memorabilia of World War II and also a tribute to Jem Mace, an old-time bare knuckle fighter who was born near the pub. There are books to browse and games to play - dominoes, cribbage, scrabble, cards - but best of all is the good conversation over a glass or two of the favourite brew; four real ales are always on tap, Greene King IPA and three regularly rotating guests, including perhaps the excellent Mallard, Augustinian and Wolf. Julie is in charge in the kitchen, using local produce to provide splendid traditional English dishes that include pheasant and pigeon in season; meals are served in the 30-40 cover non-smoking restaurant as well as in the bar.

Regular events include quiz nights and folk music sessions. Two double bedrooms provide a fine base for exploring the scenic and historic delights of the region; children are very welcome, pets too - and there's a friendly greeting for one and all from the owners and their very waggy border-cum-Lakeland terrier Aggie. The first stopping place on a local tour might be the 14th century Church of St Mary, which stands a mile outside the village on a little hill by a farm. There's fishing at Litcham Lakes, grandeur and woodland walks at the lovely moated Oxburgh Hall and a wealth of history and lovely old buildings in Dereham and Swaffham. The pub has ample car parking space and a huge beer garden.

Opening Hours: 11.30-2.30 & 6-11, Sun 12-10.30

Food: A la carte and bar meals

Credit Cards: Mastercard, Visa

Accommodation: 2 double rooms

Facilities: Car park

Entertainment: Quiz and folk music nights

Local Places of Interest/Activities:
Litcham Lakes (fishing), Dereham 7 miles, Swaffham 10 miles

Internet/Website:
website: www.theploughshare.co.uk

The Queens Head | **75**

The Street,
Long Stratton,
Norfolk
NR15 2XG
Tel: 01508 530164

Directions:

Long Stratton is on
the A140 about ten
miles south of
Norwich.

Built in the 16th
century and a public
house since early
Victorian days, the
Queens Head
presents an attractive
period frontage on
the main A140 at Long Stratton, about ten miles south of Norwich. Inside, the bar, lounge
and restaurant are full of character, with a warm, cosy ambience and an friendly greeting
from the new tenants Carole and Joe Taylor. New to the trade, they arrived here in the summer
of 2002 and are very enthusiastic about this splendid old hostelry.

Open all day, every day, it makes an ideal break on a journey along the busy main road,
and the Taylors have the services of a chef who is just as keen as they are to put the inn firmly
on the map. Fine food cooked with passion and without pretension is his forte, and his
appetising dishes are served from 11 in the morning right through to 8.30 in the evening
(bar snacks only on Monday). The Queens Head's main road location puts Norwich to the
north and Diss to the south within easy reach, while in the immediate vicinity are little lanes
and quiet villages to explore, and some notable Norfolk churches, including those at Pulham
and Shelton.

Opening Hours: 11-11, Sun 12-10.30

Food: Traditional Home Cooked, Vegetarian
& Gluten Free meals on request

Credit Cards: None

Accommodation: None

Facilities: None

Entertainment: Occasional

Local Places of Interest/Activities:
Norwich 10 miles, Diss 8 miles

76   The Red Lion

The Green, Caston,
Nr Attleborough,
Norfolk
NR17 1DB
Tel/Fax: 01953 488236

Directions:

Caston is a tiny hamlet about 6 miles west of Attleborough. From Attleborough (A11) take the B1077 for about 5 miles; Caston is signposted down a minor road to the left. From Watton, turn left off the A1075 after about 2 miles.

Stephen and Anna Blackwood arrived in the tiny hamlet of Caston in the spring of 2002 to take over the reins at the **Red Lion** overlooking the green. Full of enthusiasm, they are breathing new life into this grand old inn, whose oldest parts date from the 17th century. Behind the rough stone frontage with classic tiled roof the public rooms are neat, bright and lively, with a rural feel that is absolutely in keeping with the rest of the lovely little village. The bar and plush lounge are perfect spots to unwind over a glass of beer and a chat (and if the chat is about golf, that's fine by the hosts - they're very keen golfers!).

In the attractive restaurant, with its brick and beam features and comfortable banquette seating, home-cooked food is served every session. The choice caters for all appetites, from a quick bar snack to full meals making excellent use of locally sourced meat and poultry - the pork and cider pie is a particular favourite with the regular customers. The inn has abundant off-road parking and a beer garden with a children's play area. Tuesday is quiz night. The quiet, unspoilt village of Caston has a picture postcard appeal and is a delightful place for a stroll. The nearest communities of any size are Watton, which has a very unusual clock tower, and Attleborough, whose Church of St Mary is one of the finest in the county. Even closer to the Red Lion is the Tropical Butterfly Garden and Bird Park, home to hundreds of exotic butterflies, with a falconry centre and a garden centre.

Opening Hours: 12-3 & 6-11, Fri, Sat & Sun all day

Food: A la carte + bar snacks

Credit Cards: Mastercard, Visa.

Accommodation: None

Facilities: Car park

Entertainment: None

Local Places of Interest/Activities:
Watton 3 miles, Butterfly Garden 5 miles, Attleborough 6 miles

The Reedham Ferry Inn | 77

Ferry Road, Reedham,
Norfolk Broads,
Norfolk NR13 3HA
Tel: 01493 700429
Fax: 01493 700999

Directions:

Reedham can be reached from the south via the A146 (leave at the B1136 junction on the B1140 road to Reedham) or from the north (leave the A47 Great Yarmouth-Norwich road at Acle and pass through Moulton St Mary and Freethorpe on the B1140 road to Reedham.

A prime location overlooking the River Yare and the little car ferry is one of the many attractions of the **Reedham Ferry Inn**. The inn has a very extensive frontage enabling visitors to watch the comings and goings of the pleasure boats on the river and the Ferry, which links the counties of Norfolk and Suffolk. This splendid little ferry is one of the smallest in the country, carrying up to three cars; it plies daily from 7.30am (8 at the weekend) to 10pm. A slipway is available for trailed boats just upstream of the Ferry. The inn has been owned for more than 50 years by David and Julia Archer, whose staff cope with friendly efficiency with the large numbers who pass through the doors. Drinks served at the busy bar include traditional ales from local breweries, and food is served in The Archers restaurant from 12 to 2.30 and from 7 to 9.30 Monday to Saturday and all day on Sunday.

The owners have the services of an excellent chef leading the kitchen brigade, and the menus offer a wide choice of dishes, from light lunches to fresh fish from Lowestoft, local game in season, steaks, roast dinners and daily specials from the English and French repertoires. Two of the most popular dishes are steak & ale pie and a flavour-packed of fish and shellfish stew. Regular food theme nights feature specific cuisines such as Greek or Mexican. Vegetarian, diet-conscious and children's menus are also available, and special dietary needs can be catered for with prior arrangement. Beside the inn is a 4-acre touring park, a landscaped site open from March to October with pitches for touring caravans and tents. Coarse fishing (carp, bream and rudd) is available on a stocked private water.

Opening Hours: 11-11, Sun 12-10.30

Food: A la carte

Credit Cards: Mastercard, Visa.

Accommodation: None

Facilities: Car park

Entertainment: Live music weekly

Local Places of Interest/Activities:
Norfolk Broads

78   The Robert Kett

Lime Tree Avenue, Wymondham, Norfolk NR18 0HH
Tel:
01953 602957

Directions:
On the northern outskirts of Wymondham off the B1135.

The Robert Kett is a long, low, modern building decked out with flowers and shrubs and shaded by trees on a private development on the edge of town. Inside, the open plan layout gives plenty of carpeted floor space, and concealed lighting produces a cosy, inviting effect. The pub is in the capable hands of Sarah Rogers, an experienced Greene King employee who is enhancing its reputation as a place for all the family. Everyone is equally welcome, from senior citizens to babes in arms - there's even a mothers' room with a baby changing facility. In the 70-cover dining area, fresh, wholesome food is served every lunchtime and evening; the choice offers something for everyone, and the printed menu is supplemented by daily specials chalked up on the board.

Tuesday is quiz night at the Robert Kett, which is situated on the northern outskirts of Wymondham in Lime Tree Avenue, running south off the B1135 (Tuttles Lane East). Robert Kett, a native of Wymondham, was one of the leaders in the notorious Norfolk Rebellion of 1549, when he and his brother marched at the head of 20,000 supporters protesting against the lot of agricultural workers. Wymondham (call it Windham) is a town with many attractions for the visitor. First and foremost is the magnificent twin-towered Abbey, but other places not to be missed include Becket's Chapel, the Heritage Museum and the historic railway station of 1845.

Opening Hours: 12-3 & 5-11, Fri, Sat & Sun all day

Food: A la carte

Credit Cards: Mastercard, Visa.

Accommodation: None

Facilities: Car park

Entertainment: None

Local Places of Interest/Activities:
Wymondham Abbey, Norwich 7 miles

The Ship Inn

Main Road,
Narborough,
Nr King's Lynn,
Norfolk
PE32 1TB
Tel: 01760 337307

Directions:

Narborough lies off
the A47 5 miles
northwest of
Swaffham, 10 miles
south

Built as a drovers' inn around 1740, the **Ship Inn** overlooks the green in the village of Narborough a short drive northwest of Swaffham. The traditionally styled bar is very comfortable and inviting, with beams, panelled walls, open fires and a mixture of bench seating and bar stools. There's a separate tap room which doubles as a games room, with pool and darts. Regular events include quiz nights and live music evenings. The pub is owned and run by Yorkshireman Paul Ross and his locally born wife Michelle. Paul does the cooking, putting locally sourced produce to excellent use on a menu that sticks mainly to superior versions of well-tried classics such as battered cod, chicken Kiev, chilli, lasagne and steaks.

One dish that is less familiar is his speciality of fresh Narborough trout stuffed with paté. Sweets end a meal on a scrumptious note with the likes of pear and raspberry pie, chocolate sponge puddings and banana fritters. On the drinks side, there's a variety of wines and three real ales - two IPAs, John Smith's Cask and a rotating guest. The pub has a most delightful riverside garden as well as outside tables on patios at the front and sides, and ample parking space. Comfortable, well-appointed overnight accommodation is available in six letting bedrooms - four en suite twins, a double and a single. This is a good area for fishing, notably on Narborough trout lakes, and among the places of interest in the locality are the splendid ruins of Castle Acre Priory.

Opening Hours: 12-3 & 6.30-11

Food: A la carte

Credit Cards: None

Accommodation: 6 rooms (4 en suite)

Facilities: Car park

Entertainment: Quiz nights, occasional live music

Local Places of Interest/Activities:
Nar River walk, trout lakes, Castle Acre 4 miles, Swaffham 5 miles

Internet/Website:
e-mail: narboroughship@aol.com

80   The Spread Eagle

Erpingham,
Norfolk
NR11 7QA
Tel: 01263 761591
Fax: 01263 768609

Directions:

Turn off the main
Norwich-Cromer
road (A140) signed
Erpingham, just
before Alby Crafts.

Landlady Billie Carder, who has been in the trade for 25 years, runs the **Spread Eagle** with her son Kristian, the barman, her daughter Sara, the chef, five other staff and everybody's favourite, Dylon the basset hound. The brick and flint pub just off the A140 Norwich-Cromer road dates from the 17th century, and the outbuildings were once the home of the Woodforde Brewery (now based in Norwich). In the main building there's a long bar with plenty of comfortable seating, a games room with pool and darts, and a non-smoking dining area overlooking the lovely enclosed garden, which has equipment to keep the children happy and room to play badminton or football.

Six real ales - Adnams Broadside, Woodforde's Wherry and four regularly changing guests - present a splendid choice for beer-lovers, and in the restaurant there's an excellent selection of wines to accompany a meal. Restaurant and bar menus, plus a specials board, offer a really impressive choice of dishes, including a particularly good selection of vegetarian meals. Sandwiches, burgers, jacket potatoes and salads provide quicker or lighter meals, but this is the sort of place where it's nice to relax over a leisurely that could end with something wicked like a treacle steam pudding with custard. Live music is a popular attraction every Saturday night, when the entertainment could be folk, blues, Irish, country or rock - or even the odd karaoke. The pub is a popular venue for functions and private parties, and the plan is to make overnight accommodation available for 2003.

Opening Hours: 11-3 & 6.30-11, Sun 12-3 & 7-10.30

Food: A la carte

Credit Cards: Diners, Mastercard, Visa

Accommodation: Planned for 2003

Facilities: Car park

Entertainment: Live music every Saturday

Local Places of Interest/Activities:
Alby Crafts, Aylsham (Blickling Hall, Bure Valley Railway) 5 miles, Cromer 7 miles

Internet/Website:
e-mail: billie@spreadeagle.freesrve.co.uk

The Suffield Arms   **81**

*Church Road
(opposite Gunton
Station),
Thorpe Market,
Norfolk
NR11 8UE
Tel: 01263 833461*

Directions:

Thorpe Market lies
on the A149
between North
Walsham and
Cromer. The inn is
on a road to the
right, opposite
Gunton Station.

'Good Pub, Good Grub' says the sign outside the **Suffield Arms**, and what the sign says, the sign means. Owner Paul Mason bought the free house in 1994 and runs it in fine style with his partner Mary Haggith. Built in the mid-19th century, the pub is about to reveal its original redbrick facade to the world after it was covered by a coat of cream paint for many years. The bar and lounge are built for space and comfort, and Paul recently added an 80-cover restaurant in a redbrick extension. A good selection of cask ales is always available, and while Paul looks after his thirsty customers, Mary takes care of the inner man with her very enjoyable home cooking.

Meals are served every lunchtime and evening, and the menus cater for varied tastes and appetites: some customers pop in for a quick light lunch, while others relax over a leisurely evening meal. Every year from April to October Paul pitches a huge marquee next to the pub, which is used as an overflow and for parties and other special occasions. The Suffield Arms is named after a local bigwig, Lord Suffield of Thorpe Market, who in 1796 commissioned the village's Church of St Mary. The pub is located opposite Gunton railway station, just off the A149 and with easy access to the north to the delightful seaside town of Cromer and to the south to the market town of North Walsham, where Horatio Nelson went to school.

Opening Hours: 12-3 & 6-11

Food: A la carte and snacks

Credit Cards: Mastercard, Visa.

Accommodation: None

Facilities: Car park

Entertainment: None

Local Places of Interest/Activities:
Cromer 5 miles, North Walsham 4 miles

82 | The Walpole Arms

The Common,
Itteringham,
Nr Norwich,
Norfolk
NR11 7AR
Tel: 01263 587258
Fax: 01263 587074

Directions:

Itteringham is located 6 miles northwest of Aylsham. Take the B1354 out of Aylsham, and turn right about 1 mile after Blickling Hall on to a minor road signposted Itteringham.

Hidden is the operative word here, and never was there a pub more worth taking a little trouble to find - and once found, the return visits that will surely follow will be much easier! **The Walpole Arms** is owned and run by Richard Bryan, who for ten years produced the Masterchef programme on national television and who is a prolific writer and broadcaster on food. His business partner is Keith Reeves, a widely respected wine merchant. Between them, and with the expertise of head chef Andy Parle and his team, they have made the Walpole Arms the leading pub restaurant in the region, and a worthy winner of the Norfolk Country Pub of the Year Award for 2001.

Norfolk produces some of the best seafood, game, fruit and vegetables in the land, and nothing but the best will do for Andy, whose previous posts have included the Michelin-starred Adlard's in Norwich and Terence Conran's Pont de la Tour in London. Everything is fresh and seasonal, almost all of it local, and the pub has built up a network of the top suppliers. If mussels appear on the menu, they are the best from Morston; venison is reared, slaughtered and hung at Gunton Hall; organic beef comes from the herd at the National Trust's Fellbrigg Estate. Food service - be sure to book - is from 12 to 2 (to 3 on Sunday) and from 7 to 9. Fine food and wine bring visitors to Itteringham from far and wide, but the Walpole Arms is also a delightful village local, where a glass of locally brewed ale can be enjoyed in the 18th century beamed bar or out in the garden.

Opening Hours: 12-3 & 6-11.00

Food: A la carte

Credit Cards: Mastercard, Visa.

Accommodation: None

Facilities: Car park

Entertainment: None

Local Places of Interest/Activities:
Mannington Hall 1 mile, Blickling Hall 4 miles, Bure Valley Railway 6 miles

Internet/Website:
e-mail: goodfood@thewalpolearms.co.uk
website: www.thewalpolearms.co.uk

The Waveney Inn 83

Waveney River Centre,
Burgh St Peter Staithe,
Nr Beccles,
Norfolk NR34 0BT
Tel: 01502 677343
* or 01502 677217*
Fax: 01502 677566

Directions:

From Beccles, A146
then A143 at
Gillingham; first right
follow signs to Burgh
St Peter; from Great
Yarmouth, leave the

In the heart of the Waveney Valley between Beccles and Lowestoft, the Waveney River Centre is the premier boating and leisure centre on the Norfolk Broads. At its heart is the **Waveney Inn**, run by Mr and Mrs Martin and serving excellent food and drinks in a friendly, relaxed atmosphere enhanced by glorious views of the River Waveney. The bar has a selection of real ales among the usual range of drinks, to enjoy on their own or to accompany bar snacks or light meals. In the evening, the elegant restaurant offers seasonally changing menus to suit all tastes, from light meals and children's dishes to grills, Thai dishes and a wide à la carte selection. At the weekend there are theme nights from around the world and a traditional carvery for Sunday lunch.

The Waveney is well worth a detour in its own right, but many visitors also come to enjoy the facilities of the Centre, including boating (hiring by the hour or day), moorings for people with their own craft, a children's adventure area and an indoor complex with pool, sauna, spa bath and gym. There are also facilities for caravaners and campers, and the Centre is an ideal base for taking to the water or exploring the Broadland landscape. The market town of Beccles, with shops and two museums, is an easy drive away, and to the east is the sizeable seaside town and holiday resort of Lowestoft, the most easterly town in Britain, whose attractions include its harbour and fish market, maritime and other museums, golden sands and a splendid pier. This is an area for water-borne activity, but many an old bus-spotter has shed a nostalgic tear at the East Anglia Transport Museum at Carlton Colville, south of Lowestoft.

Opening Hours: 12-2 & 6.30-10

Food: Bar snacks and evening à la carte

Credit Cards: Mastercard, Visa.

Accommodation: Static caravans in the Centre

Facilities: Car park, moorings, marina berths, caravan and camp site, swimming pool, spa bath, sauna, gym, children's adventure area

Entertainment: All the amenities of the Centre

Local Places of Interest/Activities: Boating from the Centre, Beccles 6 miles, Lowestoft 8 miles

Internet/Website:
e-mail: info@waveneyrivercentre.co.uk
website: www.waveneyrivercentre.co.uk

84   The Weavers Arms

Swanton Abbot,
Nr Aylsham,
Norfolk
NR10 5AH
Tel: 01692 538655

Directions:

Swanton Abbot is
signposted off the
B1150 Norwich-
North Walsham
road about 10 miles
north of Norwich.

Largely unchanged in appearance from its 17th century origins, the **Weavers Arms** has certainly changed in its role and its clientele. As its name suggests, it was closely linked to the weaving trade, and it originally served as a brothel for the local weavers. The sins of the flesh have long since made way for the pleasures of the palate, and under award-winning chef-patron Spencer Hills the inn has become one of the very best eating places in the region. The interior is furnished in a pleasantly straightforward style that lets the customers concentrate on the main reason for their visit - a fine meal to be enjoyed in neat, spotless surroundings.

Spencer's British cuisine combines the best of traditional and contemporary elements, and his menu ventures far beyond the bounds of the usual pub menu with such irresistible choices as lamb steak wrapped in Parma ham with wild mushrooms à la crème and a red wine and shallot jus. These splendid dishes are served lunchtime and evening Tuesday to Saturday and Sunday lunch, and booking is advisable for all meals. Food may be uppermost in the thoughts of visitors to the Weavers Arms, but the opportunity should not be missed of exploring the area: among the many attractions are the village of Worstead (which gave its name to the hard-wearing cloth produced in the region), and the steam-hauled Bure Valley Railway, which runs between Aylsham and Wroxham.

Opening Hours: 12-3 & 5.30-11, Sun 12-3 & 7-10

Food: A la carte

Credit Cards: Mastercard, Visa.

Accommodation: None

Facilities: Car park

Entertainment: None

Local Places of Interest/Activities:
North Walsham 4 miles, Worstead 3 miles, Bure Valley Railway 4 miles

White Horse At Longham 85

Wendling Road,
Longham,
Nr Dereham,
Norfolk NR19 2RD
Tel: 01362 687464
Fax: 01362 687484

Directions:

Turn off A47
Swaffham-Dereham
road for Wendling
and Longham. First
left to Bittering,
follow for about 2½
miles to sign for
Longham.

The welcome from partners Barry White and Chrissie Sandford is warm and genuine at the **White Horse,** a substantial redbrick village pub with a 350-year record of providing hospitality. Woodforde's and two changing guest ales are on tap to be enjoyed in the spacious lounge bar or out in the beer garden and there are three separate areas laid up for meals, two of them non-smoking, and one a delightful conservatory overlooking the lawned garden. Chrissie's menus offer plenty of choice to suit all appetites and tastes, from sandwiches and light snacks to full meals.

This quintessentially English country pub is definitely a place in which to linger, and for guests staying the night, or longer, the White Horse has three very well-equipped en suite letting bedrooms - a single and two doubles - with trouser press and access to washing, drying and iron facilities. Due to come on stream by the end of 2002 are four more rooms, one of which will have full facilities for disabled guests. The pub is closed Monday lunchtime. Longham is tucked well away in the Norfolk countryside north of the A47, which runs to King's Lynn in the west and Great Yarmouth (by-passing Norwich) in the east. The next village to Longham is Gressenhall, where the Norfolk Rural Life Museum is a much visited attraction. The nearest community of any size to the White Horse is Dereham, whose twin-towered Church of St Nicholas, the second largest in Norfolk, has many treasures, including a rare and beautiful Seven Sacrament font.

Opening Hours: 12-2.30 & 6.30-11 (closed Mon lunchtime)

Food: A la carte and bar snacks

Credit Cards: Diners, Mastercard, Visa

Accommodation: 3 en suite (more planned)

Facilities: Car park

Entertainment: None

Local Places of Interest/Activities:
Gressenhall (Norfolk Rural Life Museum) 3 miles, Dereham 4 miles, Swaffham 10 miles

Internet/Website:
e-mail: whitehorse@tiscali.co.uk
website: www.longhamwhitehorse.co.uk

3 Suffolk

PLACES OF INTEREST:

PUBS AND INNS:

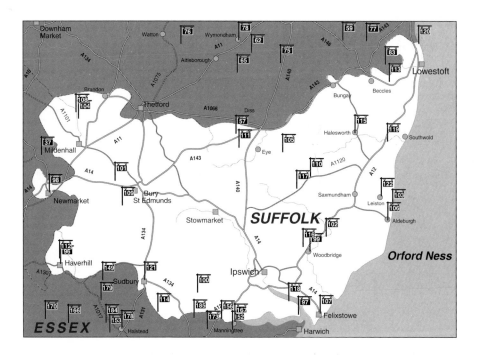

96	The Australian Arms, Haverhill		**110**	The Queens Head, Dennington
97	The Bristol Arms, Shotley Gate, Ipswich		**111**	The Railway Tavern, Mellis, Nr Eye
98	The Cherry Tree, Newmarket		**112**	The Scarlet Pimpernel, Haverhill
99	The Cherrytree Inn, Woodbridge		**113**	The Swan Inn, Barnby, Nr Beccles
100	The Cock Inn, Polstead		**114**	The Swan Inn, Bures
101	The Crown & Castle, Risby		**115**	The Triple Plea, Halesworth
102	The Dog & Duck Inn, Campsea Ashe		**116**	The Turks Head, Hasketon
103	The Dolphin Inn, Thorpeness		**117**	The Venture, Chelmondiston
104	The Half Moon, Lakenheath		**118**	The Victoria, Earl Soham
105	The Ivy House, Stradbroke		**119**	The White Hart Inn, Blythburgh
106	The Mill Inn, Aldeburgh		**120**	The White Horse, Corton, Nr Lowestoft
107	The Ordnance Hotel, Felixstowe		**121**	The White Horse, Sudbury
108	The Plough, Lakenheath		**122**	The White Horse Hotel, Leiston
109	The Plough, Rede, Nr Bury St Edmunds			

Please note all references refer to page numbers

88   Suffolk

While inland Suffolk has few equals in terms of picturesque countryside and villages, Suffolk is also very much a maritime county, with more than 50 miles of coastline. The area between the heathland and the coast is a delightful place for getting away from the urban rush to the real countryside, with unchanged ancient villages, gently flowing rivers, rich farming land, markets and fairs, churches and museums, and some of the best preserved windmills and watermills in the country. The whole of the coastal stretch is a conservation area, with miles of waymarked walks and cycle trails and an abundance of birdlife and wildlife, and the coast has long been a source of inspiration for distinguished writers, artists and musicians. The sea brings natural dangers and the coast has for centuries been under threat from storms and high tides; it also brings danger in human form, and it was against the threat of a Napoleon invasion that Martello Towers were built. At least 80 of these forts were constructed, the most northerly being at Slaughden (Aldeburgh), the most southerly at Shoreham in Sussex. The main communities in Central and East Suffolk are Aldeburgh, Southwold and Lowestoft on the coast, and Woodbridge, Stowmarket, Halesworth, Beccles and Bungay inland.

Suffolk Punch Horses

Much of Suffolk's character comes from its rivers, and in the part of the county surrounding Ipswich the Orwell and the Stour mark the boundaries of the Shotley Peninsula. Much of the countryside is largely unspoilt, with wide-open spaces between scattered villages, and the relative flatness of the terrain gives every encouragement for leaving the car and taking to walking or cycling. John Constable, England's greatest landscape painter, was born at East Bergholt in 1776 and remained at heart a Suffolk man throughout his life, painting the scenes he knew and loved in his childhood. The Suffolk tradition of painting continues to this day, with artists drawn particularly to the coast and to the beautiful Constable country. Cambridgeshire, Norfolk, the A14 and the A134 frame the northern part of West Suffolk, which includes Bury St Edmunds and Newmarket. The former is a gem of a town that is rich in archaeological treasures and places of religious and historical interest, the latter one of the major centres of the horseracing world. Towards the Essex border, the county offers some of its most attractive and peaceful countryside. In the south, along the River Stour, stand the historic wool towns of Sudbury, Long Melford, Cavendish and Clare.

PLACES OF INTEREST

ALDEBURGH

Another of the coastal towns that once prospered as a port with major fishing and shipbuilding industries. The town's role gradually changed into that of a holiday resort, and the Marquess of Salisbury, visiting early in the 19th century, was one of the first to be attracted by the idea of sea-bathing without the crowds. By the middle of the century the grand houses that had sprung up were joined by smaller residences, the railway arrived, a handsome water tower was put up (1860) and Aldeburgh prospered once more. The **Aldeburgh Festival**, started in 1948 by Benjamin Britten and others, has nearby Snape Maltings as its main venue, but many performances take place in Aldeburgh itself. The maritime connection remains very strong and the very modern lifeboat station is one of the town's chief attractions for visitors. The town has several interesting buildings, notably the 16th century timber-framed **Moot Hall** and the parish Church of **St Peter and St Paul**. The church, which stands above the town as a very visible landmark for mariners, contains a memorial to the local poet George Crabbe and a beautiful stained-glass window, the work of John Piper, depicting three Britten parables for church performance, *Curlew River*, *The Burning Fiery Furnace* and *The Prodigal Son*. Britten and his companion Peter Pears are buried in the churchyard, part of which is set aside for the benefit of wildlife.

BECCLES

The Saxons were here, the Vikings were here, and at one time the market was a major supplier of herring (up to 60,000 a year) to the Abbey at Bury St Edmunds. The contents of the **Beccles & District Museum** include 19th century toys and costume, farm implements, items from the old town jail and memorabilia from the sailing wherries. Beccles is a printing town, and has its own printing museum at the Newgate works of printer William Clowes.

BLYTHBURGH

Blythburgh's Church of **Holy Trinity** is one of the wonders of Suffolk, a stirring sight as it rises from the reed beds, visible for miles around and floodlit at night to spectacular effect. This 'Cathedral of the Marshes' reflects the days when Blythburgh was a prosperous port with a bustling quayside wool trade.

BRANDON

On the edge of **Thetford Forest** by the Little Ouse, Brandon was long ago a thriving port, but flint is what really put it on the map. The town itself is built mainly of flint, and flint was mined from early Neolithic times to make arrowheads and other implements and weapons of war. The

Heritage Centre, in a former fire station in George Street, provides visitors with a splendid insight into this industry, while for an even more tangible feel a visit to **Grimes Graves**, just over the Norfolk border, reveals an amazing site covering 35 acres and 300 pits.

BURY ST EDMUNDS

A gem among Suffolk towns, rich in archaeological treasures and places of religious and historical interest. The town takes its name from St Edmund, who was born in Nuremberg in 841 and came here as a teenager to become the last king of East Anglia. He was a staunch

Christian, and his refusal to deny his faith caused him to be tortured and killed by the Danes in 870. His remains found a resting place here, and the shrine built in his honour was incorporated into the Norman Abbey Church after the monastery was granted abbey status by King Canute in 1032. The town soon became a place of pilgrimage and for many years St

Norman Tower, Bury St Edmunds Abbey

Edmund was the patron saint of England, until replaced by St George. Growing rapidly around the great abbey, which became one of the largest and most influential in the land, Bury prospered as a centre of trade and commerce, thanks notably to the cloth industry.

Rebuilt in the 15th century, the Abbey was largely dismantled after its dissolution by Henry VIII, but imposing ruins remain in the colourful Abbey Gardens beyond the splendid Abbey Gate and Norman Tower. **St Edmundsbury Cathedral** was originally the Church of St James, built in the 15th/16th century and accorded cathedral status (alone in Suffolk) in 1914. The original building has been much extended down the years (notably when being adapted for its role as a cathedral) and outstanding features include a magnificent hammerbeam roof, whose

90

38 beams are decorated with angels bearing the emblems of St James, St Edmund and St George. **St Mary's** Church, in the same complex, is also well worth a visit.

The **Abbey Visitor Centre** is situated in Samson's Tower, part of the west front of the Abbey. The centre has displays and hands-on activities concerning the Abbey's history. The **Abbey Gardens**, which were laid out in 1831, have as their central feature a great circle of flower beds following the pattern of the Royal Botanical Gardens in Brussels. Bury is full of fine non-ecclesiastical buildings, many with Georgian frontages concealing medieval interiors. Among the most interesting are the handsome **Manor House Museum** with its collection of clocks, paintings, furniture, costumes and objets d'art; the **Victorian Corn Exchange** with its imposing colonnade; the Athenaeum, hub of social life since Regency times and scene of Charles Dickens's public readings; **Cupola House**, where Daniel Defoe once stayed; the **Angel Hotel**, where Dickens and his marvellous creation Mr Pickwick stayed; and the **Nutshell**, owned by Greene King Brewery and probably the smallest pub in the country. The **Theatre Royal**, now in the care of the National Trust, was built in 1819 by William Wilkins, who was also responsible for the National Gallery. It once staged the premiere of *Charley's Aunt* and still operates as a working theatre.

The **Bury St Edmunds Art Gallery** is housed in one of Bury's noblest buildings, built to a Robert Adam design in 1774. It filled many roles down the years, and was rescued from decline in the 1960s to be restored to Adam's original plans. It is now one of the county's premier art galleries, with eight exhibitions each year and a thriving craft shop.

Perhaps the most fascinating building of all is **Moyses Hall**, built of flint and limestone about 1180 as a rich man's residence. Now a museum, it houses some 10,000 items, from a Bronze Age hoard, Roman pottery and Anglo-Saxon jewellery to a 19th century doll's house and some grisly relics of a notorious local murder.

CAVENDISH

A most attractive village, where the Romans stayed awhile and the Saxons settled. The look is splendidly traditional, with the church, thatched cottages, almshouses, Nether Hall and

the **Sue Ryder Foundation Museum** spread around the green. The last, in a 16th century rectory by the pond, illustrates the work of the Sue Ryder Foundation, and was formally opened by Queen Elizabeth in 1979. Once a refuge for concentration camp victims, it houses abundant war photographs and memorabilia. Nether Hall is a well-restored 16th century building and the headquarters of **Cavendish Vineyards**.

CLARE

A medieval wool town of great importance. Perhaps the most renowned tourist attraction is **Ancient House**, a timber-framed building dated 1473 and remarkable for its pargeting. This is the decorative treatment of external plasterwork, usually by dividing the surface into rectangles

The Ancient House

and decorating each panel. It was very much a Suffolk speciality, particularly in the 16th and 17th centuries, with some examples also being found in Cambridgeshire and Essex. The decoration could be simple brushes of a comb, scrolls or squiggles, or more elaborate, with religious motifs, guild signs or family crests. Some pargeting is incised, but the best is in relief – pressing moulds into wet plaster or shaping by hand. Ancient House sports some splendid twining flowers and branches, and a representation of two figures holding a shield. exhibition of local history.

DUNWICH

Surely the Hidden Place of all Hidden Places! Dunwich was once the capital of East Anglia, but the relentless forces of the sea took their toll down the centuries, and all that remains now of ancient Dunwich are the ruins of a Norman leper hospital, the archways of a medieval friary and a buttress of one of the nine churches which

Dunwich Priory

once served the community. Today's village comprises a 19th century church and a row of Victorian cottages, one of which houses the **Dunwich Museum**. **Dunwich Forest**, immediately inland from the village, is one of three – the others are further south at Tunstall and Rendlesham – named by the Forestry Commission as Aldewood Forest. Work started on these in 1920 with the planting of Scots pine, Corsican pine and some Douglas fir.

South of the village lies **Dunwich Heath**, one of Suffolk's most important conservation areas. The nearby village of Westleton is the main route of access to the RSPB-managed **Minsmere Bird Sanctuary**, the most important sanctuary for wading birds in eastern England.

EAST BERGHOLT

Narrow lanes lead to this picturesque and much visited little village. The **Constable County Trail** starts here, where the painter was born, and passes through Flatford Mill and on to Dedham in Essex. **St Mary's Church**, one of the many grand churches built with the wealth brought by the wool trade, is naturally something of a shrine to Constable, his family and his friends.

St Mary's Church, East Bergholt

There are memorial windows to the artist and to his beloved wife Maria Bicknell, who bore him seven children and whose early death was an enormous blow to him. His parents, to whom he was clearly devoted, and his old friend Willy Lott, whose cottage is featured famously in *The Hay Wain*, are buried in the churchyard. A leafy lane leads south from the village to the Stour, where two of Constable's favourite subjects, **Flatford Mill** and **Willy Lott's cottage**, both looking much as they did when he painted them, are to be found.

FELIXSTOWE

Felixstowe was a little known village until the enterprising Colonel Tomline put it on the map by creating a port to rival its near neighbour Harwich. He also started work on the Ipswich-Felixstowe railway and developed the resort aspects of Felixstowe, rivalling the amenities of Dovercourt.. The town has suffered a number of ups and downs but now thrives as one of England's busiest ports, having been much extended in the 1960s. The resort is strung out round a wide, gently curving bay, where the long seafront road is prettified by trim lawns and gardens. The original fishing hamlet from which the Victorian resort was developed lies beyond a golf course north of the town. This is **Felixstowe Ferry**, a cluster of holiday homes, an inn, a boatyard, fishing sheds and a Martello tower. At the southernmost tip of the peninsula is **Landguard Point**, where a nature reserve supports rare plants and migrating birds. Just north on this shingle bank is **Landguard Fort**, built in 1718 (replacing an earlier construction) to protect Harwich harbour and now home to **Felixstowe Museum**.

FLIXTON

Javelin, Meteor, Sea Vixen, Westland Whirlwind: names that evoke earlier days of flying, and just four of the 20 aircraft on show at The **Norfolk and Suffolk Aviation Museum**, on the site of a USAAF Liberator base during the Second World War. There's a lot of associated material, both civil and military, covering the period from the First World War to the present day. The museum incorporates the Royal Observer Corps Museum, RAF Bomber Command Museum, and the Museum and Memorial of the 446th Bomb Group - the Bungay Buckeroos.

92

FRAMLINGHAM

Framlingham Castle, brooding on a hilltop, dominates this agreeable market town, as it has since Roger Bigod, 2nd Earl of Norfolk, built it in the 12th century (his grandfather built the first a century earlier but this wooden construction was soon demolished). The castle is in remarkably good condition, partly because it was rarely attacked – though King John put it under siege in 1215. Its most famous occupant was Mary Tudor, who was in residence when proclaimed Queen in 1553.

HADLEIGH

Old and not-so-old blend harmoniously in a variety of architectural styles. Timber-framed buildings, often with elaborate plasterwork, stand in the long main street as a reminder of the prosperity generated by the wool trade in the 14th to 16th centuries, and there are also some fine houses from the Regency and Victorian periods. The 15th century **Guildhall** with two overhanging storeys, the Deanery Tower and the church are a magnificent trio of huge appeal and contrasting construction – timber for the Guildhall, brick for the tower and flint for the church.

HORRINGER

Beside the Church of St Leonard on the village green are the gates of one of the country's most extraordinary and fascinating houses, now run by the National Trust. **Ickworth House** was the brainchild of the eccentric 4th Earl of Bristol and Bishop of Derry, a collector of art treasures and an inveterate traveller The massive structure is a central rotunda linking two semi-circular wings. Its chief glories are some marvellous paintings by Titian, Gainsborough, Hogarth, Velasquez, Reynolds and Kauffman, but there's a great deal more to enthral the visitor: late Regency and 18th century French furniture, a notable collection of Georgian silver, friezes and sculptures by John Flaxman, frescoes copied from wall paintings discovered at the Villa Negroni in Rome in 1777. The Italian garden should not be missed, with its hidden glades, orangery and temple rose garden, and in the Capability Brown park are designated walks and cycle routes, bird hides, a deer enclosure and play areas.

IPSWICH

History highlights Ipswich as the birthplace of Cardinal Wolsey, but the story of Suffolk's county town starts very much earlier. It has been a port since the time of the Roman occupation and by the 7th century the Anglo-Saxons had expanded it into the largest port in the country. At the beginning of the 19th century the risk from silting was becoming acute at a time when trade was improving and industries were springing up. The Wet Dock, constructed in 1842, solved the silting problem and, with the railway arriving shortly after, Ipswich could once more look forward to a safe future. The Victorians were responsible for considerable development and symbols of their civic pride include the handsome **Old Custom House** by the Wet Dock, the Town Hall and the splendid **Tolly Cobbold brewery**. **Christchurch Mansion** is a beautiful Tudor home standing in a 65-acre park. Furnished as an English country house, it contains a major collection of works by Constable and Gainsborough and many other paintings, prints and sculptures by Suffolk artists from the 17th century onwards.

The town's main museum is in a Victorian building in the High Street. Displays include a natural history gallery, a wildlife gallery complete with a model of a mammoth, a reconstruction of a Roman villa, replicas of Sutton Hoo treasures and a display of elaborately

Corn Hill, Ipswich

carved timbers from the homes of wealthy 17th century merchants.

In a former trolleybus depot on Cobham Road is the **Ipswich Transport Museum**, a fascinating collection of vehicles, from prams to fire engines, all made or used around Ipswich.

KERSEY

The ultimate Suffolk picture-postcard village, a wonderful collection of timbered merchants' houses and weavers' cottages with paint and thatch. The main street has a water splash, which, along with the 700-year-old Bell Inn, has featured in many films and travelogues. The massive Church of St Mary, which overlooks the village from its hilltop position, is testimony to the wealth that came with the wool and cloth industry. Kersey's speciality was a coarse twill broadcloth much favoured for greatcoats and army uniforms.

LAVENHAM

An absolute gem of a town, the most complete and original of the medieval 'wool towns', with crooked timbered and whitewashed buildings lining the narrow streets. More than 300 buildings are officially listed as being of architectural and historical interest, and none of them is finer than the **Guildhall**. This superb 16th century timbered building houses exhibitions of local history and the wool trade, and its walled garden has a special area devoted to dye plants. **Little Hall** is hardly less remarkable, a 15th century hall house with a superb crown post roof. The **Church of St Peter and St Paul** dominates the town from its elevated position. It's a building of great distinction, perhaps the greatest of all the 'wool churches' and declared by the 19th century

Lavenham Guildhall

architect August Pugin to be the finest example of Late Perpendicular style in the world. The Priory originated in the 13th century as a home for Benedictine monks and the beautiful timber-framed house on the site dates from about 1600.

LEISTON

For 200 years the biggest name in Leiston was that of Richard Garrett, who founded an engineering works here in 1778 after starting business in Woodbridge. The Garrett works are now the **Long Shop Museum**, and many of the Garrett machines are now on display, including traction engines, a steam-driven tractor and a road roller. The Garrett works closed in 1980 and what could have been a disastrous unemployment situation was to some extent alleviated by the nuclear power station at **Sizewell**. The coast road in the centre of Leiston leads to this establishment, where visitors can take tours, on foot with access to buildings at Sizewell A or by minibus, with guide and videos, round the newer PWR Sizewell B.

LONG MELFORD

The heart of this atmospheric wool town is a very long and, in stretches, fairly broad main street, set on an ancient Roman site in a particularly beautiful part of south Suffolk. The street is filled with antique shops, book shops and art galleries, and some of the buildings are washed in the characteristic Suffolk pink, which might originally have been achieved by mixing ox blood or sloe juice into the plaster.

Melford Hall, east of town beyond an imposing 16th gateway, was built around 1570 on the site of an earlier hall that served as a country retreat for the monks of St Edmundsbury Abbey. The variously styled rooms include the Beatrix Potter room, with some of her water colours, first editions of books and the original of Jemima Puddleduck. **Kentwell Hall** is a red-brick Tudor moated mansion approached by a long avenue of limes. Its grounds include a unique Tudor rose maze.

LOWESTOFT

The most easterly town in Britain had its heyday as a major fishing port during the late 19th and early 20th centuries, when it was a mighty rival to Great Yarmouth in the herring fishing industry. Lowestoft is still a fishing port, but is also a popular holiday resort, the star attraction being the lovely South Beach with its golden sands. The history of Lowestoft is naturally tied up with the sea, and much of that history is recorded in the **Lowestoft & East Suffolk Maritime Museum** and the **Royal Naval Patrol Museum**. At Carlton Colville, three miles southwest of Lowestoft, many an old bus-spotter has shed a nostalgic tear at the **East Anglia Transport Museum**, where children and ex-children climb aboard to enjoy rides on buses, trams and trolleybuses.

MILDENHALL

On the edge of the Fens and Breckland, Mildenhall is a town which has many links with the past. Most of the town's heritage is recorded in the excellent **Mildenhall & District Museum** in King Street. Here will be found exhibits of local history (including the distinguished RAF and USAAF base), crafts and domestic skills, the natural history of the Fens and Breckland and, perhaps most famously, the 'Mildenhall Treasure'. This was a cache of 34 pieces of 4th century Roman silverware - dishes, goblets and spoons - found by a ploughman in 1946 at Thistley Green and now on display in the British Museum. The parish of Mildenhall is the largest in Suffolk so it is perhaps fitting that it should

boast so magnificent a parish church as **St Mary's**, built of Barnack stone.

NEWMARKET

On the western edge of Suffolk, Newmarket is home to some 16,000 human and 3,000 equine inhabitants. The historic centre of British racing lives and breathes horses, with 60 training establishments, 50 stud farms, the top annual thoroughbred sales and two racecourses (the only two in Suffolk).

In 1605 James I paused on a journey north to enjoy a spot of hare coursing. He enjoyed the place and said he would be back; in moving the royal court to his Newmarket headquarters he began the royal patronage which has remained strong down the years. Charles I maintained the royal connection but it was Charles II who really put the place on the map when he, too, moved the Royal court in the spring and autumn of each year. The visitor to Newmarket can learn almost all there is to know about flat racing and racehorses and the royal connections by making the grand tour of the several establishments which are open to the public (sometimes by appointment only): the **Jockey Club**; the **National Horseracing Museum**; **Palace House**; **Nell Gwynn's house**; **Tattersalls**, where leading thoroughbred sales take place from April to December; the **British Racing School**, where top jockeys are taught the ropes; and the **National Stud**.

ORFORD

The ruins of **Orford** Castle are a most impressive sight, even though the keep is all that remains of the original building commissioned by Henry II in 1165. The walls of the keep are 10 feet deep, and behind them are many rooms and passages in a remarkable state of preservation.

St Bartholomew's Church, a wonderful sight at night when floodlit, is regularly used for the performance of concerts and recitals, and many of Benjamin Britten's works were first heard here. In summer the quayside on the river is alive with yachts and pleasure craft. On the other side of the river is **Orford Ness**, home to a variety of rare flora and fauna. Access to the spit, which is in the hands of the National Trust, is by ferry from Orford quay only. Boat trips also leave the quay for the RSPB reserve of **Havergate Island**, haunt of avocet and tern.

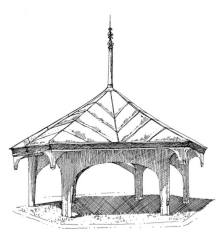

Market Cross, Mildenhall

SOMERLEYTON

Somerleyton Hall, one of the grandest and most distinctive of stately homes, is a splendid Victorian mansion built in Anglo-Italian style by Samuel Morton Peto. Its lavish architectural features are complemented by fine state rooms, magnificent wood carvings (some by Grinling Gibbons) and notable paintings. The grounds include a renowned yew-hedge maze, where people have been going round in circles since 1846, walled and sunken gardens and a 300-foot pergola.

SOUTHWOLD

A town full of character, and full of interest for both holidaymaker and historians. Though one of the most popular resorts on the east coast, Southwold has very little of the kiss-me-quick commercialism that spoils so many seaside towns. Southwold's maritime past is recorded in the museum set in a Dutch-style cottage in Victoria Street.

STOWMARKET

Much of the town's history and legacy are brought vividly to life in the splendid **Museum of East Anglian Life**, which is situated in the centre of town in a 70-acre meadowland site on the old Abbot's Hall Estate. Part of the open-air section features several historic buildings which have been moved from elsewhere in the region and carefully re-erected on site.

SUDBURY

The largest of the 'wool towns' and still home to a number of weaving concerns. Unlike Lavenham, it kept its industry because it was a port, and the result is a much more varied architectural picture. The surrounding countryside is some of the loveliest in Suffolk, and the River Stour is a further plus, with launch trips, rowing boats and fishing all available. Sudbury boasts three medieval churches, but what most visitors make a beeline for is **Gainsborough's House** on Market Hill. The painter Thomas Gainsborough was born here in 1727 in the house built by his father John. More of the artist's work is displayed in this Georgian-fronted house than in any other gallery, and there are also assorted 18th century memorabilia and furnishings and a changing programme of contemporary art exhibitions.

SUTTON HOO

A mile or so east of Woodbridge on the opposite bank of the Deben is the **Sutton Hoo burial site**, a group of a dozen grassy barrows which hit the headlines in 1939. Excavations brought to light the outline of an 80' long Anglo-Saxon ship, filled with one of the greatest hoards of treasure ever discovered in Britain. The priceless find includes gold coins and ornaments, silverware, weapons and armoury, drinking horns and leather cups; it is housed in the British Museum, but there are exhibitions, replicas and plenty of other interest at the site.

WOODBRIDGE

Standing at the head of the Deben estuary, Woodbridge is a place of considerable charm, with a considerable sense of history, as both market town and port. The shipbuilding and allied industries flourished here as at most towns on the Suffolk coast, and there's still plenty of activity on and by the river, though nowadays it is all leisure-oriented. Originally used as a corn exchange, the Shire Hall now houses the **Suffolk Horse Museum**, which is an exhibition devoted

The Tide Mill and Quay

to the Suffolk Punch breed of heavy working horse, the oldest such breed in the world. Woodbridge is lucky enough to have two marvellous mills, both in working order, and both great attractions for the visitor: The **Tide Mill**, on the quayside close to the town centre, and **Buttrum's Mill**, whose six storeys make her the tallest surviving tower mill in Suffolk.

96 The Australian Arms

Hamlet Street,
Haverhill, Suffolk
CB9 8QQ
Tel: 01440 702544

Directions:
Close to the centre
of Haverhill.

The Australian Arms is an attractive redbrick building on an elevated site a very short walk from the town centre. Glen and Jacky Boyle arrived in the middle of 2002 and immediately began applying a new broom and started to implement plans to widen the pub's appeal. First-time visitors are welcomed into a warm, spacious and comfortable ambience in which the regulars will notice the transformation made by the incoming tenants. One of the most eye-catching features is a cast-iron stove in a modern brick housing that reaches up to the ceiling in the roomy carpeted lounge. The three cask ales always available in the bar include the excellent Greene King IPA, the favourite of many a connoisseur of good beer. The changes made by the Boyles will cover all aspects of the pub. They have started to serve food, from a menu that combines traditional English and more contemporary elements.

The overnight accommodation at the pub comprises four comfortably appointed bedrooms, two of which now have en suite facilities. The pub fields a team in the local quiz league, and on Saturday night hosts a live music evening. The Australian Arms, which has a beer garden and off-road parking, is a very agreeable place to pause while exploring Haverhill, which is notable for its fine Victorian architecture. One much older building that is well worth a visit is Anne of Cleves House: after her marriage to Henry VIII (the shortest marriage of the six) she was given an allowance and spent the rest of her days here and in Richmond. With A roads leading in all directions from Haverhill, the pub is also a convenient base for excursions further afield.

Opening Hours: 11.30-2.30 & 5-11, Fri & Sat 11-11, Sun 12-10.30

Food: A la carte

Credit Cards: Mastercard, Visa.

Accommodation: 4 rooms (2 en suite)

Facilities: Car park

Entertainment: Live music Saturday

Local Places of Interest/Activities:
Haverhill: Anne of Cleves House, East Town Country Park 1 mile

The Bristol Arms **97**

Bristol Hill,
Shotley Gate,
Ipswich,
Suffolk IP9 1PU
Tel: 01473 787200
Fax: 01473 788686

Directions:

Eight miles southeast of Ipswich. Take the A137 to the southern edge of Ipswich, then turn left on to the B1456 through Woolverstone, Chelmondiston and Shotley Street to Shotley Gate at the mouth of the River Stour.

Nando Sappia, his wife Pauline and their sons Scott and Barry are the welcoming hosts at the **Bristol Arms**, which enjoys a superb setting by the River Stour, with splendid views of the river and over to the port of Harwich on the opposite bank. Dating back in part to the 12th century and once the haunt of smugglers, the inn has a particularly warm and friendly atmosphere, and behind the smart pink and red painted frontage the bay-windowed bar is a perfect spot to relax over a pint of real ale or a glass of wine. There's a strong nautical theme to the decor, with very effective use made of wood, and the theme carries through to Scott's menu, with crabs from Cromer and fish landed daily at Lowestoft among the specialities.

The non-smoking restaurant seats 80 in comfort, and when the weather is kind the patio garden, with seats for 60, really comes into its own. A pianist plays in the bar on Fridays, and the inn holds occasional other live music and karaoke evenings. The Bristol Arms has plenty of parking space and facilities for disabled visitors. An unusual and very useful amenity at the inn is a little shop-cum-off licence selling drinks, ice creams, sweets and small gifts. Almost next to the inn, at the very tip of the peninsula, is a large marina where a classic boat festival is an annual occasion. Shotley village, a little way up the road, is best known as the home of *HMS Ganges*, and a little museum records the history of the establishment.

Opening Hours: 11-11 (winter 11-2.30 & 5.30-11, Sun 12-2.30 & 6-10.30)

Food: A la carte

Credit Cards: Mastercard, Visa.

Accommodation: None

Facilities: Car park, wheelchair access + toilets

Entertainment: Pianist Friday, occasional other live music

Local Places of Interest/Activities: Ipswich 8 miles

Internet/Website: e-mail: bristolarms@aol.com

98

The Cherry Tree

Exning Road,
Newmarket,
Suffolk CB8 0EZ
Tel: 01638 663273

Directions:

The inn is about half
a mile out of
Newmarket on the
Exning road
(B1103).

Visitors to the **Cherry Tree**, a 100-year-old pub on a corner site half a mile east of Cambridge, can be sure of the warmest of welcomes from hands-on landlady Carole Streatfield. Her customers always come first, and she makes sure that no one ever stays hungry or thirsty. An excellent range of ales, lagers, ciders, wines and spirits is available throughout the all-day opening hours, and straightforward, good value bar snacks and pub meals are served lunchtime and evening Tuesday to Friday, from noon to 7 on Saturday and from 1 to 4 on Sunday. The public rooms comprise a spacious through lounge-bar and a separate dining area, and the Cherry Tree also has a beer garden.

There's always a good atmosphere here: the locals love it and they certainly love their racing, and the talk in the bar is never far away from the day's results and tomorrow's prospects. Newmarket is home to some 16,000 humans and 3,000 racehorses, and many of the Cherry Tree's regulars have connections with the industry. As well as top flat racing on its two racecourses, the town has numerous associated attractions, including the National Horseracing Museum, the Jockey Club and Nell Gwynn's House. Out of town, and just moments from the pub, Exning is an ancient village offering quiet, pleasant walks; it was originally the home of an important local market, but when the village was ravaged by a plague, the market moved a short way to the west - hence Newmarket!

Opening Hours: 11-11, Sun 12-10.30

Food: A la carte and bar snacks

Credit Cards: None

Accommodation: None

Facilities: Car park

Entertainment: Live music Friday & Saturday

Local Places of Interest/Activities:
Newmarket races, Racing Museum, National Stud, Nell Gwynn's House

The Cherrytree Inn 99

73 Cumberland Street,
Woodbridge,
Suffolk IP12 4AG
Tel: 01394 384627

Directions:
The inn lies 1½ miles off the A12 at the southern Woodbridge roundabout, opposite Notcutts Garden centre.

Since taking over as tenants of the **Cherry Tree Inn** in January 2001, Geoff and Sheila Ford have made quite an impact on the pub scene, nominated for Community Pub of the Year and a winner in the Woodbridge in Bloom competition. The 17th century building has a charming, characterful interior of wood panelling, twisting oak beams, low ceilings and open fires. Adnams real ales and various guests have earned a Cask Marque Award 'for the perfect pint', and a wide range of food is served, mainly cooked on the premises, and using local suppliers as much as possible. There's a choice of traditional roasts for Sunday lunch, and home-made puddings round off a meal in style.

Apart from the good food and drink, the Cherry Tree Inn is very much a social hub of the neighbourhood, with an appeal that extends to the whole family. There are swings and other amusements for children and picnic tables for everyone in the lawned garden, which is partly sheltered by a Grade II listed barn (the Fords plan to convert that barn to provide guest accommodation from early 2003). In the bars, most of the classic board games are played, several teams assemble for the Thursday night quiz (free plate of chips for every team!), and on Friday there's live music, with different performers every week. The splendid town of Woodbridge is a place of many attractions, including a pedestrianised street of excellent shops, two museums and two fine old mills Buttrum's Mill, the tallest surviving tower mill in Suffolk, and the 18th century Tide Mill on the quayside close to the town centre. A mile or so east of town is one of the county's, if not the country's, most interesting visitor attractions, the Sutton Hoo burial site. The River Deben, with a harbour and yacht chandler's, is close by, and a cycle route runs very near the pub.

Opening Hours: 11-11.

Food: A la carte

Credit Cards: Amex, Mastercard, Visa.

Accommodation: Planned for early 2003

Facilities: Car park, children's play area

Entertainment: Quiz night Thursday, Live music Friday

Local Places of Interest/Activities:
Woodbridge town centre ¼ mile, River Deben (yacht harbour) ¼ mile, Sutton Hoo 1 mile, Rendlesham Forest 5 miles, Butley Priory 5 miles, Ipswich 6 miles

Internet/Website:
e-mail: cherrytree.woodbridge@btinternet.com
website:
www.cherrytree.woodbridge.btinternet.co.uk

100

The Cock Inn

The Green, Polstead,
Suffolk CO6 5AL
Tel/Fax: 01206 263150

Directions:

Polstead is 11 miles
southwest of Ipswich off
the B1068 (A12 then
B1068); or A1071
beyond Hadleigh, then
minor road marked
Polstead. From
Colchester, take the
A134 to Nayland, then
B1087 to Stoke-by-
Nayland, then minor
road to Polstead.

The Cock Inn is a pretty pink-washed public house on the equally pretty village green in Polstead. The main part of the inn dates from the 17th century, while the restaurant is housed in a Victorian extension. The inn is run with great dedication and efficiency by sisters Jo and Karen Leafe, who have been the leaseholders here since 1999. Both are trained chefs, but Karen does most of the cooking, with Jo looking after front of house. Three real ales are always on tap in the bar, and there's an excellent choice of other beers and lagers, cider, wines and spirits. Visitors come from far and wide to sample the excellent fare on offer, which includes salmon fishcakes and a splendid steak & kidney pudding. A popular choice for a satisfying lunchtime snack is the Suffolk huffer, a triangular roll with a choice of several fillings.

The menu, which changes monthly to make the best use of the pick of the season, provides plenty of choice, but, as the girls say, 'if you can't see what you want on the menu - ask'. Everything is freshly prepared and attractively presented, and the sisters' expertise was rewarded in 1998, 1999, 2000 and 2001 with an AA rosette for culinary excellence. That was thoroughly deserved, as was the 2002 award as regional runner-up in the Green Apple Heritage search to find Britain's prettiest pub. The pleasure of a meal is enhanced by the decor and the furnishings in the restaurant, including exposed brickwork, beamed ceiling and open fire. There are more seats in the bar, and when the sun shines the picnic benches on the front lawn come into their own. Families are very welcome at this friendly place, and children have a play area where they can romp.

Opening Hours: 11-3 & 6-11 (closed Mon except Bank Holidays)

Food: A la carte and bar snacks

Credit Cards: Mastercard, Visa, Switch, Solo

Accommodation: None

Facilities: Car park

Entertainment: None

Local Places of InterestActivities:
Stoke-by-Nayland 2 miles, Hadleigh 5 miles

Internet/Website:
e-mail: enquiries@the-cock-inn-polstead.fsbusiness.co.uk

website: www.geocities.com/cockatpolstead

The Crown & Castle

South Street, Risby,
Nr Bury St Edmunds,
Suffolk IP28 6QU
Tel: 01284 810393

Directions:

Risby lies 3 miles west
of Bury St Edmunds
half a mile from the
A14.

In a pretty village off the A14 west of Bury, the **Crown & Castle** is a traditional pub restaurant with an attractive Georgian frontage in brick and flint. Inside, there are two pleasant bars done out in blue and plum, with cosy settees. Pool and darts are played in the back bar. In one of the passages is a deep well going down 110 feet to running water. In the non-smoking restaurant area an excellent selection of food is prepared by landlord Malcolm Missing, who runs the pub with his wife June. Sandwiches, jacket potatoes, omelettes and burgers are popular lunchtime snacks, while for full meals the choice runs from whitebait, paté, prawn cocktail and deep-fried brie for starters to main courses like scampi, cod, Thai chicken green curry, cottage pie and steaks. There are always vegetarian dishes, and children can choose from their own menu.

Two real ales head a good variety of beers and lagers, and there's also a fair choice of wines. Picnic benches at the front let visitors take the sun, and a patio will be developed at the back for 2003. Risby is a very agreeable place for a stroll, with a church, a garden centre, antique centre and a blacksmith's shop among the attractions. The historic town of Bury St Edmunds, with its abbey, cathedral, St Mary's Church and numerous other sights, is a short drive away. Country roads to the north lead to Hengrave Hall, a rambling Tudor mansion where the greengage was first imported, while to the south is the National Trust's Ickworth House. The historic town of Newmarket is only about 10 miles away.

Opening Hours: Mon-Sat 12-3 & 5-11; Sun 12-3 & 7-10.30

Food: Served 12-2 & 7-9

Credit Cards: Mastercard, Visa, Maestro, Electron, Switch, Solo and JCB

Accommodation: None.

Facilities: Car park

Entertainment: Occasional quiz

Local Places of Interest/Activities: Bury St Edmunds 3 miles, West Stow Country Park 3 miles, Lark Valley Park 4 miles, Lackford (Suffolk Wildlife Trust Reserve) 5 miles

102 The Dog & Duck Inn

Station Road,
Campsea Ashe,
Nr Woodbridge,
Suffolk IP13 0PT
Tel: 01728 748439

Directions:

From the A12 Ipswich-Lowestoft road take the B1078 2½ miles to Campsea Ashe. The inn is on the left in the centre of the village, opposite Wickham Market station.

The Dog & Duck is an early-19th century inn with a friendly, mellow atmosphere generated by Terry and Barbara Burgess. This is their first venture into the licensed trade, and in their two years here they have built up a strong local following. Barbara is an excellent cook, and her home-made steak & kidney pies are always in demand. Real ales feature in a wide selection of liquid refreshment. With the A12 close by, Campsea Ashe is a good base for touring this pleasant part of the country, and the Dog & Duck offers a choice of overnight guest accommodation - five Bed & Breakfast chalets, all en suite doubles, and two of these are for up to four guests. One of the chalets is wheelchair accessible. Children and pets are welcome, and there's ample car parking space.

Pool, darts and boules are all played keenly at the pub, which attracts a wide spectrum of guests - locals, walkers, cyclists, motorists, small coach parties; there's even a hitching post for guests arriving on horseback! In the village itself, the Church of St John is well worth a visit, and other attractions include the towns of Woodbridge and Aldeburgh, Tunstall Forest, the Anglo-Saxon burial site at Sutton Hoo and walks by the River Orde in the bracing East Coast air.

Opening Hours: 11-2.30 (not Wed) & 7-11, Sun 12-2.30 & 7-10

Food: Bar meals

Credit Cards: Mastercard, Visa

Accommodation: 5 en suite chalets

Facilities: Car park.

Entertainment: Monthly quiz, occasional music nights

Local Places of Interest/Activities:
Woodbridge 5 miles, Orford 7 miles, Aldeburgh 10 miles

The Dolphin Inn **103**

Peace Place,
Thorpeness, Suffolk
IP16 4NA
Tel: 01728 454994
Fax: 01728 454971

Directions:

In the centre of
Thorpeness, which
lies on the coast 6
miles east of
Saxmundham and 2
miles north of
Aldeburgh on the
coast road.

In the heart of the unique holiday village of Thorpeness, the **Dolphin** is a redbrick, tile-roofed inn that combines the spirit of the old with the facilities expected of a modern establishment. The ambience is friendly and relaxing in the two bars, and in the light, cheerful dining room lunches and dinners are served from a menu that changes frequently; not surprisingly, seafood is something of a speciality. In the summer months the garden, with a bar and a barbecue, comes into its own. The restaurant is open Tuesday to Saturday; at other times alternative dining arrangements can be made at the Thorpeness Hotel and Golf Club. For guests staying overnight the Dolphin has three en suite bedrooms with twin or double beds; extra beds and a travel cot can be provided. The rooms have won the coveted Sunday Times Golden Pillow Award for comfort and value.

Dolphin guests can enjoy a discount on green fees at the golf course and on charges for tennis at the club. A walk round Thorpeness reveals the true eccentricity of the place, which was created in the 1910s and which has a droll charm that is all its own. Among the many unusual buildings an 85ft water tower disguised as a house stands above the rest - it is known as the House in the Clouds. From the Dolphin it's just a short stroll to the sea, and an even shorter one to the Meare, a shallow boating and pleasure lake. Thorpeness is a fascinating place to visit at any time, but it really comes to life in the summer, and in the week following the late-August Aldeburgh Carnival a regatta is held on the Meare, culminating in a splendid fireworks display.

Opening Hours: 11-3 & 6-11 (longer hours in summer months)

Food: A la carte Tues-Sat

Credit Cards: All the major cards except Amex

Accommodation: 3 en suite rooms

Facilities: Car park, large garden, patio, outside bar and barbeque.

Entertainment: None

Local Places of Interest/Activities:
Aldeburgh 2 miles, Sizewell 1 mile, Saxmundham 6 miles, Snape Maltings 6 miles

Internet/Website:
e-mail: info@thorpeness.co.uk
website: www.thorpeness.co.uk

104

The Half Moon

4 High Street,
Lakenheath,
Suffolk IP27 9JX
Tel: 01842 861484

Directions:

The pub is on the main street of Lakenheath, 12 miles northwest of Bury St Edmunds. A1101 from Bury to Icklingham, then B1112.

With its distinctive grey flintstone frontage and prominent pub sign, the **Half Moon** is easy to find on the main street of Lakenheath, a sizeable village that stretches along the B1112 north of Mildenhall. Inside, the pub has traditional decor and an intimate, inviting feel, and visiting eyes are drawn upwards to the ceiling, where all the planets in the solar system are depicted. Landlord Rupert Sandells takes excellent care of his customers with a good choice of things to eat and drink. The Greene King range is on hand to satisfy thirsts, and the unusually extensive menu offers an outstanding choice for diners in the 32-cover non-smoking restaurant. The specials board, with the day's home-made pies, curry, pasta and other daily goodies, supplements a printed menu that takes its inspiration from around the world: Mediterranean tuna fishcke, Chinese pancakes and stir-fries, filled Jalapeno peppers, pork schnitzel, ostrich steak, Cajun cod fillet, grilled haddock with a cheese and Dijon mustard cream sauce, Italian meatballs and garlic sausage on a bed of pasta. For more traditional tastes, prawn cocktail, trout with almonds, roast shoulder of lamb and rump, sirloin, fillet and T-bone steaks in various sizes fit the bill.

Food is served lunchtime and evening every day except Monday; Sunday lunch centres round a popular carvery, there's another carvery option on Thursday, and Wednesday is curry night. Karaoke and live bands provide regular entertainment, and there's an area where children can play in the patio garden behind the pub. The area is great for walking, and local attractions include a nature reserve at Hockwold, Grimes Graves and Thetford Forest. Church historians will find plenty of interest in Lakenheath's Church of St Mary, whose treasures include medieval wall paintings and intricately carved bench ends.

Opening Hours: 12-3 and 6-11 Mon-Fri; 12-11 Sat; 12-10.30 Sun.

Food: Extensive à la carte and bar meals menu.

Credit Cards: Diners, Mastercard, Visa

Accommodation: None

Facilities: Car park, children's play area

Entertainment: Karaoke and live music nights

Local Places of Interest/Activities: Aircraft watching, Thetford (Forest, Grimes Graves etc) 4 miles, Hockwold Nature Reserve 4 miles, Mildenhall 8 miles

The Ivy House 105

Wilby Road,
Stradbroke,
Suffolk IP21 5JN
Tel:
01379 384634

Directions:

Stradbroke is on
the B1118
Framlingham
road 5 miles east
of Diss.

Situated in the lovely village of Stradbroke, **The Ivy House** is a classic country inn, a 16th century house that has been a pub for more than 100 years. During that time it has had only five owners, the latest being John and Brenda Huby, who provide a welcome along with Charlie, their loveable West Highland terrier. The pink-washed facade, topped by a steeply raked thatched roof, is a very pretty sight, and the spotless interior is no less appealing, with beams and brasses and jugs hanging above the bar counter. Darts and cribbage are played in the public bar, where Adnams bitter comes straight from the barrel and Indian Cobra lager is an increasingly popular choice.

Happy hour from 6.30 to 7.30 Tuesday to Saturday sees reductions on the price of beers and wines. There are seats for 32 in the dining area, whose walls are hung with attractive watercolours. John does the cooking, a task that he greatly enjoys, and his menu offers a good choice of dishes, from British classics such as prawn cocktail, scampi or steak & kidney pudding to halloumi cheese with smoked pork loin, Mediterranean chicken or enchiladas filled with chilli beef. The inn has plenty of parking spaces and a lawned garden with picnic tables and a pond. Every month John organises special theme evenings featuring perhaps steaks or the cuisines of Italy, Spain or India. The B1118 runs north to Diss and south to Framlingham with its marvellous castle.

Opening Hours: 12-2 & 6.30-11, Sun 12-3 & 7-10.30. Closed Monday

Food: A la carte

Credit Cards: All the major cards

Accommodation: None

Facilities: Car park

Entertainment: None

Local Places of Interest/Activities:
Local vineyards, Wingfield College 2 miles, Diss 5 miles

106   The Mill Inn

Market Cross Place,
Aldeburgh, Suffolk
IP15 5BJ
Tel: 01728 452563

Directions:

The Mill Inn is on
the seafront,
opposite the Moot
Hall. Aldeburgh lies
on the coast at the
end of the A1094,
off the A12.

Right on the seafront in the delightful town of Aldeburgh, the **Mill Inn** is a traditional public house with a cosy, welcoming atmosphere. It has been run for the last ten years by Sheila and Ted Fleming, who greet familiar faces and first-timers with equal friendliness, and behind the black-and-white frontage with its tiny-paned windows, the timbered bar is a perfect place to relax with a glass or two of the famous Adnams Ale. There are plenty of other beers available, along with a good selection of wines and spirits, and the Mill's home-cooked food is guaranteed to satisfy appetites sharpened by the bracing East Coast air. Fresh fish is always recommended, and fresh really means just that, as the fishermen's huts are literally a few seconds away on the beach. For those who want to enjoy a longer stay in this charming spot, the Mill offers Bed & Breakfast accommodation in four guest bedrooms - two doubles, a twin and a single. Guests wake to the sound of waves breaking on the beach, and a good traditional breakfast provides the drive for a day in the Suffolk air.

The ancient Moot Hall, which incorporates a small museum, is on the doorstep, and other places of interest a short stroll away include the striking modern lifeboat station and the Church of St Peter and St Paul with its beautiful stained glass window by John Piper of three Benjamin Britten parables - Britten spent much of his life in Aldeburgh and is buried in the churchyard. In season, Aldeburgh buzzes with activity, particularly around the time of the August carnival; outside season, it's quiet and peaceful. The town is a joy to visit at any time of the year, and the Mill Inn makes the ideal base.

Opening Hours: 11-3 & 6-11 (all day in summer)

Food: Bar meals

Credit Cards: All the major cards

Accommodation: 4 B&B rooms

Facilities: None

Entertainment: None

Local Places of Interest/Activities:
Thorpeness 2 miles, Sizewell 3 miles, Snape Maltings 3 miles

Internet/Website:
e-mail: tedmillinn@btinternet.com
website: www.themillinn.com

The Ordnance Hotel   107

1 Undercliff Road West,
Felixstowe,
Suffolk IP11 2AN
Tel: 01493 273427
Fax: 01493 282513

Directions:

The hotel is 200 yards
from the beach at
Felixstowe, which lies at
the eastern end of the A14.

Purpose-built in 1880, the **Ordnance Hotel** takes its name from the army quarters and stables that previously occupied the site. It is the first hotel on driving on to the seafront and stands well back from the road shaded by attractive trees. The day rooms comprise a large and comfortable carpeted bar furnished in traditional style; an equally roomy residents' lounge; and a restaurant with seats for 100. The function room is also of generous proportions, and the hotel has applied for a licence to hold civil wedding ceremonies. Overnight accommodation consists of 16 en suite bedrooms with all the usual facilities. The main menu in the restaurant features mostly traditional British dishes, and there's a bar menu for smaller appetites. Packed lunches can be provided with a little notice for guests spending the day exploring the local sights. The choice of real ales changes weekly, and the hotel has a very good wine list.

Entertainment at the Ordnance comes in the shape of regular quiz, live music and karaoke nights. Felixstowe has good shops, a pier, frequent bus and train services to Ipswich and the largest container port complex in Britain. To the north of the town is Felixstowe Ferry, a popular sailing centre, while to the south, at the tip of the peninsula, is Landguard Point, a nature reserve; close by is Landguard Fort, home to a fascinating museum of local history. Beyond the fort is an excellent viewing point for watching the comings and goings of the ships. The Ordnance Hotel is managed by Neil Quigley for the Lohan family, who also have the White Horse in Leiston.

Opening Hours: All day

Food: A la carte and bar snacks

Credit Cards: All the major cards

Accommodation: 16 en suite rooms

Facilities: Car park, function room

Entertainment: Quiz, live music and karaoke nights

Local Places of Interest/Activities:
Landguard Point 1 mile, Ipswich 6 miles

108 The Plough

*Mill Road,
Lakenheath,
Suffolk IP27 9DT
Tel: 01842 860285*

Directions:

Lakenheath is 12
miles northwest of
Bury St Edmunds.
A1101 from Bury to
Icklingham, then
B1112.

2002 saw the 200th birthday of the **Plough**, an attractive inn with a flintstone frontage. The bars and candlelit restaurant are cosy and inviting, and the inn has a large rear garden. Bar and restaurant menus provide plenty of choice for all appetites. Bar snacks and the lunch menu include BLT and Club sandwiches, tasty bratwurst with potato salad, scampi or cod with chips and salad, pizza and rack of ribs (half or full). The main menu starts with familiar favourites like garlic mushrooms or prawn cocktail, or the more unusual couscous stuffed pepper, while main dishes wines are mainly of German inspiration: porkhaxe with sauerkraut, jaegerschnitzel with mushroom sauce, wienerschnitzel (meat or vegetarian) with peas and carrots. The dessert menu tempts with the likes of alabama chocolate or luvable lemon lush pie. Food is served every session except Monday lunchtime.

The short wine list is also mainly German, and other drinks include Budweiser on tap and Greene King IPA. The German influence comes from tenant Linda Mueller, who runs the Plough with her husband Gary. Linda grew up in Germany and met Gary on the airbase at Lakenheath. They are both very fond of Germany and its food, so when they took over the Plough in June 2002 it was only natural that they should open a German restaurant. The Plough has parking spaces front and rear, and the garden is a popular spot when the sun shines.

Opening Hours: 11-2 & 6-10.30

Food: A la carte and bar meals

Credit Cards: Mastercard, Visa

Accommodation: None

Facilities: Car park

Entertainment: None

Local Places of Interest/Activities: Aircraft watching, Thetford (Forest, Grimes Graves etc) 4 miles, Hockwold Nature Reserve 4 miles, Mildenhall 8 miles

The Plough 109

Rede,
Nr Bury St Edmunds,
Suffolk IP29 4BE
Tel: 01284 789208

Directions:

Rede is 6 miles south
of Bury St Edmunds
off the A143.

The village of Rede, the highest point in the county of Suffolk, is the picturesque setting for a truly delightful inn. **The Plough** is a 16th century inn, its roof part thatched, part tiled, that has been run for the past 20 years by Brian and Joyce Desborough, now assisted by their daughter Amy. The location at one edge of the village green is one of unspoilt rural splendour: the inn is sheltered by a large and elegant willow, and wooden benches shaded by white parasols provide a perfect spot for enjoying a drink and something to eat on a fine summer's day. An ancient hand plough completes the idyllic scene at the front of the inn, while at the back the gardens include an aviary and a dovecote. Inside, all is old-world charm, with classic beams and plush, comfortable seats.

The Plough has built up a fine reputation for its outstanding hospitality and for its excellent ales and super home cooking by Joyce. The choice runs to some 20 dishes daily, and fresh produce, much of it local, is the input to tasty, satisfying dishes on a menu that changes daily; typical offerings might include venison sausage, calves' liver, monkfish creole and bobotie, a spicy lamb dish from South Africa. Game appears in season, and, although the portions are very hearty, room should definitely be kept for one of Joyce's desserts. Bury St Edmunds, an easy drive up the A143, was once one of the most important centres of pilgrimage in Europe, and now attracts tourists from near and far who come to see the ruins of the great Abbey and its gardens. Just before Bury, at Horringer, is another great visitor attraction, the National Trust's Ickworth House, an elegant treasure-filled Italianate building in a Capability Brown landscape.

Opening Hours: 12-3 & 6.30-11

Food: A la carte

Credit Cards: Amex, Mastercard, Visa.

Accommodation: None

Facilities: Car park

Entertainment: None

Local Places of Interest/Activities: Ickworth National Trust 5 miles, Bury St Edmunds 6 miles,

110 The Queens Head

*The Square,
Dennington,
Suffolk IP13 8AB
Tel: 01728 638241*

Directions:

Dennington lies on
the A1120 Yoxford-
Stowmarket road.
The inn is next to
the church. From
Framlingham, take
the B1116 (2 miles).

Built in 1528 and once a monastery, the **Queens Head** has all the atmosphere that its age
suggests, and with newly arrived Peter Mills and Hilary Cowie at the helm, the inn's reputation
for hospitality and good food will surely be enhanced. The pub stands in its own grounds,
with a large gravelled car park and an enclosed garden with a children's play area. The bar,
with its brick counter and hearth, old beams and country furniture, is a fine setting for
socialising over a pint of Adnams or a guest ale, and bar snacks and sandwiches are always
available. Food is an important part of the Queens Head's business, and home-cooked food is
served lunchtime and evening seven days a week. Steaks are a popular option on the extensive
menu, and there's a wide range of tempting desserts to round off a meal in style.

The pub has two separate dining areas, one for families, the other for adults only which
is non smoking. The pretty village of Dennington has a very interesting church and one of
the oldest Post Offices in the country. There are many places of interest to visit nearby, including
the superb Framlingham Castle and the amazing 18th century post mill at Saxtead Green.
There are several golf courses in the vicinity and numerous hiking trails, and the coast is 15
miles away. The Queens Head has no guest accommodation of its own, but there are several
Bed & Breakfast establishments close by.

Opening Hours: 12-2.30 & 6.30-11

Food: A la carte and bar snacks

Credit Cards: All the major cards

Accommodation: None

Facilities: Car park.

Entertainment: Background music

Local Places of Interest/Activities:
ramlingham Castle 2 miles, Saxtead Green 3
miles, Sibton Abbey 4 miles

The Railway Tavern 111

The Common,
Yaxley Road,
Mellis, Nr Eye,
Suffolk IP23 8DU
Tel: 01379 783416

Directions:

Mellis lies 3 miles southwest of Diss off the A143 or A140.

The Railway Tavern stands on the largest common in Suffolk, a conservation area noted for wild flowers. Colourful cultivated flowers adorn the spruce black-and-white outside of the tavern, and within, the two bars have the comfortable feel of a much-loved local; one of the bars has a piano and a pool table. Licensees Ruth and Denny Newman have a warm welcome for all their customers, and their springer spaniel Jess is equally friendly. Real ale enthusiasts are catered for in fine style with a choice of six brews, including Adnams Broadside, Greene King IPA and Woodforde's Wherry. Traditional pub dishes are served every day except Monday, and the Sunday roasts are always very popular.

Most of the classic pub games are played here, and the tavern fields pool, cricket and football teams. A quiz is held one Monday a month, and on the first Thursday of each month there's an evening of folk music. The Thornham Walks and Field Centre, with 12 miles of walks and a herb garden and nursery, is one of several attractions in the vicinity, and the tavern is an excellent base for exploring the countryside. Its three double bedrooms, all with en suite showers, tv and tea/coffee-making facilities, provide very comfortable Bed & Breakfast accommodation. The Railway Tavern was built in 1840 and for many years served passengers arriving at Mellis station, once an important stop on the Ipswich to Norwich main line. The station was closed in 1966, and the trains now rush through, but the unused station buildings and the signal box still stand.

Opening Hours: Mon & Tues 3.30-11, rest of the week from 12

Food: Home cooked fayre

Credit Cards: None

Accommodation: 3 en suite rooms

Facilities: Car parking, small function room

Entertainment: Quiz one Monday a month, live blues music, folk music 1st Thursday of the month

Local Places of Interest/Activities:
Diss 3 miles, Thornham Walks and Field Centre 2 miles, Yaxley 2 miles

112 The Scarlet Pimpernel

Millfield Way,
Haverhill,
Suffolk CB9 0JB
Tel/Fax:
  01440 705888

Directions:

The inn is half a
mile from
Haverhill on the
A143 road
towards Bury St
Edmunds.

The Scarlet Pimpernel is a pub for all the family, a big modern concept pub in yellow brick, with hanging flower baskets and a little tiled awning over the door. It stands on a neat private estate half a mile north of the town centre by the A143 Bury St Edmunds road, and though not right on the main road it is not nearly as elusive as the man after whom it is named - turn right into Millfield Way off the A143 and you'll see it. Behind the bricks the pub has considerable floor space, with partitioned sections adding intimacy, full carpeting and a nod to tradition given by wood panelling and some brass ornaments.

The pub is run with cheerful enthusiasm by chef and landlord Glenn Roberts and his partner Julie Light. Glenn's cooking is one of the major draws to this convivial place, and his wholesome, tasty dishes - curries are one of his specialities - are available from 12 to 3 and 6 to 9 Tuesday to Thursday, from 1 to 9 on Friday, from 12 to 9 on Saturday and from 12 to 6 on Sunday (no food on Monday). The real ales, which include residents and regularly changing guests, are kept in excellent order, and there's a good range of other beers, lagers, wines and spirits. The Scarlet Pimpernel has a beer garden and plenty of off-road parking. It's a very sociable and convivial place, and once a month it buzzes to the sound of live music on Friday and Saturday nights.

Opening Hours: 12-11, Fri & Sat 11-11, Sun 12-10.30

Food: A la carte

Credit Cards: Mastercard, Visa.

Accommodation: None

Facilities: Car park

Entertainment: Live music Sat & Sun once a month

Local Places of Interest/Activities: Haverhill (Anne of Cleves House, East Town Country Park 1 mile), Kedington Church of St Peter and St Paul 2 miles

The Swan Inn

113

Swan Lane, Barnby,
Nr Beccles,
Suffolk NR34 7QE
Tel: 01502 476646
Fax: 01502 711698

Directions:

Barnby is located on
the A146 4 miles east
of Beccles. The Swan
is situated just off
this road.

The Swan Inn is a neat pink-washed building located just off the A146 between Beccles and Lowestoft. Its front is adorned in summer with window boxes, and the picnic benches at the front are fringed by little bushes in tubs. Very much the centre of village life, it also attracts tourists who join the locals for anything from a convivial drink to a full meal. The Swan is much more than a village inn, it's also a top-notch restaurant specialising in seafood. Owner Don Cole, a former naval officer, is a successful fish merchant, and this fine old inn is his 'hobby'. His passion is very evident in both the decor and the menu. The bar areas and the Fisherman's Restaurant are filled to the gunwales with nautical articles and artefacts (note the boat in the ceiling!) and the menu majors on the best and freshest of the fruits of the sea.

The restaurant, managed in fine style by Charles Hall, is deservedly very popular, so booking is essential whether it's for lunch or dinner. But the Swan is even more than a village inn and top-notch restaurant, it's also a great place to stay when exploring the scenic and historic delights of the region. The accommodation is a self-contained flat for up to six people, with three bedrooms, bathroom, kitchen and lounge/dining room. While in Barnby, visitors should take time to stroll round the garden centre and look in at the handsome Church of St John; dating in part from around 1200, the church contains some notable wall paintings. Among the many places of interest within a short drive are the Transport Museum and the Nature Reserve at Carlton Colville, just south of Lowestoft.

Opening Hours: 11-11.

Food: A la carte

Credit Cards: All the major cards

Accommodation: 3-bedroom flat with bathroom, kitchen, lounge/diner

Facilities: Car park

Entertainment: None

Local Places of Interest/Activities: Waveney River Centre 3 miles, Beccles 4 miles, Carlton Colville (Transport Museum) 3 miles, Lowestoft 5 miles

114

The Swan Inn

*Station Hill, Bures,
Suffolk CO8 5DD
Tel: 01787 228121*

Directions:

Bures is on the
B1508 about
halfway between
Colchester and
Sudbury.

Ian and June Scott are the popular tenants of the **Swan Inn**, a traditional hostelry in a pleasant village on the River Stour. Window boxes and hanging baskets make a colourful display on the long frontage. To the rear there is an attractive walled garden and small car park. Inside the pub boasts two bars, both with real log fires. The Public bar has a tiled floor and is popular with walkers, farmers and local villagers alike. Traditional Pub games are also enjoyed here. The Lounge bar retains all its cosy old world charm with beamed ceilings, an abundance of bric-a-brac and photographs of Bures in days gone by. The Pub also has a rather unique bottle and Jug off sales. Locally brewed Greene King, Cask IPA and Abbot Ale are available along with a couple of lagers, Guinness and Cider. The Menu is traditional and unpretentious offering good value for money. Filled Baguettes and Jacket potatoes make satifying snacks whilst main meals include Steak and Guinness Pie, various Curries and the English favorite Cod, Chips and Mushy Peas.

Bures lies at a point where the Stour takes a sharp turn to the East, making a natural boundary between Essex and Suffolk; Bures is partly in each county, and the river is crossed by a new foot bridge that opened in 2002. A stroll round the village is rewarded with the sight of fine half-timbered houses and an elegant church, and a mile outside the village to the northeast is the thatched St Stephen's Chapel, which contains splendid medieval effigies of the Earls of Oxford. Also in the vicinity is the Paradise Centre at Lamarsh, with a garden centre, lots of animals and an area set out for children to play.

Opening Hours: Mon-Sat 11.30am to 11.00pm. Sun 12.00 to 10.30pm.

Food: Traditional Pub Fayre & Bar Snacks Mon-Sat 12.00-2.30pm and 6.00pm to 9.00pm Sun 12.00 to 2.30pm (Roast lunch only) Tea & Coffee available all day

Credit Cards: Mastercard, Visa, Switch, Solo.

Accommodation: None

Facilities: Parking at rear and on street. Local Train Station.

Local Places of Interest/Activities: Millennium footbridge opened 2002, River Stour boat trips, Lamarsh 2 miles, Colchester 6 miles, Sudbury 6 miles

The Triple Plea
115

Broadway,
Halesworth, Suffolk
IP19 8QW
Tel: 01986 874750

Directions:

From the A12 take the A144 Halesworth road. Go through Halesworth towards Bungay. At the fourth roundabout after Halesworth the pub is on the righthand side.

The Triple Plea is a handsome hostelry just north of the town on the A144 Bungay road. The exterior is very appealing, with hanging baskets adorning the cream-painted brick frontage topped by a roof in patterned tiles. Completing the summery scene are picnic benches under parasols, and there are more of these at the back on a lawn that leads down to open countryside. The bars are neat and cheerful, with black beams contrasting with creamy white walls, and a pool table in one corner. Proprietor James Martin, once a Weights and Measures inspector, now works on the other side of the bar, where he dispenses a good choice of drinks that include real ales from local as well as national breweries. The variety of the liquid refreshment is matched by the choice of food, which runs from hot and cold snacks and light lunches to three-course evening meals.

Top local suppliers ensure the freshness and quality of the ingredients, and the selection is always boosted by daily specials chalked up on boards. The chef is a particularly dab hand at soups - cream of parsnip, French onion, ham with lentils - and other daily specials could include macaroni cheese and a hearty lamb casserole. Steaks are great favourites, and Friday is special steak night. Other weekly events are the quiz on Tuesday and live music on Saturday. The area is very popular with walkers and cyclists, and two en suite guest bedrooms make the Triple Plea a good base for exploring the region. There's plenty to see in Halesworth itself, including two museums and an art gallery, and among other local attractions are the magnificent 'Cathedral of the Marshes' at Blythburgh and the Earsham Otter Trust on the banks of the Waveney, with a large colony of otters and many other creatures, from waterfowl to wallabies.

Opening Hours: 11-11 (Sun 12-10.30)

Food: Bar meals and à la carte

Credit Cards: All the major cards

Accommodation: 2 en suite double rooms

Facilities: Car park

Entertainment: Quiz Tuesday, live music Saturday

Local Places of Interest/Activities: Cycle and hiking paths nearby, Halesworth and District Museum, Earsham Otter Trust 10 miles, Blythburgh 6 miles, Southwold 8 miles

116

The Turks Head

Low Road, Hasketon,
Nr Woodbridge,
Suffolk IP13 6JG
Tel: 01394 382584

Directions:

Hasketon is situated
on the A12 2 miles
north of Woodbridge,
7 miles north of
Ipswich.

The Turks Head is a charming redbrick public house with friendly family owners Kirsty and Steve. Both are accomplished chefs with experience at leading local establishments, so it is not surprising that food is an important part of the business here. Using the best local suppliers as much as possible, they produce a good choice of dishes ranging from bar snacks to a full à la carte menu. Creeper adorns the frontage of the pub, and the bars are delightfully traditional, with tiled floors, a mighty inglenook fireplace and ancient beams hung with cups, mugs, glasses and ornamental brasses. Six real ales, including Greene King, Adnams and guests, are always on tap, and when the sun shines the food and drink can be enjoyed in the beer garden, which has a children's play area.

Dominoes is the favourite game in the bar, and visitors are encouraged to watch the experts at work - one of the locals has been playing here for more than 50 years! The Turks Head also promotes events such as horse shows and car rallies and can cater for horse and carriage operators. The pub has no letting bedrooms, but caravan and camping facilities are available. There's plenty to see and do in the vicinity, including shopping in Woodbridge and Ipswich, the amazing Sutton Hoo Anglo-Saxon burial site, Butley Priory and Rendlesham Forest, once famous for UFO sightings. The coast is easily reached, offering bracing walks in the East Coast air.

Opening Hours: 12-3 (not Mon except Bank Holidays) & 6-11, Sun 12-4 & 7-10.30

Food: A la carte and bar snacks

Credit Cards: All the major cards

Facilities: Car park

Accommodation: None (caravan and camping facilities)

Entertainment: Occasional live music

Local Places of Interest/Activities: Woodbridge 2 miles, Sutton Hoo 4 miles, Rendlesham Forest 4 miles, Ipswich 7 miles, Orford 8 miles

Internet/Website: website: www.turkshead.info

The Venture

Main Road,
Chelmondiston,
Nr Ipswich,
Suffolk IP9 1DX
Tel: 01473 780327
Fax: 01473 780327

Directions:

The inn is on the main street of Chelmondiston, 5 miles south of Ipswich on the B1456.

Dating from the 18th century, the **Venture** presents an attractive pink-painted front on the main street of Chelmondiston. Kay and Robert Davies, who took over in July 2002, are very warm and friendly hosts, and their dogs Fudge and Shannon are equally affable. Real ales from local and national breweries are on tap in the bar, which features a striking carved wooden counter and an open log fire. Food is an important part of the business here, and Kay specialises in dishes featuring local fish. Robert contributes with his own recipes for chilli and chicken curry, the latter based on a dish from Sri Lanka that he enjoyed while on holiday there. A daily specials board adds to the choice, and fish and chips are available to take away.

Pool, darts and cribbage are played in the pub, and there's live music every other Friday. Children are welcome, and they have a play area in the garden. The village of Chelmondiston has no bank, so the Venture's cashback service is particularly useful. The Venture takes its present name from a barge built locally in the early 1900s. The original name board of the barge stands on display outside the pub, while the rest of the barge - now a wreck - can be seen at Pin Mill, a well-known sailing centre that was once a major manufacturer of barges. Once a year veteran barges gather for a race that starts at Pin Mill and ends at Harwich. Another popular annual occasion is the classic boat festival held at Shotley Marina, on the very tip of the peninsula.

Opening Hours: 11-11, Sun 12-10.30 (winter 11-3 & 5-11, Sat & Sun all day)

Food: Traditional pub food + takeaway fish & chips

Credit Cards: Diners, Mastercard, Visa

Accommodation: None

Facilities: Car park, children's play area, cashback service

Entertainment: Live music every other Friday

Local Places of InterestActivities:
Pin Mill 1 mile, Ipswich 5 miles, Shotley 3 miles

118

The Victoria

The Street,
Earl Soham,
Nr Stowmarket,
Suffolk IP13 7RL
Tel: 01728 685758

Directions:

Earl Soham is on
the A1120 3 miles
east of
Framlingham.

Paul and Clare Hooper, ably assisted by Paul's parents, have run the **Victoria** in fine style since taking over in 1997. Flower tubs and climbing greenery adorn the immaculate white outside of the pub, while inside all is cosy and old-fashioned, with tiled or wooden floors, open log fires, pictures and memorabilia of Queen Victoria and a display of locally made clocks for sale. Food is an important part of the business here, served every lunchtime and every evening. Everything is fresh, wholesome and full of good honest flavours, and the day's choice could include casseroles and curries, goulash, fish specials, seasonal game and excellent salads. Toasted sandwiches and ploughman's platters are popular for quicker snacks, but no one should leave without sampling one of Paul's mother's super desserts - perhaps cheesecake, steamed pudding or treacle and walnut tart.

Locally brewed beers, Suffolk cider and interesting wines are on tap or on hand to accompany the food or to enjoy by themselves. When built as an alehouse in the middle of the 19th century, the Victoria was adjacent to a brewery. The brewery moved in 2000 to a new site 100 yards up the road, where it now produces a mild beer and three bitters. Visitors can take a guided tour of the brewery by arrangement. Parking is available front and rear at the Victoria, where occasional Tuesdays bring folk music, sometimes with morris dancing. Tourist attractions in the vicinity include the village's 13th century church and the splendid Saxtead windmill.

Opening Hours: 12-3 & 6-10.30

Food: A la carte

Credit Cards: None

Accommodation: None

Facilities: Car park

Entertainment: Folk music some Tuesdays

Local Places of Interest/Activities: Earl Soham 13th century church, birdwatching, Framlingham Castle 3 miles, Saxtead Windmill 2 miles, Stowmarket 12 miles

The White Hart Inn 119

London Road,
Blythburgh,
Nr Halesworth,
Suffolk IP19 9LQ
Tel/Fax:
  01502 478217

Directions:

The inn lies right
on the London
Road (A12) at
Blythburgh.

A former courthouse dating back to the 16th century, the **White Hart Inn** retains a number of fine original features, including ornate beams in the bar area and a large, handsome inglenook fireplace. The inn, whose facade is adorned in spring and summer with cheerful hanging baskets, has been owned since early 1999 by Mike and Julie Davis, who offer their customers an impressive range of food and drink. Traditional ales from Adnams head a long list of beers, lagers and ciders, and the choice of home-cooked dishes spans the whole range from quick bar snacks to a children's menu and a full à la carte selection served in the separate restaurant. Dishes of the day widen the options still further, and the seafood specials are definitely not to be missed.

Blythburgh's Church of Holy Trinity, almost cathedral-like in its scale and grandeur, is one of the great landmarks of the county, a stirring sight as it rises above the marshy Blyth estuary, visible for miles around and floodlit at night to spectacular effect. This is also splendid walking country, and bird-watchers will head for the sanctuary at nearby Walberswick. The A12 provides quick and easy access north and south, while a short distance to east and west respectively are the resort of Southwold, equally interesting to the holidaymaker and the historian, and the fine old market town of Halesworth. With so much exploring to be done and sights see, this is not a part of the world to rush through in a hurry, and the White Hart makes an ideal base for touring. Its four en suite chalets, twins or doubles, offer comfort, modern amenities and lovely views over the estuary. Children and pets are welcome, and the inn has a patio and beer garden.

Opening Hours: 11-11, Sun 12-10.30

Food: Bar meals and à la carte

Credit Cards: All the major cards

Accommodation: 4 en suite chalets

Facilities: Car park

Entertainment: None

Local Places of Interest/Activities:
Blythburgh Church of Holy Trinity,
Halesworth 5 miles, Southwold 4 miles,
Walberswick 4 miles

120

The White Horse

The Street, Corton,
Nr Lowestoft,
Suffolk
NR32 5HP
Tel: 01502 730294

Directions:

Corton is situated
on the coast road
B1385 3 miles
north of Lowestoft.

The White Horse is a very appealing inn on the main street of Corton. Built in 1850, it recently acquired a conservatory extension, and the whole place looks spick and span after repainting. Inside, the bar and lounge are pleasant and relaxing, with a straightforward, uncluttered look and a relaxed ambience that is just right for the mature client base and for tourists who take a break on their journey along the coast. The inn is run by the Brighty family, who are on hand throughout the day to welcome old friends and greet first timers and to attend to their thirsts and appetites. Two experienced chefs produce a decent choice of value-for-money dishes using fresh wholesome ingredients. Everything is good, but the savoury pies and the sweets have won particular favour with the regulars.

The food is served from 12 to 2.30 and from 6.30 to 9 every day. The pub quiz has really caught on at the White Horse, with cash prizes available for sharp brains no fewer than three times each week - Wednesday, Friday and Sunday. Less taxing to the brain cells but equally popular is the inn's version of Play Your Cards Right, which takes place on Wednesday and Friday. The inn has ample off-road parking, with two slots for disabled visitors. It's almost on the sea, in a fairly secluded setting between the sizeable towns of Lowestoft and Great Yarmouth. The A12, just minutes away, provides ready access north and south, while a few miles inland from Corton are two important visitor attractions - the magnificent Somerleyton Hall and the beautiful Herringfleet Windmill, the last survivor of the Broadland wind pumps used to assist in draining the marshes.

Opening Hours: 11-11, Sun 12-10.30

Food: A la carte

Credit Cards: Mastercard, Visa.

Accommodation: None

Facilities: Car park

Entertainment: Quiz Wed, Fri, Sun; Play Your Cards Right Wed, Fri

Local Places of Interest/Activities:
Lowestoft 3 miles, Great Yarmouth 6 miles

The White Horse   **121**

North Street,
Sudbury, Suffolk
CO10 1RF
Tel: 01787 371063

Directions:

In the centre of
Sudbury. Parking at
rear, off Girling
Street.

The White Horse is a fine traditional coaching inn with beer gardens at the rear and side, floodlit at night and with heaters to allow alfresco sipping even on cool evenings. Inside, the inn has an inviting period appeal with lots of wood panelling in evidence. It has been run for the past 15 years by the Martin family - Anne and her two sons Nick and Steve. Anne's food is an important part of the inn's attraction, served from 11.30 to 3 and from 5 to 8 except Monday and Sunday evening. There's plenty of seating throughout the inn, and the fare on offer ranges from Simply Snax to the full Nosebag Menu. The former consists of sandwiches with hot or cold fillings, toasties, jacket potatoes and burgers, while the latter runs the gamut from ploughman's platters, omelettes and salads to pasta, seafood, curries (chicken, beef, vegetable), lasagne, gammon and steaks. The Naughty But Nice dessert menu tempts with the likes of sherry trifle, Bramley apple pie, sticky toffee pudding and pancakes filled with lemon & sugar, cherry or golden syrup - scrumptious and very hard to resist!

Greene King IPA and Old Speckled Hen are among the beers on tap, and there are some well-priced house wines. Sudbury is a hospitable market town of great appeal, whether it's for interesting shops, cruises on the River Stour or walks along its banks, the three splendid medieval churches or the house where the painter Thomas Gainsborough was born.

Opening Hours: 11-11.

Food: A la carte

Credit Cards: None

Accommodation: None

Facilities: Parking at rear

Entertainment: None

Local Places of Interest/Activities: Sudbury (Gainsborough's House, Corn Exchange etc), Long Melford 3 miles

122 The White Horse Hotel

Station Road, Leiston,
Suffolk IP16 4HD
Tel: 01728 830694
Fax: 01728 833105

Directions:

Leiston is situated 4 miles east of Saxmundham off the B1119. Saxmundham lies just off the A12 between Woodbridge and Southwold.

At the centre of Leiston life for 250 years, the **White Horse** is a handsome redbrick building with striking blue window surrounds and shutters. Managed by George and Linda Howe for the owning Lohan family, the hotel has 12 well-appointed en suite bedrooms, two bars, a good restaurant and a small meeting room. Several real ales are always available, and an extensive wine list complements the accomplished French/English cuisine that offers both traditional and modern dishes. Families are very welcome, and children have an excellent outdoor play area in the spacious garden. The hotel hosts regular live music and karaoke evenings, and there's a popular quiz every Tuesday. A large screen tv in one of the bars shows the major sporting events.

The White Horse is an ideal base for exploring the Suffolk Heritage Coast, which runs for 34 miles from Kessingland in the north to Felixstowe in the south. Dunwich Heath, Minsmere Bird Reserve, Orford Castle and the lovely old town of Aldeburgh are among the many places of interest on the coast. Inland, there are also many attractions, including Framlingham, famous for its school and its castle, and Snape Maltings, home of the Aldeburgh Music Festival. This is one of many hostelries built in the mid-18th century with the name of the White Horse. The owners of the time were eager to show their loyalty to the new royal dynasty by using the Hanoverian badge of a galloping white horse on their inn sign. The Lohan family also have the Ordnance Hotel in Felixstowe.

Opening Hours: 11-11, Sun 12-10.30

Food: A la carte and bar food

Credit Cards: All the major cards

Accommodation: 12 en suite rooms

Facilities: Car park, children's play area, small function and conference facilities

Entertainment: Quiz Tuesday, live music and karaoke nights

Local Places of Interest/Activities
Leiston Abbey, Long Shop Museum, Sizewell 1 mile, Aldeburgh 3 miles, Snape 4 miles, Minsmere 4 miles

Internet/Website:
website: www.whitehorsehotel.co.uk

4 Essex

PLACES OF INTEREST:

PUBS AND INNS:

The Hidden Inns of East Anglia

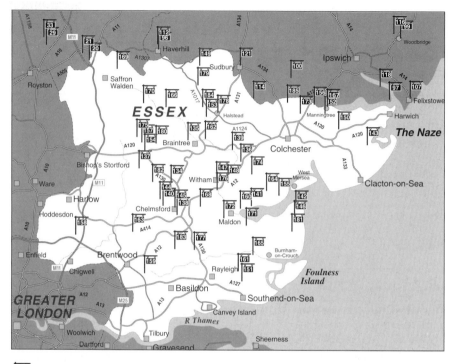

The Beehive, Great Waltham

The Bell, Panfield, Nr Braintree

The Bell Inn, Feering, Nr Colchester

The Black Lion, High Roding

The Carpenters Arms, Great Baddow

The Chapel Inn, Coggeshall

The Chequers, Writtle

The Chequers Inn, Goldhanger

The Cricketers, Bradwell-on-Sea

The Crown, Thorpe-le-Soken

The Duck Inn, Writtle, Nr Chelmsford

The Fox & Hounds, Chelmsford

The Fox & Hounds, Tillingham

The George, Witham

The Green Man, Little Braxted

The Half Moon, Belchamp St Paul

The Hedgerow Restaurant & Bar, Horsley Cross, Nr Manningtree

The Horse & Groom, Rochford

The Kings Arms, Lawford

The Kings Head, Gosfield

The Kings Head, Great Dunmow

The Kings Head, Tollesbury

The Kings Head Inn, Flatford

The Lion & Lamb, Little Canfield

The Moletrap, Tawney Common

The Old Dog, Herongate Tye

The Old Ship Inn, Heybridge Basin, Maldon

The Old Ship Inn, Rochford

The Onley Arms, Stisted, Nr Braintree

The Prince Albert, Blackmore

The Queens Head, Tolleshunt d'Arcy

125

Please note all references refer to page numbers

Essex

Northeast Essex has the true feel of East Anglia, particularly the area that has become known as Constable Country. The inland villages and small towns are notably historic and picturesque, offering very good walking and touring opportunities, and the half-timbered medieval buildings, farms and churches mark out this region as of particular historic interest. Monuments to engineering feats past and present include Hedingham Castle, Chappel Viaduct and the postmill at Bocking Church Street. Truly lovely villages abound, rewarding any journey to this part of the county. There are also many fine gardens to visit, and the region's principal town, Colchester, is full of interesting sights and experiences.

Saffron Walden

The North Essex coast has a strong maritime heritage, as exemplified in towns like Harwich, Manningtree and Mistley. Further examples are the fine Martello Towers along the coast at Walton, Clacton, Jaywick and Point Clear. The Tendring Peninsula has a rich and varied heritage ranging from prehistoric remains to medieval churches and Victorian villas, and along the coast is an interesting mix of extensive tidal inlets, sandy beaches and low cliffs. The Stour Estuary, Hamford Water and Colne Estuary are all renowned for seabirds and other wildlife, and many areas are protected nature reserves.

The part of the county known as the 'sunshine holiday coast' is where the traditional holiday resorts of Clacton, Frinton and Walton are to be found. The small northwest Essex towns of Saffron Walden, Thaxted, Great Dunmow and Stansted Mountfichet are some of the most beautiful and interesting in the country, and in this area can be seen the typical features of weatherboarding and pargeting, as well as historic preserved windmills. Visitors to southwest Essex and Epping Forest will find a wealth of woodland, nature reserves, superb gardens and rural delights. Also here are Audley End House and Waltham Abbey, both major attractions. On the north bank of the Thames, the borough of Thurrock encompasses huge swathes of green belt country, and along its 18 miles of river frontage there are many important wildlife habitats.

There's history here, too: Henry VIII built riverside block houses at Tilbury, and it was at West Tilbury that Queen Elizabeth I gave the famous speech to her troops, gathered to meet the Spanish Armada threat. At the southeast tip of the county, Southend is a popular resort with all the amenities of a traditional seaside holiday, including a world-famous pier. The area surrounding the Blackwater and Crouch rivers contains much ancient woodland, and this corner of Essex is ideal for enthusiasts of water-borne activities, as well as walking, cycling, birdwatching and other nature pursuits.

PLACES OF INTEREST

AYTHORPE RODING

Aythorpe Roding Windmill is the largest remaining post mill in Essex. Built around 1760, it remained in use up until 1935. It was fitted in the 1800s with a fantail which kept the sails pointing into the wind. It is open to the public on the last Sunday of each month from May to September, 2-5 p.m.

BRAINTREE

This town and its close neighbour Bocking are sited at the crossing of two Roman roads and were brought together by the cloth industry in the 16th century. Flemish weavers settled here, followed by many Huguenots. One, Samuel Courtauld, set up a silk mill in 1816 and, by 1866, employed over 3,000 Essex inhabitants. The **Working Silk Museum** on South Street features demonstrations of silk production - from start to finish - in a former mill building that has been faithfully restored. The original hand looms, some over 150 years old, are still used to weave silk fabrics for many of the royal houses throughout the world.

The **Braintree District Museum** on Manor Street tells the story of Braintree's diverse industrial heritage and traditions. The **Town Hall Centre** is a Grade II listed building housing the Tourist Information Centre and the Art Gallery, which boasts a continuous changing programme of exhibitions and works.

BRENTWOOD

Brentwood Cathedral on Ingrave Road was built in 1991 in classical style, incorporating the original Victorian church that stood on this spot. It was designed by the much-admired architect Quinlan Terry, with roundels by Raphael Maklouf (who also created the relief of the Queen's head used on current coins).

Brentwood Museum at Cemetery Lode in Lorne Road, in the Warley Hill area of Brentwood, is a small and picturesque cottage museum concentrating on local and social interests during the late 19th and early 20th centuries. It is set in an attractive disused cemetery, which is in itself of unique interest.

BRIGHTLINGSEA

Brightlingsea enjoys a long tradition of shipbuilding and seafaring and has the

Jacobes Hall, Brightlingsea

distinction of being the only limb of the Cinque Ports outside Kent and Sussex. The 13th century **Jacobes Hall** in the town centre is one of the oldest occupied buildings in Essex, and **All Saints Church**, which occupies the highest point of the town on a hill about a mile from the centre, is also mainly 13th century. Here are to be found some Roman brickwork and a frieze of ceramic tiles commemorating local residents whose lives were lost at sea. **Brightlingsea Museum** offers an insight into the lives, customs and traditions of the area with a collection of exhibits relating to the town's maritime connections and the oyster industry.

BURNHAM-ON-CROUCH

Burnham-on-Crouch is an attractively old-fashioned yachting station, lively in summer and packed around August Bank Holiday Monday for its regatta. In Tudor times sailing barges thronged the estuary, where now yachts ply to and fro. Seafarers still come ashore to buy provisions, following a tradition that goes right back to medieval times when Burnham was the market centre for the isolated inhabitants of Wallasea and Foulness Islands. The whole area was, and still is, famous for its oyster beds.

CANVEY ISLAND

Canvey Island is a peaceful and picturesque stretch of land overlooking the Thames estuary with views to neighbouring Kent.

The island boasts two unusual museums: **Dutch Cottage Museum** is an early 17th century eight-sided cottage built by Dutch workmen for Dutch workmen and boasting many traditional Flemish features. **Castle Point Transport Museum** is housed in a 1930s bus garage. It houses a fascinating collection of historic and modern buses and coaches, mainly of East Anglian origin.

CASTLE HEDINGHAM

This town takes its name from its Norman **Castle**; one of England's strongest fortresses in the 11th century, it is impossible even now not to sense its power and strength. The village itself is a maze of narrow streets radiating from Falcon Square, named after the half-timbered Falcon Inn. Attractive buildings include many fine Georgian and 15th century houses comfortably vying for space, and the **Church of St Nicholas**, built by the de Veres, which avoided Victorian

'restoration' and is virtually completely Norman, with grand masonry and interestingly carved choir seats.

Castle Hedingham

At the **Colne Valley Railway and Museum**, a mile of the Colne Valley and Halstead line between Castle Hedingham and Great Yeldham has been restored and now runs steam trains operated by enthusiasts. These lovingly restored Victorian railway buildings feature a collection of vintage engines and carriages; short steam train trips are available. **Colne Valley Farm Park**, set in 30 acres of traditional river meadows, is open from April to September.

CHAPPEL

Here, on a 4 acre site beside Chappel and Wakes Colne Station, is the **East Anglian Railway Museum**, a comprehensive collection of period railway architecture, engineering and memorabilia in beautifully restored station buildings. For every railway buff, young or old, this is the place to try your hand at being a signalman and admire the handsome restored engines and carriages. There is also a delightful miniature railway. Special steam days and other events are held throughout the year. The dramatic 32-arched Chappel Viaduct standing 75 feet above the Colne Valley and a designated European Monument, was begun in 1846 and opened in 1849.

CHELMSFORD

The town has always been an important market centre and is now the bustling county town of Essex. It is also directly descended from a new town planned by the Bishop of London in 1199. At its centre are the principal inn, the **Royal Saracen's Head**, and the elegant **Shire Hall** of 1791. Three plaques situated high up on the eastern face of the Hall overlooking the High Street represent Wisdom, Justice and Mercy. The building now houses the town magistrates court.

Chelmsford Cathedral in New Street dates from the 15th century and is built on the site of a church constructed 800 years ago. The cathedral, which is noted for the harmony and unity of its perpendicular architecture, has memorial windows dedicated to the USAAF airmen who were based in Essex from 1942-5.

The Marconi Company, pioneers in the manufacture of wireless equipment, set up the first radio company in the world here in Chelmsford in 1899, and exhibits of those days of wireless can be seen in the **Chelmsford and Essex Museum** in Oaklands Park, as can interesting displays of Roman remains and local history. The **Essex Regiment Museum** is also situated in Oaklands Park. Together these two fine museums exhibit temporary and permanent displays exploring local and social history from prehistoric times up until the present.

CLACTON-ON-SEA

Clacton is a traditional sun-and-sand family resort with a south-facing, long sandy beach, lovely gardens on the seafront and a wide variety of shops and places to explore. Settled by hunters during the Stone Age, the town grew over the centuries from a small village into a prosperous seaside resort in the 1800s, when the craze for the health benefits of coastal air and bathing was at its peak. The Pier was constructed in 1871; at first paddle steamers provided the only mode of transport to the resort, the railway arriving in 1882. **The Pier** was widened from 30 to over 300 feet in the 1930s. On the pier, apart from the marvellous traditional sideshows, big wheel, restaurants and fairground rides, there is the fascinating **Seaquarium and Reptile Safari**.

There are three Martello Towers along this bit of the Essex coast. Just south of the town, **Jaywick Sands** is the ideal spot for a picnic by the sea, boasting one of the finest natural sandy beaches in the county.

COGGESHALL

This medieval hamlet, a pleasant old cloth and lace town, has some very fine timbered buildings. **Paycocke's House** on West Street, a delightful timber-framed medieval merchant's home dating from about 1500 with unusually rich panelling and wood carvings, is owned by the National Trust. Inside there's a superb carved ceiling and a display of Coggeshall lace. The

National Trust also own the restored **Coggeshall Grange Barn**, which dates from around 1140 and is the oldest surviving timber-framed barn in Europe.

COLCHESTER

England's oldest recorded town, it has over 2,000 years of history to discover. Roman walls - the oldest in Britain - still surround the oldest part of the town, which is today presided over by its lofty town hall and enormous Victorian water tower, nicknamed 'Jumbo' after London Zoo's first African elephant, controversially sold to P T Barnum in 1882. The tower has four massive pillars of one and a quarter million bricks, 369 tons of stone and 142 tons of iron, which work to support the 230,000 gallon tank.

A good place to start exploring the town is **Colchester Castle** and its museum. The castle boasts the largest Norman keep ever built in Europe, which now houses the Castle Museum, one of the most exciting hands-on historical attractions in the country. Among its fascinating collection of Iron Age, Roman and medieval relics there are tombstones carved in intricate detail and exquisite examples of Roman glass and jewellery. Visitors can try on Roman togas and helmets, touch some of the 2,000-year-old pottery unearthed nearby, and experience the town's murkier past by visiting the Castle prisons, where witches were interrogated by the

Tymperleys Clock Museum

notorious Witchfinder General Matthew Hopkins.

Hollytrees Museum in the High Street is located in a fine Georgian home dating back to 1718. This museum on the edge of Castle Park houses a wonderful collection of toys, costumes, curios and antiquities from the last two centuries. Also nearby, housed in the former All Saints' Church, is the **Natural History Museum**, with exhibits and many hands-on displays illustrating the natural history of Essex from the Ice Age right up to the present day. Around the corner on Trinity Street, another former church, Holy Trinity - the only Saxon building left in Colchester - is home to the Museum of Social History, containing displays of rural crafts and country life. An arch opposite this museum leads to **Tymperleys Clock Museum**, the 15th century timber-framed home of William Gilberd, who entertained Elizabeth I with experiments in electricity. Today this fine example of architectural splendour houses a magnificent collection of 18th and 19th century Colchester-made clocks. Dutch Protestants arrived in Colchester in the 16th century, fleeing Spanish rule in the Netherlands, and the houses of these Flemish weavers stand in the **Dutch Quarter** to the west of the castle.

Colchester Zoo, just off the A12 outside the town, stands in the 40-acre park of Stanway Hall, with its 16th century mansion and church dating from the 14th century. Founded in 1963, the zoo has a wide and exciting variety of attractions. The zoo has gained a well-deserved reputation as one of the best in Europe. Its award-winning enclosures allow visitors closer to the animals and provide naturalistic environments for the 170 species. Colchester has been famous in its time for both oysters and roses. This legacy is remembered in the annual Oyster Feast and Colchester Rose Show. Colchester oysters are still cultivated on beds in the lower reaches of the River Colne, which skirts the northern edge of town. A visit to the **Oyster Fisheries** is a fascinating experience, and the tour includes complimentary fresh oysters and a glass of wine.

DEDHAM

This is true Constable country, along the border with Suffolk, the county's prettiest area. The village has several fine old buildings, especially the 15th century flint church, its pinnacled tower familiar from so many Constable paintings. There's also the school Constable went to, and good walks through the protected riverside meadows of Dedham Vale to **Flatford**, where **Bridge Cottage** is a restored thatched 16th century building housing a display about Constable, who featured this cottage in several of his paintings (his father's mill is across the river lock).

Dedham Vale Family Farm on Mill Street is a 16-acre farm boasting a comprehensive collection of British farm animals, including many different breeds of livestock such as pigs, sheep, cattle, Suffolk horses, goats and poultry. The **Art and Craft Centre** on the High Street is well worth a visit, as is the **Toy Museum** with its fascinating collection of dolls, teddies, toys, games, doll houses and other artefacts of childhoods past.

At Castle House, on the corner of East Lane and Castle Hill, The **Sir Alfred Munnings Art Museum** is housed in the former home, studios and grounds of the famous painter, who lived here between 1898 and 1920.

EAST TILBURY

Coalhouse Fort is considered to be one of the best surviving examples of a Victorian Casement fortress in the country, and as such it is a protected Scheduled Ancient Monument. Open to the public, it contains reconstructions of period guns and other displays, and also houses the **Thamesside Aviation Museum**, with a large collection of local finds and other aviation material.

FRINTON-ON-SEA

Once a quiet fishing village, this town was developed as a select resort by Sir Richard Cooper, and expanded in the 1880s to the genteel family resort it is today. Situated on a long stretch of sandy beach, Frinton remains peaceful and unspoilt. The tree-lined residential avenues sweep elegantly down to the Esplanade and extensive clifftop greensward. Along its main shopping street in Connaught Avenue, the 'Bond Street' of the East Coast, shopkeepers maintain a tradition of friendly and courteous service.

HALSTEAD

Halstead was once an important weaving centre, and **Townsford Mill** is the most picturesque reminder of its industrial heritage. Built in the

130 1700s, this white, weather-boarded three-storey mill across the River Colne at the Causeway was once a landmark site for the Courtauld empire; today, the Mill is an antiques centre.

HARLOW

This lively town has a great deal more to offer than excellent shopping facilities. The **Gibberd Collection** in Harlow Town Hall in The High offers a delightful collection of British watercolours, featuring works by Blackadder, Sutherland, Frink, Nash and Sir Frederick

Gibberd, Harlow's master planner and the founder of the collection. **Harlow Museum** occupies a Georgian manor house set in picturesque gardens which includes a lovely pond and is home to several species of butterfly. The museum has extensive and important Roman, post-medieval and early 20th century collections, as well as a full programme

Gibberd Gardens, Harlow

of temporary exhibitions. **Mark Hall Cycle Museum and Gardens** in Muskham Road offers a unique collection of cycles and cycling accessories illustrating the history of the bicycle from 1818 to the present day.

HARWICH

During the 14th and 15th century French campaigns Harwich was an important naval base, and it remains popular as a vantage point for watching incoming and outgoing shipping in the harbour and across the waters to Felixstowe. Nowadays, lightships, buoys and miles of strong chain are stored along the front, and passengers arriving on North Sea ferries at Parkeston Quay see the 90 foot high, nine-sided **High Lighthouse** as the first landmark. Now housing the **National Vintage Wireless and Television Museum**, it was built in 1818 along with the **Low Lighthouse**. The latter is now the

town's **Maritime Museum**, with specialist displays on the Royal Navy and commercial shipping.

Two other worthwhile museums in the town are the **Lighthouse Museum** and the **Ha'penny Pier Visitor Centre** on the Quay.

KELVEDON HATCH

A simple bungalow in the rural Essex village of Kelvedon Hatch is the deceptively simple exterior for the **Kelvedon Secret Nuclear Bunker**. Built in 1952, 40,000 tons of concrete were used to create a base for up to 600 top Government and civilian personnel in the event of nuclear war. Visitors can explore room after room to see communications equipment, a BBC studio, sick bay, massive kitchens and dormitories, power and filtration plant, government administration room and the scientists' room, where nuclear fall-out patterns would have been measured.

MALDON

The steep winding streets of Maldon are full of intriguing shops and welcoming inns. The town's High Street, of which the **Moot Hall** is a distinctive feature, runs right down to the River Blackwater estuary. Filled with craft of all shapes and sizes, the quayside is overlooked by the Queen's Head pub, which organises an annual mud race across the river at low tide.

Hythe Quay, Maldon

Just outside the town lies the spot where this decisive battle of England's early history took place. At the Battle of Maldon in 991, the English leader, Byrthnoth, was killed by the invading Danes after a fierce three-day battle. As a result of this defeat the English king, Ethelred the Unready, was obliged to pay an annual tribute to his conquerors. The Danes soon tired of this arrangement, however, and overthrew Ethelred, putting Canute on the throne. Maldon is also famous for its sea salt, produced for generations in the traditional manner of letting sea water evaporate naturally, leaving just the mineral-rich salt behind.

MISTLEY

The **Essex Secret Bunker** in Mistley, former county nuclear war headquarters, is now a public museum offering a fascinating insight into the postwar world of top-secret preparations against nuclear attack. Operational from 1951, it was 'declassified' in 1993 and opened to the public in 1996. Interesting things to see and do, include the giant underground operations room, office and dormitories, telephone exchange communications centre and radio room, powerhouse and filtration plant.

MOUNTNESSING

This village has a beautifully restored early 19th century windmill as its main landmark, though the isolated church is also well worth a visit. **Mountnessing Post Mill** was built in 1807 and restored to working order in 1983.

NORTH WEALD

North Weald Airfield Museum is a small, meticulously detailed museum displaying the history of North Weald from 1916 to the present. Collections of photos and artefacts such as uniforms and the detailed records of all flying operations are on display. There is also a video exhibit recounting a day to day account of North Weald history. Guided tours of the airfield can be arranged for large groups.

SAFFRON WALDEN

A great deal of Saffron Walden's medieval street plan survives, as do hundreds of fine buildings, many timbered with overhanging upper floors and the decorative plastering known as pargeting. At the **Saffron Walden Museum**, visitors can try their hand at corn grinding with

a Romano-British quern, see how a medieval timber house would have been built, admire the displays of Native American and West African embroidery and come face to face with Wallace the Lion, the museum's faithful guardian.

On the local **Common**, once Castle Green, is the largest surviving Turf Maze in England, believed to be some 800 years old.

Audley End House is one of England's most impressive Jacobean mansions, its distinguished

Audley End House, Saffron Walden

stone facade set off perfectly by Capability Brown's lake. The state rooms retain their palatial magnificence and the exquisite state bed in the Neville Room is hung with the original embroidered drapes. The silver, the Doll's House, the Jacobean Screen and Robert Adam's painted Drawing Room are just among the many sights to marvel at. There are paintings by Holbein, Lely and Canaletto, and the natural history collection features more than 1,000 stuffed animals and birds.

ST OSYTH

This pretty little village centres around its Norman church and the ancient ruins of **St**

St Osyth Priory

Osyth Priory. Little of the original 12th century Priory remains, except for the magnificent late 15th century flint gatehouse, complete with battlements. Within the gatehouse building there is an interesting collection of ceramics and jade. Other attractions include the Fitzwilliam art collection in the Georgian wing, with paintings by Reynolds, Stubbs and Van Dyck.

SOUTHEND-ON-SEA

The town is one of the best loved and most friendly resorts in Britain, featuring the very best ingredients for a break at the seaside. **Southend Pier and Museum** brings to life the fascinating past of the longest Pleasure Pier in the world. The Pier itself is 1.3 miles long; visitors can either take a leisurely walk along its length or take advantage of the regular train service that plies up and down the pier.

Central Museum and Planetarium on Victoria Avenue is the only planetarium in the southeast outside London, and also features local history exhibits. **Beecroft Art Gallery** boasts the work of four centuries of artistic endeavour.

The Sealife Centre employs the most advanced technology to bring visitors incredibly close to the wonders of British marine life. The Centre offers fun ways of exploring life under the waves, with concave bubble windows helping to make it seem you're actually part of the sea creatures' environment. Just west of Southend, the picturesque fishing village of **Old Leigh** has a long and distinguished history. The pilgrim ship *The Mayflower* restocked here en route to the New World of America, and the Dunkirk rescue embarked from here, as commemorated in a framed poem on the wall of the local pub, The Crooked Billet.

STANSTED MOUNTFICHET

Though rather close to Stansted Airport, there are plenty of reasons to visit this village. These include a **Norman Village**, complete with domestic animals, and the reconstructed motte and bailey **Mountfichet Castle**. The original castle was built after 1066 by the Duke of Boulogne, a cousin of the Conqueror. Siege weapons on show include two giant catapults. Visitors can take a trip to the top of the siege tower and tiptoe into the baron's bed chamber

while he sleeps! Next door to the castle is **The House on the Hill Toy Museum**, where children of every age are treated to a unique and nostalgic trip back to their childhood. **Stansted Windmill** is one of the best preserved tower mills in the country. Dating back to 1787 and in use until 1910, most of the original machinery has survived.

THAXTED

Thaxted has numerous attractively pargeted timber-framed houses, and a magnificent **Guildhall**, built as a meeting-place for cutlers around 1390. The demise of the cutlery industry in this part of Essex in the 1500s led it to becoming the administrative centre of the town. Restored in Georgian times, it became the town's Grammar School, as well as remaining a centre of administration. The town's famous **Tower Windmill** was built in 1804 by John Webb. In working order until 1907, it fell into disuse and

Thaxted Tower Windmill

disrepair but has now been returned to full working order. It contains a rural life museum, well worth a visit. **Thaxted Church** standing on a hill and soaring cathedral-like over the town's streets, has been described as the finest parish church in the country. The composer Gustav Holst lived in Thaxted from 1914-1925, and often played the church organ. To celebrate his connection with the town, there is a month-long music festival in late June/early July which attracts performers of international repute.

TILBURY

Tilbury Fort is a well-preserved and unusual 17th century structure with double moat. Owned by English heritage, the site was used for a military Block House during the reign of Henry VIII and was rebuilt in the 17th century. It remains one of Britain's finest examples of a star-shaped bastion fortress. Extensions were made in the 18th and 19th centuries, and the Fort was still being used in the Second World War.

WALTHAM ABBEY

The early Saxon kings maintained a hunting lodge here; a town formed round this, and the first church was built in the 6th century. By the 8th, the town had a stone minster church with a great stone crucifix that became the focus of pilgrims seeking healing. One of those cured of a serious illness, Harold Godwinsson, built a new church, the third on the site, which was dedicated in 1060 - and it was this self-same Harold who became king and was killed in the battle of Hastings six years on. Harold's body was brought back to Waltham to be buried in his church. The church that exists today was built in the first quarter of the 12th century; once three times its present length, it incorporated an Augustinian Abbey, built in 1177 by Henry II. The town became known for the Abbey, which was one of the largest in the country and the last to be the victim of Henry VIII's dissolution of the monasteries, in 1540.

Along the Cornhill Stream, crossed by the impressive stone bridge, the town's **Dragonfly Sanctuary** is home to over half the native British species of dragonflies and damselflies. A Tudor timber-framed house forms part of the **Epping Forest District Museum** in Sun Street. The wide range of displays includes exhibits covering the history of the Epping Forest District from the Stone Age to the 20th century. Tudor and Victorian times are particularly well represented, with some magnificent oak panelling dating from the reign of Henry VIII, and re-creations of Victorian rooms and shops.

To the west of town, the **Lee Navigation Canal** offers opportunities for anglers, walkers, birdwatching and pleasure craft. Once used for transporting corn and other commercial goods to the growing City of London, and having associations with the town's important gunpowder industry for centuries, the canal remains a vital part of town life.

133

Gunpowder production became established in Waltham as early as the 1660s; by the 19th century the **Royal Gunpowder Mills** employed 500 workers, and production did not cease until 1943, after which time the factory became a research facility. Of the 175 acres the site occupies, approximately 80 have been designated a Site of Special Scientific Interest, and the ecology of the site offers a rare opportunity for study. in 2001, the site was opened to the public for the first time in its 300-year history.

WALTON-ON-THE-NAZE

Walton is a traditional, cheerful resort with a good sandy beach and colourful seafront gardens. The Backwaters to the rear of Walton are made up of a series of small harbours and saltings, which lead into Harwich harbour.

The Pier, first built in 1830, was originally constructed of wood and measured 330 feet long. It was extended to its present length of 2,610 feet in 1898, at the same time as the electric train service began.

The wind-blown expanse of **The Naze** just north of Walton is an extensive coastal recreation and picnic area, pleasant for walking, especially out of season when the visitor is likely to have all 150 acres virtually to him- or herself, with great views out over the water.

WEST THURROCK

Immortalised by the film *Four Weddings and a Funeral*, little **St Clement's church** occupies a striking location and is one of a number of picturesque ancient churches in the borough. Although this 12th century church is now deconsecrated, it was in its day a stopping point for pilgrims; visitors can see the remains of its original round tower.

134

The Beehive

Barrack Lane, Great Waltham, Essex
Tel: 01245 360356

Directions:
Off the B1008 3 miles north of Chelmsford.

In a cosy chocolate box village north of Chelmsford, **The Beehive** attracts a broad cross-section of local customers and also motorists in the know who are very happy to take a short trip into the countryside from the bustle of Chelmsford. Holly Clayton, Andy Ives and Holly's father, Stuart Clayton, recently took over all the duties and the chores at this top-notch village pub, whose original 18th century main section has been added to down the years to produce the handsome, comfortable and very civilised pub that serves today's customers so well. A fine selection of real ales is always on offer, and the hosts provide an excellent choice of pub grub and traditional Sundayroasts. Whilst the bar is open all day, food is available during the lunchtime sessions.

The Beehive has a beer garden and a capacious car park. There is entertainment every weekend, be it live music, quiz, karaoke or disco. Great Waltham is a good place for a quiet stroll, and it's a short drive into Chelmsford, with its shops, cathedral and museums, or west to High Easter, where the Aythorpe Post Mill is a magnificent sight. The largest surviving mill of its type in the county, it is four storeys high. Venturing a little further afield, Great Dunmow attracts with many historic buildings and the superb gardens of Easton Lodge.

Opening Hours: All day.

Food: Pub grub.

Credit Cards: Mastercard, Visa

Accommodation: None

Facilities: Car park

Entertainment: Every weekend

Local Places of Interest/Activities:
Chelmsford 3 miles, Aythorpe Post Mill 3 miles, Great Dunmow 8 miles

Internet/Website:
e-mail: hollyclayton@hotmail.com website: www.pickapub.co.uk

The Bell 135

Panfield,
Nr Braintree,
Essex CM7 5AQ
Tel:
 01376 324641

Directions:
Panfield is off the
B1053 2 miles
northwest of
Braintree.

The 16th century building that is home to **The Bell** occupies a substantial site in the peaceful village of Panfield, a short drive northwest of Braintree. It has been a public house since 1772 and has all the qualities of a classic English country inn - and a few more! The front is a mass of colourful flowers in spring and summer, and the bars and dining area are comfortably old-fashioned. Landlord Robert Dorking took over at The Bell in 2001 after several years in other Ridleys outlets. The Essex based Ridleys Brewery provides IPA and other excellent cask ales, while catering for different tastes are a selection of wines and a very good choice of malt whiskies. In the 24-seat restaurant tasty home-cooked dishes are served lunchtime and evening every day except Monday (but the pub is open all day for drinks seven days a week).

The inn is a popular venue for functions and special celebrations, for which a marquee can be pit up just outside the door. Many pubs have a beer garden, and quite often this will include a play area for children. The Bell has both of these, but it also has what very few can claim: it has its own football pitch, and also a caravan site with space for 30+ touring vans. Well worth a visit at any time of day, The Bell is only a few minutes' drive from the A120 and Braintree. This town still has reminders of its past as a centre of the cloth and silk industries, a magnificent Town Hall and an award-winning museum. Close by in the country are the fine post mill at Bocking and Saling Hall Garden at Great Saling.

Opening Hours: 11-11, Sun 12-10.30

Food: Good pub food

Credit Cards: None

Accommodation: None

Facilities: Car park, children's play area, football pitch, caravan site

Entertainment: None

Local Places of Interest/Activities:
Braintree 2 miles, Bocking Post Mill 1 mile, Halstead 6 miles

136

The Bell Inn

The Street, Feering,
Nr Colchester,
Essex CO5 9QQ
Tel: 01376 570375
Fax: 01376 572862

Directions:

Feering is on the
B1024 (off A12) 5
miles west of
Colchester.

Alan and Carole Nash are devoted to the **Bell Inn**, which they have run since 1986. Dating from the early 16th century, the inn stands on an elevated site overlooking the green in the village of Feering, five miles west of Colchester on the B1024. Behind the neat cream painted frontage with a steeply raked tiled roof the owners keep the whole place in immaculate order, and in the comfortable, traditional lounge bar - note the beams and dark oak - the loyal regulars meet over a glass or two of cask ale - some of them swear that the Greene King IPA is the best pint in Essex! If the beer deserves its high praise, so too does the food, all prepared and cooked on the premises by Carole and her chef.

They use the best local supplies of meat, fish and vegetables in their dishes, which cover an excellent choice and are served every session except Sunday and Monday evenings in the 34-cover restaurant. If golf's your game, Alan's your man - he'll happily chat about the birdies and the eagles for as long as you like! If it's karaoke you want, that's on Sunday evening, while on Saturday a pianist entertains. Close to Feering is the grand Feeringbury Manor, whose grounds include ponds, streams, bog gardens and old-fashioned plants. The next village to Feering is Kelvedon, where the Feering and Kelvedon deals with local history from Roman times and has displays that include old agricultural implements. Coggeshall, with its Grange Barn and Paycocke's House, is also nearby, and Britain's oldest recorded town of Colchester is an easy drive away.

Opening Hours: 11.30-2.30 (Sat till 3) & 6-11, all day Sunday

Food: A la carte

Credit Cards: Mastercard, Visa.

Accommodation: None

Facilities: Car park

Entertainment: Pianist Saturday, karaoke Sunday

Local Places of Interest/Activities: Kelvedon 1 mile, Coggeshall 3 miles, Marks Tey 4 miles, Colchester 5 miles

Internet/Website:
e-mail: alannash9@aol.com

The Black Lion

The Street,
High Roding,
Nr Great Dunmow,
Essex CM6 1NT
Tel: 01371 872847

Directions:

High Roding is on
the B184 5 miles
south of Great
Dunmow.

The Black Lion is an ancient and atmospheric coaching inn whose history dates back as far as the 14th century. In classic style, with a smartly painted black and white exterior, the inn has all the style and charm to be expected by its age, and the bars and dining room feature black beams, blockwood floors, mellow red brick, old oak tables and chairs and a wealth of pictures and assorted bric-a-brac. Ridleys IPA is the best seller among the cask ales, and tenant Fiona Day satisfies her customers' appetites with a good selection of freshly cooked, good-value dishes that include a daily fish special and beef from an excellent local butcher. Food is served from 11.30 to 2.30 and 6.30 to 9 Monday to Friday and all day Saturday and Sunday.

The Black Lion is a very sociable place, with quiz and darts teams and occasional live music evenings. It stays open all day in the summer, and when the sun shines the beer garden is a popular spot. High Roding lies about 5 miles south of Great Dunmow on the B184, which follows the route of an old Roman road. To the north, Great Dunmow appeals with its many splendid old buildings. Little Easton has the Harold Peto Gardens and a wonderful old tithe barn used for theatre performances and many other events, and to the south lies Aythorpe Roding, whose windmill is the largest surviving post mill in Essex.

Opening Hours: 11-3 & 6-11, Sun 12-4 & 6-10.30. Open all day in summer

Food: A la carte (Good Pub Food)

Credit Cards: Mastercard, Visa.

Accommodation: None

Facilities: Car park

Entertainment: Occasional live music

Local Places of Interest/Activities: Great Dunmow 5 miles, Aythorpe Roding Windmill 2 miles

138 The Carpenters Arms

Baddow Street,
Great Baddow,
Nr Chelmsford,
Essex CM2 7QE
Tel/Fax:
   01245 491188

Directions:

Off the A12/A414
on the southern
outskirts of
Chelmsford.

It's all change at the **Carpenters Arms**, which stands on the southern outskirts of Chelmsford. The original 17th century building has long gone, and behind the redbrick frontage, the premises are being totally redeveloped into a pub/motel due to open in its new form in October 2002. 14 letting bedrooms, all en suite, will constitute the major part of the work, with 4 rooms offering access and facilities for wheelchair users. Other plans coming to fruition include the construction of a beer garden. The interior of the existing pub will receive a facelift that will not alter its traditional character, and the Carpenters Arms will still be open all day, every day for drinks and well-priced, straightforward bar food, with roasts for Sunday lunch.

With its overnight accommodation, the Carpenters Arms will be a practical and convenient base both for business people with appointments in Chelmsford and for tourists exploring a part of the country that offers the delights of town, country, canal and river. Great Baddow itself is best known for its splendid antiques centre, while among other nearby attractions are the astonishing Spanish oak tree at Sandon and the country park at Danbury.

Opening Hours: 12-11.

Food: Bar snacks, Sunday roast

Credit Cards: None

Accommodation: 5 rooms + motel planned

Facilities: Car park

Entertainment: Live music Fri, Sat & Sun

Local Places of Interest/Activities: Great Baddow Antiques Centre, Chelmsford 1 mile, Hanningfield Reservoir 5 miles

The Chapel Inn 139

Market Hill,
Coggeshall,
Essex
Tel: 01376 561655
Fax: 01376 561852

Directions:

In the centre of
Coggeshall, which is
off the A120 4 miles
west of Colchester.

The Chapel Inn is a handsome old pub sandwiched between elegant period buildings in the centre of Coggeshall. Behind the neat cream and black painted frontage it stretches back to the large main public car park. The Chapel's interior has considerable character, with oak floors and sturdy oak furniture, and proprietor George Coulwill has created a splendidly relaxed, laid-back ambience - he knows all about Irish pubs, and in Coggeshall he has managed to recreate something of the feel of a traditional Irish pub. Cask ales are on tap to quench country thirsts, and there's an excellent list of wines to accompany the wide variety of food served in the 60-seat restaurant lunchtime seven days a week and every evening except Sunday.

The long menu covers pasta, seafood and meat and vegetarian dishes, and one of the most popular orders is Moby Dick - a more than generous piece of cod served with all the trimmings. The pleasant old cloth and lace town of Coggeshall has plenty to interest the visitor, with two National Trust properties, the timber-framed Paycocke's House and the great Grange Barn, heading the attractions. A road sign outside the Chapel Inn points motorists in the direction of the Marks Hall Country Estate, a centre with native plants and wildlife, an ornamental lake and an arboretum with a collection of trees from all around the world. The towns of Braintree and Colchester, both with plenty of historic interest, are a few miles away along the A120 to the west and east respectively.

Opening Hours: 11-3.30 & 5.30-11, all day Sat & Sun

Food: A la carte

Credit Cards: None

Accommodation: None

Facilities: Public car park

Entertainment: Quiz and Play Your Cards Right Sunday night

Local Places of Interest/Activities: Grange Barn and Paycocke's House in Coggeshall, Braintree 5 miles, Colchester 5 miles

Internet/Website:
website: www.thechapelinn.co.uk

140

The Chequers

Chequers Road,
Writtle, Essex
CM1 3MG
Tel: 01245 422515

Directions:

The pub is in Writtle, about 3 miles west of Chelmsford off the A414.

The Chequers is a splendid little village pub dating from the 18th century. In spring and summer the white-painted outside is a riot of colour from flower tubs running all the way along the front at first-floor level, and the interior is no less appealing; from the bright, cheery bar to the attractive, intimate lounge and the small, comfortably furnished dining area, the Chequers is a fine example of what an English country inn should be. Landlord Lance Middleditch, at the helm since 2000, is not only the bubbly, enthusiastic host, he's also the chef and the head waiter. His good wholesome cuisine, with honest, natural flavours to the fore, is served from 12 to 3 and from 7 to 9 every day of the week; everything is prepared and cooked by Lance in his kitchen, and it's all very much recommended. Pool and darts are played in the bar, where three real ales and a fine selection of other draught beers, lager and cider are on tap to quench thirsts; there's live music at the weekend. A couple of picnic benches are set outside at the front, and the pub has off-road parking at the side.

Writtle is the village from where Britain's first regular service originated - a 15-minute programme put out nightly by Marconi's engineers. Ducks swim on the main village green, which is surrounded by lovely Tudor and Georgian houses. Chelmsford is almost literally on the doorstep, but this lovely old village has managed to preserve its own identity.

Opening Hours: 11-11, Sun 12-10.30

Food: Bar meals

Credit Cards: Mastercard, Visa

Accommodation: None

Facilities: Car park.

Entertainment: Live music weekends

Local Places of Interest/Activities:
Chelmsford (museums, cathedral) 3 miles, Great Leighs Maze 6 miles, Danbury Country Park 6 miles, Maldon 12 miles

The Chequers Inn 141

*The Square,
Goldhanger, Essex
CM9 8AS
Tel: 01621 788203
Fax: 01621 788500*

Directions:

Off the B1026 5 miles
south of Maldon.

Philip Glover and Dominic Davies make an excellent team in charge of the **Chequers Inn**, a classic village pub with an exterior that has graced many a chocolate box lid. Behind the cream-painted facade with quaint, tiny-paned windows and red-tiled roof, the bars are no less appealing, with ancient beams, carpeted wooden floors, a huge brick hearth adorned with old farming implements, black and white photographs and a hatch-type servery bar. In this most atmospheric of settings Philip dispenses cask ales of the highest quality, while Dominic prepares a good variety of wholesome dishes which customers can enjoy every lunchtime and every evening. Everything he cooks is recommended, but it's his home-made pies that he's become famous for.

A paved beer garden with plenty of chairs set at parasol-shaded tables makes the most of the long summer days (the pub is open all day at the weekend), but it's inside on Thursday night for the weekly quiz. For guests staying overnight the Chequers has three Bed & Breakfast bedrooms that share a bathroom. To find the Chequers, leave Maldon on the B1026 Colchester road and take the minor road to Goldhanger after about 5 miles. In Church Street, Goldhanger, the Maldon District Agricultural & Domestic Museum is well worth a visit. It's a short stroll south from Goldhanger to the estuary of the River Blackwater; Maldon lies a short drive to the west, Tolleshunt d'Arcy and Tollesbury Marina are to the west, and in the estuary itself are Northey and Osea Islands.

Opening Hours: 10.30-3 & 6-11. All day Sat & Sun (April to September only)

Food: Traditional pub food - contemporary à la carte

Credit Cards: Mastercard, Visa, Switch and Delta

Accommodation: 3 rooms

Facilities: Car park

Entertainment: Quiz Thursday night

Local Places of Interest/Activities: Maldon 5 miles, Tollesbury Marina 4 miles

Internet/Website:
e-mail: chequersgoldhang@aol.com

142

The Cricketers

*East End Road,
Bradwell-on-Sea,
Essex*
Tel: 01621 776013

Directions:

Bradwell is situated 9 miles north of Burnham-on-Crouch off the B1021.

If not quite hidden, the **Cricketers** is certainly a destination pub that needs seeking out, and visitors venturing into this far-flung part of Essex will be rewarded with a very warm welcome and an agreeably relaxed atmosphere in which to unwind. Since taking over in the spring of 2002, Tracey and Mick McCulloch have made many important little changes to this late 19th century hostelry outside the village, enhancing its appeal as a really pleasant place to seek out and linger awhile. It's an excellent base for walkers and cyclists, with well-priced overnight accommodation available in four rooms with shared facilities. The carpeted bar/lounge/dining area is bright and cheerful, with brick and wood panelling features and ample comfortable chairs and tables for diners.

Mick looks after liquid refreshments, while Tracey does sterling work in the kitchen, producing food to satisfy fresh-air appetites at realistic prices, from snacks to full meals; everything is good, but the seafood specials and home-made pies are particular favourites. The marina at Bradwell-on-Sea bustles in the summer, but visitors to this remote village can also feel that they are hundreds of miles away from the more crowded parts of the county. Essex between Blackwater and Crouch is an isolated and sometimes wild part of the county, with bracing walks the order of the day and the salty tang of the sea in the air. There are also some unexpected sights and some striking contrasts. Half a mile across fields from the nearest road lies what might be the oldest church in the country, St Peter-on-the-Wall, dating from the 7th century, while to the north of the village Bradwell's nuclear power station looms over a nature reserve.

Opening Hours: 12-3 & 6-11, all day Fri, Sat & Sun

Food: A la carte and snacks

Credit Cards: None

Accommodation: 4 single rooms with shared facilities

Facilities: Car park

Entertainment: None

Local Places of Interest/Activities: Bradwell Marina, Church of St Peter-on-the-Wall, Southminster 7 miles, Burnham-on-Crouch 9 miles

The Crown

High Street,
Thorpe-le-Soken,
Nr Clacton-on-Sea,
Essex CO16 0DY
Tel: 01255 861296

Directions:

Thorpe-le-Soken is 4
miles north of
Clacton on the
B1033.

Occupying a prominent site on Thorpe-le-Soken's main street, the **Crown** is a fine early 19th century pub with a lawned beer garden, a children's play area and a huge car park. The place has great atmosphere and a genuine feeling of warmth throughout the public and lounge bars and the dining area. Ian and Angie Barker, who took over at the Crown at the beginning of 2002, put a lot of hard work into running this very likeable pub, dividing the tasks and making all their customers feel very welcome. Two cask ales and a good selection of beers, lagers, ciders and wines are always available throughout the long opening hours, and straightforward home-from-cooking produces a variety of tasty, satisfying dishes.

It's well worth strolling round the little village of Thorpe, which lies at the crossroads on the B1033 and B1414, as it has a number of historic buildings and a fine parish church; there's also plenty to see and explore in the area round the village. A minor road north of Thorpe off the B1414 leads to the Landermere Creek of Hamford Water, with views of Horsey and Hedge End Islands in the creek. Also close by, near the seashore, is Holland Haven Country Park, a 100-acre open space that's ideal for watching the seabirds and the other wildlife of the region. Here and elsewhere by the coast there's excellent walking, with many marked trails, while for those who enjoy the amenities of a traditional seaside resort, Frinton, Walton and Clacton are all easily reached.

Opening Hours: 11-11, Sun 12-10.30

Food: A la carte

Credit Cards: Mastercard, Visa.

Accommodation: None

Facilities: Car park, children's play area

Entertainment: None

Local Places of Interest/Activities: Clacton 4 miles, Frinton 4 miles, Walton 4 miles

Internet/Website:
e-mail: ianabarker@thorpepub.co.uk

144

The Duck Inn

Newney Green,
Writtle,
Nr Chelmsford,
Essex CM1 3SF
Tel: 01245 421894
Fax: 01245 420855

Directions:

On the A414 about 3 miles west of Chelmsford.

Simon Edwards, hardworking host and chef, sets great store by the quality and freshness of the food he cooks at the **Duck Inn**. Everything is prepared and made on the premises, even the ice cream, and the chalk board menus always offer plenty of choice to enjoy in the 82-cover restaurant. Simon's signature duck dishes are famed throughout the county, whether as rillettes for starters or roasts for main courses, and other options on a list that tours the world for its inspiration - the choice changes constantly - might include trout quenelles, chicken noodle soup, seared salmon fillet, ratatouille tart, avocado and mozzarella salad, tuna steak, pan-fried calves' liver, sea bass, beef stroganoff and a smoked meat platter. Food is served from 12 to 2.30 and from 6 to 10 seven days a week. The first-class food is complemented by a wine list that runs to 80+ bottles, or for those who prefer ale, there are always three cask ales available.

The inn, which dates from the early 18th century, is a classic of its kind, with great period character and a tremendous ambience that comes not only from the host and the regulars but from the decor and the furnishings - oak tables and 'country' chairs, exposed beams, and a huge feature brick fireplace that links the two bars. Everything is kept in apple pie order, and outside there are more delights in the shape of a garden with lawns, a play area for children and a fish pond with ornamental carp.

Opening Hours: 12-3 & 6-11

Food: A la carte.

Credit Cards: Mastercard, Visa.

Accommodation: None

Facilities: Car park, children's play area

Entertainment: None

Local Places of Interest/Activities:
Chelmsford 3 miles, Blackmore (Church of St Laurence) 5 miles

Internet/Website:
e-mail: theduckwrittle@aol.com

The Fox & Hounds 145

Cock Clarks,
Chelmsford,
Essex CM3 6RF
Tel/Fax:
  01621 829662

Directions:

Cock Clarks is a
village about 6 miles
east of Chelmsford.
From Chelmsford,
take the A414
through Danbury,
then the B1010 very
briefly; first right on
minor road
signposted Cock
Clarks.

The Fox & Hounds is the social hub of a lovely little village in the countryside east of Chelmsford. The structure has been altered considerably since its 17th century origins, but inside, the bar has all the ambience and character expected from a good country pub, with well-spaced seating, attractive decor and the relaxed, welcoming feel generated by the family who run it. And it really is very much a family affair, with Ann doing the cooking, Russ the jack of all trades and the sons helping out behind the bar. Russ takes great pride in the way he keeps his cask ales, and his regulars will tell you that he pulls the best pint of Ridley's IPA in the Chelmsford area.

Ann's food, which is served every session except Monday evening, offers good value and plenty of variety, from the ever popular basket meals to excellent meat dishes using top local suppliers. The Fox & Hounds has a large car park and a beer garden with a children's play area. The village and the vicinity provide pleasant walking opportunities, and there's plenty more for the active visitor within an easy drive. At Danbury, the Common and the Country Park are very agreeable places to stretch the legs on the nature trails, while at Maldon the quayside, the museum and Promenade Park are among the many attractions.

Opening Hours: Mon-Sat 12-11; Sun 12-10.30

Food: A la carte

Credit Cards: Mastercard, Visa

Accommodation: None

Facilities: Car park, children's play area

Entertainment: None

Local Places of Interest/Activities:
Danbury 2 miles, Maldon 4 miles,
Chelmsford 6 miles

146 The Fox & Hounds

12 The Square,
Tillingham,
Essex CM0 7SU
Tel/Fax:
 01621 779416

Directions:

Tillingham is located on the B1021 4 miles north of Southminster.

Peter Fenn, for many years a National Sales Manager in Medical Supplies, had an ambition to own a pub, and in October1999 his dream became a reality when he took over the **Fox & Hounds** overlooking the village green in Tillingham. Dating from the early 1800s, the pub has a very smart and handsome facade in red brick, with the doors and windows edged in gleaming white paint, and flowers and greenery adding to the appeal. There's a lovely "villagey" feel to the bar, lounge and dining area, with its splendid tropical fish tank, where everything is kept as neat as a new pin. Friendly, mature staff dispense hospitality and well-kept ales and lagers, and Peter himself is in charge of culinary matters.

An enthusiastic cook, he always tries to vary the menus, using top-quality local produce to provide interesting dishes at very kind prices - the food is served every lunchtime and evening. The owner, the staff and the locals make for a very pleasant, relaxed ambience, and the pub hosts two regular special events - live music every three or four weeks on a Saturday evening and a charity quiz on the second Tuesday of every month.

The attractive little village of Tillingham is located in the least populated and least spoilt part of Essex on the Dengie Peninsula between the Crouch and Blackwater estuaries. To the east are wild and sometimes windy marshes; to the north, the village of Bradwell-on-Sea, with the contrasting attractions of a bustling marina, a lapsed nuclear power station and the oldest church in the land at St Peters-on-the-Wall; to the south, the former market town of Southminster and the busy town of Burnham-on-Crouch with its popular marinas and regular sailing events .

Opening Hours: 11.30-3 & 6-11, all day Sat & Sun

Food: A la carte

Credit Cards: None

Accommodation: None

Facilities: Car park

Entertainment: Charity Quiz 2nd Tuesday of every month; live music every 3/4weeks on Saturdays (phone for details). Pool, Darts, Dominoes, Cribbage and Shove Ha'penny.

Local Places of Interest/Activities:
Bradwell 2 miles, Southminster 6 miles

The George

Newland Street,
Witham,
Essex CM8 2AQ
Tel: 01376 511098
Fax: 01376 514236

Directions:

The George is in the centre of Witham, very close to the exit from the A12.

A live contender for the title of friendliest pub in Essex, the **George** enjoys a convenient town centre very close to the exit from the A12. The cheerful, relaxed ambience is generated by the young, go ahead landlord Paul Thatcher, who has transformed the place since taking over the reins in January 2002. The pub, which dates from the 17th century, stands on a prime corner site and is open long hours for the service of both food and drink. Liquid refreshment is provided by excellent cask ales and an impressive choice of lagers, while on the food front the 'sizzlers' are popular choices among the well-priced dishes served in very generous portions from opening time right through the day.

The bar, with its deep pile red carpeting and red upholstery, is particularly warm and inviting, and a separate function suite makes an ideal venue for small private parties, wedding reception and the like. Witham is a delightful place for a stroll, and to that end a continuous walk has been created along the banks of the river. Also well worth a visit are the Church of St Nicholas and the Dorothy L Sayers Centre, whose contents include a reference collections of books by and about her. And when the walking and the sightseeing are done, the George and its landlord are always ready with a friendly greeting and something good to eat and drink.

Opening Hours: 10-11, Sun 12-10.30

Food: A la carte

Credit Cards: Amex, Mastercard, Visa

Accommodation: None

Facilities: Car park, function suite

Entertainment: None

Local Places of Interest/Activities:
Dorothy L Sayers Centre Witham, Kelvedon 5 miles, Maldon 6 miles, Chelmsford 6 miles

148 The Green Man

Kelvedon Road,
Little Braxted,
Essex CM8 3LB
Tel: 01621 891659

Directions:

Little Braxted is north east of Chelmsford. Sign posted off the A12 after the Witham bypass on the B1389. Follow the small country lane for about 2-3 miles. Be patient!

Neil Pharaoh and Amanda Yelland make a great team at the **Green Man**, an exceptional country inn overlooking the green in the village of Little Braxted. Peaceful, civilised and relaxing, the inn dates from 1728 and was originally a farmhouse; it has been an inn since the mid-19th century. Behind the cream-painted, slate-roofed frontage, an interesting assortment of memorabilia adorns the walls, including carpenter's tools, horse brasses and artefacts associated with the Royal Marines. In the public bar are old photographs of the inn down the years and a collection of model cars in glass display cases.

This is a Ridleys inn, well known for the excellent condition of it's ales, including IPA and Rumpus. The inn also keeps a good selection of wines to enjoy on their own or to accompany the home-cooked food served throughout the pub or garden from 12 to 2 and 7 to 9 every day of the week. Fresh produce, much of it local, is handled with much skill to create the imaginative menu; everything is worth trying, but when the steak and ale pies are on the menu the regular customers look no further. The Green Man has a delightful tree-fringed garden with flower beds, a lawn, a pretty pond and tables. The village itself has been a frequent winner of the Best Kept Village awards - the first in 1973 and most recently in 2002. Little Braxted's Church of St Nicholas, mentioned in the Domesday Book and famous for its murals, is well worth a visit, and among other nearby places of interest are the Dorothy L Sayers Centre at Witham and the splendid medieval barns at Cressing.

Opening Hours: 11.30-3 & 6-11, Sun 12-3.30 & 7-10.30

Food: A la carte

Credit Cards: Mastercard, Visa.

Accommodation: None

Facilities: Car park, garden

Entertainment: Occasional quiz nights in the winter months on a Sunday evening.

Local Places of Interest/Activities: Little Braxted Church of St Nicholas, Maldon 4 miles, Witham 3 miles, Hatfield Peverel 3 miles, Kelvedon 4 miles, Cressing Temple Barns 4 miles.

The Half Moon   149

Cole Green,
Belchamp St Paul,
Nr Sudbury,
Essex CO10 7DP
Tel/Fax:
   01787 277402

Directions:

Belchamp St Paul
is located off the
A1092 2 miles
south of Clare

The quiet village of Belchamp St Paul, off the A1092 south of Clare, is home to the **Half Moon**, a pretty, cottage thatched inn dating from the 16th century and overlooking the village green. Outside, the inn has a garden and plenty of parking space, while inside is a beamy bar, an area for pub games, a restaurant and a 'confession nook' in the old inglenook fireplace. In this most pleasant setting Shirley and Martin welcome visitors with genuine hospitality and a good range of cask ales (Greene King IPA and guests), draught and bottled beers and lagers, wines and a selection of malt whiskies.

Shirley's son Laurence takes equally good care of appetites with a choice of menus. The snack menu comprises sandwiches, baguettes, salads and some light hot dishes, while the full menu runs from paté, whitebait and garlic mushrooms to lasagne, liver & bacon, beef cobbler and specials such as sole meunière; sea bass; steak, stilton and Guinness pie; or duck with a red wine, port and cranberry sauce. Food is served Tuesday to Sunday lunchtimes and all evenings. Several short walks start from the inn, and within a short drive are numerous visitor attractions, including the Colne Valley Railway, the Ancient House and the Priory at Clare and the Sue Ryder Foundation Museum at Cavendish.

Opening Hours: 12-2.30 & 6-10.30

Food: A la carte and snacks

Credit Cards: Diners, Mastercard, Visa

Accommodation: None

Facilities: Car park

Entertainment: None

Local Places of Interest/Activities: Short walks starting from the pub, Clare 2 miles, Cavendish 4 miles

150 The Hedgerow Restaurant & Bar

Horsley Cross,
Nr Manningtree,
Essex CO11 2NR
Tel: 01206 395585

Directions:

Horsley Cross lies on
the B1025, off the
A120 2 miles south of
Manningtree.

The Hedgerow is a substantial roadside inn on the B1025 a short drive from Manningtree. Its appeal is twofold - it's both a village local and a top-notch dining place. Adjoining the bar is an immaculately appointed restaurant overlooking the garden, open for food from 11.30 to 3 and from 7 to 10, with service all day Sunday, when booking is recommended. Partners Paul Chenery and Denis Brosnan lease the catering arrangements from the pub's tenant; these two accomplished chefs take it in turns to man the stoves, and both are equally passionate about what they put on their customers' plates. Their dishes range from the simple to the more elaborate and sometimes the exotic, and there are often French or Italian influences in the cooking.

The menu changes frequently, so any return visit - and there are many - is certain to produce a new range of delights. The ingredients are as far as possible top-quality British, many of them locally sourced, and the distinguished food is complemented by well-priced wines and a good choice of cask ales, draught and bottle beers, lagers and cider. Horsley Cross is located at the junction of the A120 and the B1035. Manningtree and Mistley are a short drive to the north, Ramsey and Harwich to the east, and Thorpe-le-Soken, Walton and Frinton to the south. So before or after a leisurely meal in this excellent place there's plenty to do and see, including walks in the country or by the sea, sailing, craft workshops, museums, churches, country parks and all the fun of traditional seaside resorts.

Opening Hours: 11.30-3 & 7-11, closed Monday

Food: A la carte

Credit Cards: Mastercard, Visa.

Accommodation: None

Facilities: Car park

Entertainment: None

Local Places of Interest/Activities:
Manningtree 2 miles, Mistley 3 miles

Internet/Website:
e-mail: chenerypaul@hotmail.com

The Horse & Groom

Southend Road,
Rochford,
Essex SS4 1HA
Tel/Fax:
  01702 544318

Directions:

Rochford is
signposted off the
A127 on the
outskirts of
Southend, close to
Southend Airport

The Horse & Groom is a classic roadside pub dating from the early 18th century and run by since the beginning of 2002 by newlyweds Carol and Colin Crowne. The whole place is looking very smart after top-to-toe refurbishment, and with the upgrading of the restaurant there will be more choice and different opening times for food (Carol is the cook). This will add to the choice of straightforward snacks and basket meals served lunchtime from 12 to 3 Monday to Saturday and the traditional roasts served from 12 to 4 on Sunday. The public bar is neat, bright and roomy, and the lovely little lounge, with decor themed in blue, features plush carpets, fine drapes and inviting, well-upholstered seating. A separate function room has seats for up to 75. Sunday night is quiz night. The beer garden contains a children's play area, and the pub has ample car parking space in its extensive grounds.

Rochford is close to Southend Airport and just three miles from Southend itself, one of the most popular and friendly of all seaside resorts. But for a quieter life, there's good walking by the River Roach and out towards the coast, while on the other side of Rochford, Hockley Woods is an ancient woodland that supports a wide variety flora and fauna. An hour or two's healthy exercise will build up a thirst and an appetite that the Horse & Groom is ready and waiting to satisfy.

Opening Hours: 12-11, Sun to 10.30

Food: A la carte and snacks

Credit Cards: None

Accommodation: None

Facilities: Car park, children's play area

Entertainment: Quiz Sunday

Local Places of Interest/Activities:
Southend 3 miles, Rayleigh 4 miles

152   The Kings Arms

Wignall Street,
Lawford,
Nr Manningtree,
Essex CO11 2JL
Tel: 01206 392758

Directions:

Lawford is on the
A137 1 mile west of
Manningtree

The Kings Arms is a pink-painted 16th century village pub in a small community on the A137 a short drive west of Manningtree. The decor inside is particularly appealing, and the atmosphere very warm and friendly - a credit to the new proprietors. These are the husband and wife team of Gary and Eve Phillips, who took over in the spring of 2002. Gary is always ready at the bar with a cheerful greeting and a choice of two cask ales, including Greene King IPA. Eve does sterling work in the kitchen, producing a variety of traditional pub fare including a top-notch steak & kidney pie. Quoits is a popular diversion to the bar, and Wednesday is dominoes night. On Sundays in winter, the weekly quiz is something the regulars look forward to.

    The Kings Arms is more than just a lovely, lively local, it's also a good place for an overnight (or longer) stay, its main road access making an ideal base for business with appointments in nearby towns and for tourists visiting this beautiful part of the world. Manningtree, a mile away, is an interesting place for a stroll and is also a centre of leisure sailing, while the world famous area known as Constable Country is very close by. The Constable Country Trail starts at East Bergholt and visits Flatford Mill and Willy Lot's Cottage, both looking much as when Constable painted them. At Mistley, just beyond Manningtree, the Essex Secret Bunker, the craft workshops and the Animal Rescue Centre are among the attractions.

Opening Hours: 11.45-3 & 6-11, Sun 12-4 & 6.30-10.30

Food: A la carte

Credit Cards: None

Accommodation: 3 rooms sharing facilities

Facilities: Car park

Entertainment: Quiz Sun in winter, dominoes Wed, quoits

Local Places of Interest/Activities: Manningtree 1 mile, Ardleigh 1 mile, Dedham 2 miles, East Bergholt 4 miles

The Kings Head   **153**

The Street, Gosfield,
Essex CO9 1TP
Tel/Fax:
   01787 474016

Directions:

On the main street of
Gosfield, which lies
on the A1017 5 miles
north of Braintree.

In the heart of the picturesque village of Gosfield, the **Kings Head** is a fine country inn dating from the 16th century. Hosts Alyson Keep and Tony Wickert always have the welcome mat out, and the ambience is warm and inviting in the public bar and the lounge bar with its open log fire and handsome black oak furnishings. There's a separate conservatory dining room. Cask ales and a wide selection of other beers, lagers, cider and wine are always available, to enjoy on their own or to accompany the food that is served every session. Alyson and Tony share the cooking, and the customers have an excellent choice, from bar snacks to a full à la carte menu supplemented by dishes of the day chalked up on a board. The speciality of the house is a very tasty and satisfying mixed grill. Senior citizens can take advantage of a special deal on Tuesday lunchtime.

There are regular theme food nights throughout the year, and the inn can cater for private functions and group bookings. Food for thought is provided by the popular quiz on the last Sunday of each month. Guest accommodation is among the plans of the go-ahead landlords at the Kings Head, which has a patio and an ample car park. Gosfield Lake is the county's largest freshwater lake and is now a leisure resort. It stands in the grounds of Gosfield Hall, built by Samuel Courtauld, like many of the mock-Tudor houses in the village. The inn is situated on a corner site on the A1017 5 miles north of Braintree, which has two fascinating museums and a magnificent town hall (another Courtauld gift).

Opening Hours: 12-3 & 6-11, all day Sat and Sun (summer only)

Food: A la carte and specials board

Credit Cards: Mastercard, Visa.

Accommodation: Planned

Facilities: Car park, disabled facilities (separate toilets, parking, access ramp)

Entertainment: Quiz last Sun each month

Local Places of Interest/Activities: Gosfield Lake Leisure Resort 1 mile, Braintree 5 miles, Halstead 3 miles

Internet/Website:
e-mail: enquiries@kingsheadgosfield.co.uk

154   The Kings Head

30 North Street,
Great Dunmow,
Essex CM6 1BA
Tel: 01371 872052

Directions:

Close to the centre of
Great Dunmow, which
lies on the A120
halfway between
Bishops Stortford and
Braintree.

The Kings Head is a 16th century village inn overlooking a duck pond. Behind a classic frontage with a roof of red tiles, the inn has a good-sized bar and an attractive restaurant permanently set for meals, with pink napkins and gleaming cutlery and glassware. The menus, available lunchtime and evening Tuesday to Saturday and from 12 to 6 on Sunday, offers traditional pub cuisine as well as some less familiar dishes such as chicken parcels or tomatoes Rossini. Drinks to accompany include cask ales and an extensive wine list, and Lynn organises regular food and drink theme nights. The inn is owned by a partnership who in the spring of 2002 employed Lynn Long as the manager. This was an excellent move, as Lynn has a lifetime's experience in the licensed trade; among the plans they have are the creation of letting bedrooms for Bed & Breakfast accommodation.

The new Stanstead-Braintree motorway will by-pass the historic town of Great Dunmow, where the numerous visitor attractions include the parish church and the Maltings. The Flitch Way is a 15-mile country walk along the former Bishops Stortford-Braintree railway tracks. A walk along a stretch offers impressive views and a wealth of woodland wildlife and will generate a thirst and an appetite that the Kings Head is just waiting to satisfy. Hatfield Forest is another excellent spot for gentle exercise, and other places to visit in the vicinity include the famous Aythorpe Roding Windmill, the largest remaining post mill in the county.

Opening Hours: 12-3 & 6-11, Sat & Sun all day

Food: A la carte

Credit Cards: Mastercard, Visa.

Accommodation: Planned

Facilities: Car park

Entertainment: None

Local Places of Interest/Activities: Hatfield Forest 3 miles, Aythorpe Roding Windmill 4 miles

The Kings Head | 155

*1 High Street,
Tollesbury, Essex
Tel: 01621 869203*

Directions:

Tollesbury is on the B1023 6 miles east of Maldon

The Kings Head is a substantial, no-nonsense village square pub that is one of the most popular in the region, attracting a clientele of local residents, tourists and those messing about on the nearby rivers. The straightforward, traditional appeal of this 17th century inn has been maintained and enhanced for the past ten years by owner Paul Yull. He removed the fruit machines as soon as he arrived, and he won't stock alcopops or fancy designer beers, but supplements the resident and guest British beers with specialist beers from Eastern Europe. In this way he attracts beer connoisseurs as well as those who like the occasional sip in convivial company, and his regular clientele ranges from the good people of Tollesbury and the neighbouring towns and villages to the Tollesbury Motorcycle Club.

He also provides his customers with solid nourishment, often claiming to feed the village with a range of good-value dishes that includes very tasty home-made pies. Sailors, workers and tourists are among those who take advantage of the Kings Head's overnight accommodation - the two letting bedrooms are planned to become three by 2003. The last Saturday of every month is a big live music night, and the pub also has regular quiz evenings.

Opening Hours: 11-11, Sun 12-10.30

Food: Home cooking

Credit Cards: Mastercard, Visa.

Accommodation: 2 rooms (1more planned)

Facilities: Car park

Entertainment: Regular quiz nights, live music monthly on a Tuesday

Local Places of Interest/Activities: Tollesbury Marina, Maldon 6 miles

156   The Kings Head Inn

Burnt Oak, Flatford,
East Bergholt,
Essex CO7 6TL
Tel: 01206 298190

Directions:

2 miles north of
Manningtree: A137
then B1070.

Close to Flatford Mill in the heart of Constable Country, the mid-17th century **Kings Head Inn** nestles among pretty little cottages. The pink-washed front is a mass of colourful flowers in spring and summer, and inside all is neat, attractive and traditional in the comfortable public and lounge bars and the 30-seat restaurant. Phil and Angie Woodend have been here since 1994, Phil in the kitchen and Angie looking after her mature regular customers and visitors who come from around the world to see the villages and scenes that John Constable made famous in his paintings. Most notable among these is the mill itself, which appears in one of his best loved works, *The Hay Wain.*

Phil produces dishes for the educated palate, and if duck is on the menu it should not be missed, as it's his speciality. The carpeted dining area is inviting and intimate, with neatly set little tables, low lighting and black beams that contrast with the cream-painted walls. Food is served from 12 to 2 and from 7 to 9 (not Sunday or Monday evenings), and to complement the fine cooking are a comprehensive wine list as well as high-quality ales and lagers. The Kings Head has an ample car park and a lawned garden with picnic benches. The whole area is very popular with walkers and ramblers - the Constable Country Trail is a good one to follow - as well as tourists in cars or coaches.

Opening Hours: 12-3 & 7-11

Food: A la carte

Credit Cards: Mastercard, Visa.

Accommodation: None

Facilities: Car park

Entertainment: None

Local Places of Interest/Activities: Flatford Mill, Dedham 2 miles, Manningtree 2 miles

The Lion & Lamb 157

Stortford Road,
Little Canfield,
Nr Dunmow,
Essex CM6 1SR
Tel: 01279 870257
Fax: 01279 870423

Directions:
The inn is on the
A120, 4 miles east of
the M11 and Stansted
(Junction 8) and a
short distance west of
Great Dunmow.

Hospitality is in generous supply at the **Lion & Lamb**, which is situated on the A120 at Little Canfield, about two miles west of Great Dunmow. A coaching inn dating from the 18th century, this lovely old hostelry is run by Mike Shields, whose belief in traditional pub values has made the place such a success. Inside, the spacious bars have a delightfully old-world appeal, with masses of oak beams, open fires, red brick and rustic furniture. In this cosy, comfortable ambience Essex-brewed Ridleys ales come from the pump in perfect condition, and an outstanding international selection of wines can be enjoyed on their own or to complement the food, which is served throughout the day right up until 10 o'clock, 7 days a week.

The cooking offers restaurant quality at pub prices, and the menus provide a very good choice, with prime fresh produce used wherever possible. Salads and quiches provide wholesome light meals, while from the main menus come more substantial items such as pasta, peppered sirloin steaks with stilton or chicken supreme filled with goat's cheese, sundried tomatoes and spinach, served with a lobster sauce. The popular Sunday menu proposes a good choice of starters and desserts framing the main courses, which always includes two roasts, a fish dish and a vegetarian option. There are smoking and non-smoking areas in the restaurant, and a self-contained room with access to a patio and gardens makes an ideal venue for a private party. The inn has a large car park, and there are plenty of seats in the beer garden for summer supping. Great Dunmow, a village full of history, is a short drive along the A120, and the Lion & Lamb is also close to Stansted Airport and the M11 (junction 8).

Opening Hours: 11-11, Sun 12-10.30

Food: A la carte

Credit Cards: Amex, Mastercard, Visa.

Accommodation: None

Facilities: Large car park, disabled access, family garden, private function room.

Entertainment: Live music monthly

Local Places of Interest/Activities: Great Dunmow 2 miles, Hatfield Forest 4 miles, Braintree 6 miles, Stansted Airport 3 miles

Internet/Website:
e-mail: info@lionandlambtakeley.co.uk
website: www.lionandlambtakeley.co.uk

158

The Moletrap

Tawney Common,
Nr Epping,
Essex CM16 7PQ
Tel: 01992 522394

Directions:

Tawney Common lies
south of Epping
Forest and north of
the A113 - leave on
minor road about 2
miles east of Abridge.
From Chipping
Ongar take minor
road to Toot Hill and
Tawney Common.

Off the A113 about two miles south of Epping, the **Moletrap** is a delightful little gem of a pub
tucked away in a tiny hamlet reached down country lanes east of Epping. A luxuriant covering
of greenery decks much of the outside of the inn, while in the comfortable, cosy bars the
walls and the ancient beams are adorned with pictures, postcards, brasses and beer mats,
making a very homely and inviting ambience. In this charmingly traditional setting David
Kirtley dispenses real ales and a good variety of lagers, while in the kitchen his wife Jean
produces generous portions of appetising, tasty dishes including splendid savoury pies that
are highly recommended by all who have tried them. Food is served every lunchtime and
evening.

David and Jean have run this delightful place for the last five years and will be greatly
missed by their regular customers when they retire in 2003. They will be missed, and so will
Jean's pies, and the Kirtleys' successors will certainly have plenty to live up to. The area round
the Moletrap provides very pleasant walking (Epping Forest alone covers 6,000 acres, all
open to the public), and among the many places of interest within a short drive of the inn
are the aircraft museum at North Weald Bassett and the Church of St Andrew, reputedly the
oldest wooden church in the world, in the charmingly rural village of Greensted.

Opening Hours: 11-3 & 6-11, Sun 12-4 &
6.30-10.30

Food: A la carte

Credit Cards: None

Accommodation: None

Facilities: Car park

Entertainment: None

Local Places of Interest/Activities: Epping
Forest, Waltham Abbey 4 miles

The Old Dog

Herongate Tye, Nr Brentwood,
Essex CM13 3SD
Tel: 01277 810337
Fax: 01277 811825

Directions:
The hamlet of Herongate lies just off the A128 beyond Ingrave, 3 miles south of Brentwood.

On a bend in the road in the hamlet of Herongate Tye, the **Old Dog** - spot the faithful old chap on the prominent sign - is a fine 16th century inn with a white weatherboarded frontage and a classic tiled roof. The two-storey central part of the inn is flanked by two single storey 'wings', and the decor inside is most appealing, with black beams, open fires and leather settees helping to preserve its delightful period character. The Old Dog is lovingly looked after by the Murphy family: Sheila Murphy keeps things running smoothly front of house, while her sons James and John do a fine job in the kitchen, making the best use of prime local supplies to produce a variety of dishes every lunchtime and evening. There's off-road parking at the front, along with a couple of picnic benches.

This is an Old Dog that doesn't need to be taught new tricks - it's perfect just the way it is, as any of the many regular customers will testify. After a drink or a meal here, there are some good walks in the area, and it's only a short drive to Brentwood, Basildon and Billericay, which all offer plenty of places of interest. In Billericay, the Chantry House is one of many fine old buildings. Even closer is Thorndon Country Park and Hartswood, a former royal deer park with lakes and woods and a wildlife exhibition.

Opening Hours: 11-3 & 6-11, Sun 12-3 & 6-10.30

Food: A la carte

Credit Cards: Amex, Mastercard, Visa.

Accommodation: None

Facilities: Car park

Entertainment: None

Local Places of Interest/Activities:
Brentwood 3 miles, Thorndon Country Park 1 mile

160   The Old Ship Inn

Heybridge Basin,
Maldon, Essex
CM9 4RX
Tel: 01621 854150

Directions:

1½ miles from
Maldon town centre.
Take the B1026
towards Goldhanger.
After about 1 mile,
turn right towards
Heybridge Basin; the
pub is along the canal
bank.

From the early 18th century, **The Old Ship Inn** has served the countryside and the waterside. Built primarily for the navvies working on the construction of the Canal, it was later a haven for the seaman and bargees who plied their trade in the Basin. Today, under young, enthusiastic manager Ben Priestley, it continues to do sterling service as a village 'local' while welcoming leisure visitors from near and far. It occupies a site right on the lockside where the Chelmer and Blackwater Canal meets salt water, and beyond the myriad boats bobbing in the harbour the view takes in Northey and Osea Islands.

Always busy, cheerful and convivial, the Old Ship has a pine bar, pine tables and chairs, and log fires in winter. Sketches of local maritime characters adorn the walls. In summer, picnic tables line the lockside - a perfect spot for soaking up the sun and the lively atmosphere on a fine day. Most tables in the pub have sea views, both in the bars and in the upstairs restaurant. The pub is renowned for its well-kept real ales, and the wine list is chosen from around the world. The menu offers an imaginative à la carte selection of home-cooked dishes running from quick, simple snacks to full meals; specialities include mussels, fresh fish and big juicy steaks. Booking is advisable at weekends. The area around the canal is rich in flora and fauna, and this peaceful part of the county has long attracted birdwatchers, anglers, walkers and artists, as well as boating enthusiasts.

Opening Hours: 11-11, Sun 12-10.30

Food: A la carte

Credit Cards: Diners, Mastercard, Visa

Accommodation: None

Facilities: Car park

Entertainment: None

Local Places of Interest/Activities: Sailing, walking, angling, birdwatching, Maldon Museum & Moot Hall 1 mile, Northey Island 1 mile, Langford Museum of Power 3 miles

The Old Ship Inn 161

North Street,
Rochford,
Essex SS4 1AB
Tel: 01752 544210

Directions:

Rochford is signposted off the A127 on the outskirts of Southend, close to Southend Airport

On one of the main streets of the small town of Rochford, the **Old Ship Inn** presents a bright, cheerful face to the world, with hanging baskets and pennants festooning its long, handsome frontage. The pub dates from the mid-19th century, and the original oak floors are still in place in the spacious, uncluttered bar. The pub has been run since the middle of 2002 by Carrie Holyland and Mark Terry. Carrie's face will be familiar to the regular customers at the Old Ship, as she was the barmaid here for a few years before taking over the helm. The usual choice of drinks is on offer, and under the new regime food will now be served between 12 and 2 and from 5 to 7 Monday to Saturday and from 12 to 4 on Sunday.

The menu will stick to tried and tested pub British classics such as fish & chips or bangers & mash. The pub is open for drinks from 11 till 11 in the week, and from 12 to 10.30 on Sunday. There's live music at the weekend. After a walk around the shops and houses in Rochford itself, visitors could head for all the fun of the fair at Southend, take things gently at the smaller seaside resorts, catch their flight from nearby Southend Airport, stroll along the banks of the River Roach or strike inland to the leafy tranquillity of Hockley Woods - there's certainly no shortage of things to do hereabouts.

Opening Hours: 11-11, Sun 12-10.30

Food: Bar meals

Credit Cards: None

Accommodation: None

Facilities: Car park

Entertainment: Live music weekends

Local Places of Interest/Activities:
Southend 3 miles, Rayleigh 4 miles

162 The Onley Arms

The Street,
Stisted,
Nr Braintree,
Essex CM77 8AW
Tel: 01376 325204

Directions:

Stisted is reached by minor roads off the A131 or A120 2 miles northeast of Braintree.

Dennis and Wendy Crispin and their family welcome one and all to the **Onley Arms**, a Ridleys pub just outside Braintree reached by minor roads off the A131 or A120. Shaded by a huge tree in the front, the pub dates back to 1860 and has been kept in excellent order throughout. Comfort is the keynote in the public rooms, where the new tenants intend to keep things just the way they have always been, offering 'good food and good beer in a good place to be'. That's a motto to define the very best country inns, and the Onley Arms lives up to it with its warm, inviting atmosphere, its well-kept cask ales and its home-cooked food courtesy of Wendy.

Good value dishes range from bar snacks, served every day, to full meals served in the restaurant, which is open Friday and Saturday evenings and Sunday lunch. The inn has a beer garden for alfresco summer supping, and on occasional winter nights the Onley Arms hosts a quiz. Braintree, which is a few minutes' drive away, has shops, museums and a magnificent Town Hall; at Bocking, there's a fine old post mill, and at Coggeshall, also very close by, are two National Trust properties - Grange Barn, the oldest surviving timber-framed barn in Europe, and Paycocke's, a merchant's house dating from about 1500, with splendid panelling, wood carving and a collection of the famous Coggeshall lace.

Opening Hours: 12-3 & 7-11. Closed Monday lunchtime.

Food: A la carte (weekends) and bar snacks

Credit Cards: None

Accommodation: None

Facilities: Car park

Entertainment: Quiz nights in winter

Local Places of Interest/Activities: Braintree 2 miles, Bocking 2 miles, Coggeshall 3 miles, Halstead 6 miles

Internet/Website:
e-mail: wendycrispin@yahoo.com

The Prince Albert | 163

1 The Green,
Blackmore,
Nr Ingatestone,
Essex CM4 0RJ
Tel: 01277 821705

Directions:
Blackmore is 4 miles
north of Ingatestone
off the A12 or 3 miles
southeast of
Chipping Ongar off
the A414.

In a quiet village easily reached from Ingatestone, Chipping Ongar, Chelmsford or Brentwood, the **Prince Albert** is a redbrick roadside building dating from the early 18th century. Black beams and old oak tables assist the traditional look in the bars, where newly arrived proprietors Anne and Peter Michaels have a warm welcome for visitors of all ages. The little public bar and adjoining lounge bar are convivial, inviting spots to linger over a glass of superb Marston's Pedigree or another cask ale, and in the separate dining area there are seats for 50 for enjoying traditional home cooking that offers an excellent choice and very good value for money. Fish specials and home-made pies are always among the favourite orders, and room should definitely be kept for one of the tempting desserts. Food is served from noon to 4 and from 6 to 9 seven days a week.

Darts is the main pub game played here, and the occasional quiz nights are guaranteed to bring in a good crowd of regulars. The Prince Albert has recently extended its appeal out of doors with the opening of a beer garden. Apart from the Prince Albert, the chief attraction in Blackmore is the Church of St Laurence, whose 15th century wooden tower is one of the finest of its kind in the country. Another notable building is nearby Ingatestone Hall, home to many generations of the distinguished Petrie family.

Opening Hours: 12-11.

Food: Bar meals

Credit Cards: None

Accommodation: None

Facilities: Car park

Entertainment: Occasional quiz nights

Local Places of Interest/Activities:
Blackmore's Church of St Laurence (wooden Gothic tower), Chipping Ongar 3 miles, Ingatestone Hall (16th century mansion) 4 miles

164 The Queens Head

North Street,
Tolleshunt d'Arcy,
Nr Maldon, Essex
CM9 8TF
Tel: 01621 860262

Directions:

Seven miles
northeast of Maldon
at the junction of the
B1023 and B1026.

Jim and Angie Errington brought with them considerable experience in the licensed trade when they took over the **Queens Head** in the summer of 2001. Standing at the junction of the B1023 and B1026 about seven miles from Maldon, the 18th century pub is not only a traditional village local but also attracts visitors from further afield with its excellent food and drink. Cask ales, maintained by Jim in perfect condition, are on tap to quench thirsts, and the fine home cooking can be enjoyed from 12 to 2.30 and from 7 to 9 seven days a week. The menu changes constantly to highlight the best and freshest local produce, and many of the dishes are cooked to the Erringtons' own home recipes, providing not only variety but often a new twist on familiar favourites. Behind its traditional frontage the Queens Head has a really eye-catching old-world interior with flagstone floors, painted panelled walls and plenty of country furniture in the bars.

On a slightly lower level, the 26-seat restaurant has walls in mellow brick, wall-to-wall carpeting and comfortably upholstered chairs set at neatly laid tables. The Queens Head is a good place for families with youngsters, particularly in the summer, and in the beer garden is a children's play area with a bouncy castle and cougar mountain. The go-ahead tenants have plans to add a conservatory in 2003 and are seeking permission to create two letting bedrooms for guests staying overnight. Tolleshunt d'Arcy is a quiet, picturesque village which takes its name from the d'Arcy family, whose moated manor house can still be seen and who are commemorated in the Church of St Nicholas.

Opening Hours: 11.30-11

Food: A la carte

Credit Cards: All the major cards

Accommodation: Planned

Facilities: Car park, children's play area

Entertainment: Occasional music nights

Local Places of Interest/Activities:
Tollesbury Marina 2 miles, Goldhanger 3 miles, Maldon 7 miles

The Railway · 165

50 Hullbridge Road,
South Woodham
Ferrers,
Essex CM3 5MG
Tel: 01245 320262

Directions:

The inn is close to the railway station in South Woodham Ferrers, 6 miles east of Wickford on the A132/ B1012.

Landlord Barry Hatt is bringing fresh ideas and a wider appeal to **The Railway**, a handsome and substantial black and cream building close to the railway station in South Woodham Ferrers (the line runs from London and serves, to the east, Burnham-on-Crouch and Southminster). Behind the repainted facade Barry has brought an appealing modern look to the bars, with soft, warm colours, thick pile carpets and smart new furniture creating a lovely inviting ambience. Outside is a spacious wooded garden with a gazebo as an unusual centrepiece. Barry has introduced food at lunchtime, a straightforward selection of sandwiches, ploughman's platters, pies and the like, which can be accompanied by a glass of cask ale.

The Railway hosts a live music evening once a month, on a Sunday. South Woodham Ferrers is a 20th century new town on the Crouch estuary, developed round a traditional market square; the surrounding arcades and terraces were built in a style true to Essex tradition, with brick, tile and weatherboard. The estuary is a paradise for yachtsmen, while lovers of the rural way of life will make for Marsh Farm Country Park, a working farm and country park by the Crouch. Among other attractions in the vicinity is the Royal Horticultural Society's Hyde Hall Garden at Rettendon, where many exciting developments include the planting of 3,000 young trees.

Opening Hours: 11-11, Sun 12-10.30

Food: Lunchtime bar snacks

Credit Cards: None

Accommodation: None

Facilities: Car park.

Entertainment: Live music one Sunday a month

Local Places of Interest/Activities: Marsh Farm Country Park 1 mile, RHS Garden Hyde Hall Rettendon 4 miles, Burnham-on-Crouch 8 miles

166   The Red Lion

6 Church Hill,
Finchingfield,
Essex CM7 4NN
Tel/Fax:
01371 810400

Directions:
Finchingfield is 6
miles northwest of
Braintree off the
B1053.

Finchingfield is a really charming village with thatched cottages and other attractive buildings spread round a sloping green. One of the most picturesque and most photographed villages in the whole of Essex, it has a great deal to detain the visitor, and it's always a pleasure to spend some time at the **Red Lion Inn**. Run with great care and enthusiasm by Frank and Zahra Taylor, the inn was built in the 15th century and modernised in 1823, and for all those years has been a focal point of local community activity for Finchingfield and the neighbouring villages. The interior is a splendid mix of oak beams, brick and brass, the most striking feature being a huge brick fireplace with a cast-iron stove flanked by old cart wheels. This fireplace links two areas of the bar, where cask ales in tip-top condition have earned the inn a long-standing entry in the CAMRA Good Pub Guide.

Lunch and dinner are always available in the bar or restaurant, with salads and ploughman's platters for lighter snacks and seafood specials and big juicy steaks among the main courses. Finchingfield is not a place to leave in a hurry, and for visitors wanting a base for exploring the region the Red Lion has three well-appointed double bedrooms with beautiful pine furniture, tv and tea/coffee making facilities. Children are welcome, and dogs by arrangement. Finchingfield boasts craft and antique shops, a lovely little windmill, and, right by the Red Lion, the 15th century Guildhall and the fine Norman Church of St John the Baptist. There are some excellent walks in and around the village.

Opening Hours: 11.30-11, Sun 12-10.30

Food: A la carte

Credit Cards: Mastercard, Visa.

Accommodation: 3 en suite rooms.

Facilities: Car park, children's play area

Entertainment: Occasional live music sessions

Local Places of Interest/Activities: Finchingfield Norman church and 15th century Guildhall, Braintree 6 miles, Thaxted 6 miles

The Red Lion

42 South Street,
Manningtree,
Essex CO11 1BG
Tel: 01206 395052

Directions:

Off the main street in Manningtree.

In a narrow street just off Manningtree's busy main thoroughfare, the 16th century **Red Lion** is a great place to relax and unwind with a pint of Adnams, perhaps over a game of darts. In summer the inn is decked in colourful flower baskets and window boxes (the display is a regular award-winner), and inside, there are two bars, the neat public bar and the elegant little lounge with a homely, inviting feel. The inn is owned and run by Chris and Myrtle Elliott, who for several years lived next to the inn. They bought it at the end of 2001 and have worked hard to create the charming, spotless little inn that is building a loyal following among the citizens of Manningtree and the surrounding area.

The appeal lies not only in the atmosphere and the well-kept beer but also in Myrtle's very good home cooking. Her smoked salmon tart is the talk of the town, and there's always a good turn-out for the monthly theme nights, which could be Spanish one month, Tex-Mex the next. The monthly folk music night is another fixture in many local diaries, and the inn can host conferences and private gatherings of up to 80 in a function suite with its own bar. The owners' plans include the bringing on stream of overnight accommodation for guests. This will be a considerable boon for visitors to Manningtree and a convenient base for exploring the region, which includes the world-famous sights of Constable Country.

Opening Hours: 11.30-3 & 7-11, Sun 12-2.30 & 7-10.30

Food: A la carte

Credit Cards: None

Accommodation: Planned

Facilities: Function suite

Entertainment: Acoustic folk night once a month

Local Places of Interest/Activities: Flatford Mill 2 miles, Colchester 6 miles, Harwich 9 miles

Internet/Website:
e-mail: mmunro@aspects.net

168 The Rodney

North Hill,
Little Baddow,
Nr Chelmsford,
Essex CM3 4TQ
Tel/Fax:
   01245 222385

Directions:

5 miles east of
Chelmsford. Take
the A12, turn off at
Boreham. Little
Baddow is 3 miles
to the south.

Built around 1650 as a farmhouse and a pub for the past 150 years, the **Rodney** overlooks the tiny village of Little Baddow from its elevated site on North Hill. Flower tubs and parasols make a colourful show outside the pub in the summer, while in the bars with their original oak floors the theme is mainly maritime, with all kinds of models, documents, photographs and a display case of sailors' knots providing the interest. A painting of the pub takes pride of place above the hearth, while the service area is adorned with beer mats, brasses, mugs and other bric-a-brac. In this most appealing setting owners Peter and Lynne Smeeton, who came here in 1989, provide a comfortable village pub atmosphere in which to enjoy cask ales or a glass or two from the wine list, or to settle down to some of Lynne's accomplished home cooking. Everything on the menu is fresh, tasty and well presented, and it's all home-made, even the chips.

Sandwiches and ploughman's platters provide quick snacks, while for main meals the choice runs from jacket potatoes and salads with a range of accompaniments to omelettes, cottage pie, spare ribs, lasagne, pork in cider, chicken in red wine and rump steak served plain, peppered or Diane. Food is available lunchtime and evening and all day Sundays and Bank Holidays, but please check as times vary from opening hours. The Rodney has another delight in store - lawns and a gardens with an area where children can play. Handsome trees add to the attractive setting, and there's plenty of car parking space in front of the pub. Little Baddow lies east of Chelmsford and can be reached from either the A12 or the A414. If the latter, turn left at Danbury, perhaps after a walk on Danbury Common or in the Country Park to work up a thirst that the Rodney is waiting to satisfy.

Opening Hours: 11.30-2.30 & 6-11, Sun 12-10.30

Food: A la carte

Credit Cards: Mastercard, Visa.

Accommodation: None

Facilities: Car park, children's play area

Entertainment: None

Local Places of Interest/Activities: Danbury 3 miles, Chelmsford 5 miles, Hatfield Peverel 5 miles

Internet/Website:
e-mail: therodney@barstewards.com

The Rose & Crown

Crown Hill,
Ashdon,
Nr Saffron Walden,
Essex CB10 2HB
Tel:
01799 584337

Directions:

Ashdon is reached by a minor road signposted northeast from Saffron Walden (about 3 miles).

Owner Paul Lewis spent some time in Australia before taking over at the **Rose & Crown**, which stands in the village of Ashdon a short drive north of Saffron Walden. This cream-painted roadside pub has a very traditional and convivial bar, a small lounge bar and a neat little restaurant; a huge wood burning stove ensures that things stay snug in the cooler months. Three cask ales are on tap to quench thirsts, and the pub also keeps a good selection of wines. On the food side, which is a very important part of the Rose & Crown's business, fresh seafood, excellent local lamb and big juicy steaks are just a few of the menu options, and there's also an unusually generous selection of vegetarian dishes.

The theme food nights are always well attended, as are the live music sessions held from time to time, but the main event in the Rose & Crown's calendar is the popular beer festival held every August Bank Holiday. The inn is well placed for both town and country lovers. Saffron Walden is a wonderful old market town with delightful 15th and 16th century timber-framed buildings - some adorned with the East Anglian speciality of pargeting - and the largest church in Essex, the magnificent Church of St Mary, whose soaring 193ft spire dominates the town. Even closer to the inn is the historic site of Bartlow Hills, whose 2nd century Roman burial mounds are said to be the largest of their kind in Europe.

Opening Hours: 12-3 & 6-11

Food: A la carte

Credit Cards: None

Accommodation: None

Facilities: Car park

Entertainment: Beer Festival August Bank Holiday, occasional live music nights

Local Places of Interest/Activities: Ashdon Guildhall, Linton Zoo 3 miles, Bartlow Hills 3 miles, Saffron Walden 3 miles, Audley End 4 miles

170   The Rose & Crown

31 Mill End, Thaxted,
Essex CM6 2LT
Tel: 01371 831152

Directions:

Thaxted is on the B184
6 miles north of Great
Dunmow.

When the Rose inn joined with its neighbour the Crown inn many years ago, there was no problem in finding a name for the combined 16th century building. **The Rose & Crown** is currently thriving under the tenancy of Suzanne and George Carless, who have long-term plans to make things even better. They have completely redecorated the interior, and the resulting blend of old fittings and all new furniture works exceptionally well. Ridleys cask ales head the selection of beers, and freshly home-cooked meals are served every session except Sunday evening. Traditional Sunday roasts are guaranteed to bring in the crowds, so booking is a good idea.

The Rose & Crown has a patio and beer garden, and for guests spending the night there are two spacious en suite twin rooms. These rooms provide a comfortable and convenient base for exploring one of the most appealing of all the small 'country towns' in Essex. With a character all its own, it is full of fine old buildings, including some with timber frames and the typical decorative pargeting. The Guildhall and the Almshouses are the most notable, and also not to be missed are the famous Tower Windmill and the imposing church where Gustav Holst often played the organ. A festival of Morris dancing takes place annually in Thaxted, usually on the Spring Bank Holiday, and on most other Bank Holidays there's dancing in the streets - on such occasions the Rose & Crown definitely comes into its own!

Opening Hours: 11-3 & 5.30-11, all day Sat & Sun

Food: A la carte

Credit Cards: None

Accommodation: 2 en suite rooms.

Facilities: Car park

Entertainment: None

Local Places of Interest/Activities: Thaxted Church & Guildhall, Great Dunmow 6 miles, Little Easton 5 miles

The Round Bush | 171

Frambridge Road,
Mundon,
Nr Maldon,
Essex CM9 6NQ
Tel/Fax:
  01621 828354

Directions:

Mundon lies off the
B1018 3 miles
south of Maldon.

2003 will see the 300th birthday of the building that houses the **Round Bush**. Set in rolling countryside two miles from Maldon, it has an unpretentious rural appeal. A collection of old-fashioned, uncluttered adjoining rooms include good-sized public and lounge bars and a neat little restaurant. Proprietor Ray Ibbotson is also the chef; passionate about food, he takes great pride in what he puts on the plate, and what's on the plate encompasses a really good choice that offers something for all tastes, at very kind prices. Everything is recommended, but the curries and the steaks are perhaps the outstanding favourites. Good house wines accompany the food, and three cask ales - a resident and two guests - are always on tap. Adjoining the old building is a single-storey redbrick café open from 8.30 to 2 for breakfasts, snacks and lunches.

There's excellent walking hereabouts, and St Peter's Way passes through the village on its route from Purleigh to Maylandsea. And the surroundings provided inspiration for at least one well-known writer: the village was home for a while to Leon Tolstoy, and he wrote a chapter of his monumental *War and Peace* while living here. With some of Ray's cooking inside him, he might have stayed longer and written another chapter or two. The many and varied attractions of Maldon are a short drive away, and it's an easy drive down to the River Crouch and along to the delightful sailing centre of Burnham-on-Crouch.

Opening Hours: 11-3 & 6-11, Sun 12-3 & 6-10.30

Food: Bar meals

Credit Cards: None

Accommodation: None

Facilities: Car park.

Entertainment: Quiz one Tuesday a month

Local Places of Interest/Activities: Maldon (River Blackwater, quay, museum, All Saints Church) 3 miles, Northey Island 4 miles, Burnham-on-Crouch 6 miles

172

The Royal Oak

Chelmsford Road,
Woodham Mortimer,
Nr Maldon, Essex
CM9 6 TJ
Tel: 01245 223186

Directions:

Woodham Mortimer lies just off the A414 1 mile east of Danbury, 3 miles west of Maldon.

The Royal Oak is a handsome roadside hostelry whose classic cream-painted facade is ablaze in spring and summer with flowers in tubs and baskets and greenery that climbs up one side. Inside, the bars are open-plan yet at the same time intimate and inviting, with a stone-faced fireplace, green plush carpets and old oak tables. For the very pretty adjacent restaurant the chefs prepare a well-balanced menu of fresh, wholesome dishes served lunchtime and evening and all day on Sunday. Local produce, including seafood and excellent lamb, is featured as often as possible. To accompany the food, or to enjoy on their own, are two cask ales and a good selection of wines.

The Royal Oak has a family garden with a children's play area. On Thursdays, the pub hosts live music evenings. The owner of the Royal Oak is Marie Brewster, a young and very professional lady who worked at this delightful place before buying it in Millennium year. She is rightly proud of her purchase, and with her care and enthusiasm for her job her customers can look forward to many years of the fine hospitality that has made them loyal regulars. Woodham Mortimer is situated between Danbury and Maldon. The former offers excellent walking and nature study on the National Trust's Common and in the Country Park, while the latter has the tang of the sea and a number of interesting places to visit, including the Moot Hall and the Museum.

Opening Hours: 11-3 & 6-11, Sun 12-10.30

Food: A la carte

Credit Cards: Mastercard, Visa.

Accommodation: None

Facilities: Car park

Entertainment: Live music Thursday night

Local Places of Interest/Activities: Danbury 1 mile, Maldon 3 miles, Chelmsford 6 miles

The Shepherd & Dog

Moor Road,
Langham,
Nr Colchester,
Essex CO4 5NR
Tel: 01206 272711
Fax: 01206 273136

Directions:

Langham is situated just off the A12 about 2 miles north of Colchester.

Julian Dicks had a distinguished career on the football field with Birmingham City, West Ham United and Liverpool between 1985 and 1999. He then turned for a while to golf, and recently embarked on his third professional career when he became the owner of the **Shepherd & Dog** in June 2002. In this classic English village public house, built in 1928, he has a quality product that is one of the premier hostelries in the region. Behind the long frontage, bedecked with flowers and greenery in the summer, the lively public bar and intimate lounge are comfortable, civilised spots for enjoying one of the three cask ales that are always on tap, and when the weather allows, the scene transfers to the beer garden, which has an area where children can play.

The chefs produce an impressive range of top-quality dishes including the freshest seafood specials and meat and poultry main courses that make excellent use of the best local suppliers. They also offer vegetarian dishes and have recently added a children's menu (a limited number of high chairs are available). Food is served from noon to 2.15 and 6 to 10 Monday to Friday and all day Saturday and Sunday. The inn has seating for about 75, including 22 bookable covers in the elegant beamed restaurant; the rest is divided between the two bar areas. Booking is also essential for the regular theme nights, where the cuisine - perhaps French, Spanish or Seafood - is matched by appropriate wines. The Shepherd & Dog dominates the prosperous village of Langham, on the Essex/Suffolk border, where John Constable would climb the tower on the hill and sit and paint. Walking is a popular activity hereabouts, and motorists have easy access to the many attractive places on the Constable Country Trail.

Opening Hours: 11-3 & 5.30-11, all day Sat & Sun

Food: A la carte

Credit Cards: All the major cards

Accommodation: None

Facilities: Car park

Entertainment: None

Local Places of Interest/Activities:
Colchester 2 miles, Stratford St Mary 1 mile.

Internet/Website:
website:www.shepherdanddog.fsnet.co.uk

174

The Ship Inn

Maldon Road,
Tiptree,
Essex CO5 0PQ
Tel:
01621 817967

Directions:

Tiptree is on the B1022/B1023 7 miles southwest of Colchester.

No one travelling in this part of the world need ever be in a jam wondering where to pause for refreshment. **The Ship Inn** fits the bill admirably, open all day for both food and drink. In a prime roadside location just outside the crossroads village of Tiptree, the 17th century inn has a distinctive low profile, and tables and chairs are set outside on a lawned area. Inside, there's a public bar with a pool table, a cosy little lounge and a well-carpeted, comfortably furnished dining area with exposed black beams. Hands-on hostess Debbie Williams cooks, caters and keeps the place in apple pie order, while her husband Graham tends the cellars and the shelves.

The inn's cask ales are his pride and joy, to be enjoyed on their own over a chat in the bar or out in the beer garden, or to accompany something from Debbie's traditional menus: two of the favourites from her repertoire are shepherd's pie and an excellent quiche served with a salad accompaniment. This Ship is a very sociable vessel and is a very child friendly place. There is karaoke on Tuesday, live music on Saturday and a disco on Sunday. Once part of the great forest of Essex, the area round Tiptree is now a centre for growing fruit trees. And, of course, what Tiptree is most famous for is the jams and preserves made since 1885 by the firm of Wilkin & Son. Their combined shop, tea room and museum is well worth a visit, but visitors heading for the Ship Inn should go easy on the jam tasting - they have to leave plenty of room for Debbie's dishes.

Opening Hours: 11-11, Sun 12-10.30

Food: Bar meals

Credit Cards: None

Accommodation: None

Facilities: Car park, children's play area, 7 day a week bouncy castle.

Entertainment: Karaoke Tuesday, Live music Saturday, Disco Sunday

Local Places of Interest/Activities: Wilkin & Sons Jam Factory, Kelvedon 3 miles, Great Braxted 3 miles, Colchester 7 miles

Internet/Website:
website:
   www.pickapub.co.uk/theshiptiptree.htm

The Stag

Little Easton,
Nr Great Dunmow,
Essex CM6 2JE
Tel: 01371 870214

Directions:

Little Easton is located off the B184 2 miles north of Great Dunmow.

The 12th century church, the Barn Theatre and the lovely Harold Peto-designed gardens at Easton Hall bring visitors from near and far to the village of Little Easton, and many are delighted to find another attraction in the shape of **The Stag**. This 100-year-old double-fronted pub is kept in immaculate condition by the husband-and-wife team of Barry and June Jackson. They have transformed The Stag since taking over in 2001, and regulars and first-timers can be sure of a warm welcome and top hospitality from hosts whose motto is 'The Customer is King'. Well-kept cask ales have earned The Stag an entry in the CAMRA Good Beer Guide, and the restaurant-quality food loses nothing in comparison.

June's appetising home cooking is served lunchtime and evening Monday to Saturday and from 12 to 3 on Sunday, when the traditional roasts are eagerly anticipated by the regular customers. The Stag, which has two bars and a separate dining area, stands in lovely gardens, and in the grounds are an area where children can play and a caravan and camping site. Quiz and race nights take place from time to time. The pub is the meeting place of the local hunt. Little Easton is a really delightful place to visit, and there are many other places of interest nearby, including the historic towns of Great Dunmow and Thaxted. Stanstead Airport is about five miles to the west.

Opening Hours: 11.30-3 & 5.30-11.

Food: A la carte

Credit Cards: Mastercard, Visa.

Accommodation: None

Facilities: Car park, children's play area, caravan and camp site

Entertainment: Occasional race nights

Local Places of Interest/Activities: Little Easton 12th century church and Barn Theatre, Great Dunmow 3 miles, Thaxted 3 miles

176

The Swan Inn

THE SWAN INN

The Street,
Hatfield Peverel,
Nr Chelmsford,
Essex CM3 2DW
Tel/Fax:
  01245 380238

Directions:

On the main street of Hatfield Peverel (B1137) 5 miles northeast of Chelmsford.

Located on the main street through Hatfield Peverel, the **Swan Inn** was built in the 17th century and was once an important stopping point on the coaching run between London and Norwich. Much of its old-world appeal lives on in the spotless bar and lounge, where beams and brasses help paint a very traditional scene. In Chris Ward, the inn has a young, go-ahead landlord who is passionate about the Swan and this part of Essex, and who takes excellent care of his customers with the assistance of hardworking staff. Popular with locals, it also offers motorists the chance of a pleasant break on their journey along the nearby A12. Greene King IPA and two other real ales head the drinks list, and straightforward, no-frills bar meals and snacks are served Tuesday to Sunday lunchtimes, with evening meals available from 6 o'clock until 8.

The Swan also offers very agreeable guest accommodation in four characterful bedrooms with tv and tea/coffee makers; two of the four have en suite facilities. With the A12 only half a mile away, the inn is an excellent base both for businessmen who want a peaceful place to spend the night and for tourists visiting the sights of the area. Hatfield Peverel itself has a handsome village green and some charming architecture, and within an easy drive are the bustling town of Chelmsford, the delightful smaller town of Witham, Whetmead nature reserve and the medieval Temple Barns at Cressing.

Opening Hours: 11- 3 & 5.30-11, all day at the weekend

Food: A la carte

Credit Cards: Mastercard, Visa.

Accommodation: 4 rooms (2 en suite)

Facilities: Car park

Entertainment: Live music at the weekend

Local Places of Interest/Activities:
Chelmsford 5 miles, Baddow Antiques Centre 6 miles, Witham 2 miles

Internet/Website:
website:
  www.pickapub.co.uk/swanhatpev.htm

The Three Compasses

West Hanningfield, Nr Chelmsford,
Essex CM2 8UQ
Tel: 01245 400447

Directions:

West Hanningfield is located 6 miles south of Chelmsford on a minor road off the A130.

The Three Compasses is a 15th century roadhouse in an elevated position overlooking, indeed, commanding the village green at West Hanningfield, six miles south of Chelmsford. Rosemary Cotton and family, here for more than 30 years and the owners since 1998, has kept the pub just the way she and her long-standing regular customers would like - peaceful, civilised, and with a traditional look and feel that has changed little down the years. There's no place here for trendy modern developments - no raucous music, no noisy games, just the constant care and attention that have kept it as the lovely civilised spot it has long been and remains today.

An 'owner tree' lists all the landlords and landladies from the day it first opened, and the split bars, public and saloon, have a delightfully cosy, cluttered appeal, with comfortable cushions on solid oak furnishings; the centrepiece is a massive inglenook fireplace with an open log fire. Simple, traditional pub food is served from 12 to 2 and from 7 to 9 daily, accompanied by a choice of two cask ales and a good selection of wines. Tables and chairs are set out under parasols in the summer, and the Three Compasses has plenty of off-road parking space. West Hanningfield is a quiet, prosperous village that is off the beaten track but certainly not remote (the A130 and the A12 are both just a few minutes' drive away). The village is at the northern end of Hanningfield Reservoir, which is famous for its trout fishing.

Opening Hours: Mon-Sat 11.30-3 and 6-11; Sunday 12-3 and 7-10.30

Food: Bar meals

Credit Cards: None

Accommodation: None.

Facilities: Car park

Entertainment: None

Local Places of Interest/Activities:
Hanningfield Reservoir and Wild life Sanctuary, beautiful walking areas, Chelmsford 6 miles

178 The Three Pigeons

**Mount Hill,
Halstead,
Essex CO9 1AA
Tel: 01787 472336**

Directions:

Halstead is on the A131 6 miles north of Braintree.

Built in the 17th century and an inn since 1851, the **Three Pigeons** stands on an elevated site a short distance from the town centre. Tenant Debbie Webb, here since 1998, has stamped her bubbly, cheerful personality on the place, generating a warm, welcoming atmosphere that is apparent the moment visitors walk through the door. The bar is spotlessly clean and very comfortable, with some superb original pine flooring. Real ales, including Greene King IPA and Old Speckled Hen, are accompanied by a good selection of other draught and bottle beers, and straightforward, well-priced hot and cold bar snacks are served throughout the day.

On a lower level from the bar is a games room. Darts is played very keenly at the Three Pigeons, which fields one of the best ladies' teams in the area, but pool and dominoes also have their supporters, and the pub can boast its own rounders team. Entertainment includes regular quiz nights and race nights. The pub has a patio area and a spacious beer garden. Halstead, like Braintree and Coggeshall, was once an important weaving centre, and Townford Mill, built in the 18th century and now an antiques centre, is one of the most handsome reminders of the industrial heritage. Among the many other attractions within a short distance of the pub are Castle Hedingham, Colne Valley Farm Park and the Colne Valley Railway and Museum.

Opening Hours: 11-3 & 5-11, Sat & Sun all day

Food: Bar snacks

Credit Cards: None

Accommodation: None

Facilities: Car park

Entertainment: Regular quiz nights and race nights

Local Places of Interest/Activities: Castle Hedingham 3 miles, Colne Valley Railway 3 miles, Little Maplestead 3 miles, Gestingthorp 5 miles, Sudbury 7 miles

Internet/Website:
e-mail: deb3pigshal@aol.com

The Waggon & Horses | 179

High Street, Great Yeldham,
Nr Halstead, Essex CO9 4EX
Tel: 01787 237936

Directions:
Great Yeldham lies just off the A134 8 miles northwest of Halstead (from Halstead A1124 then A134).

Easily found just off the Halstead-Haverhill road in the lovely little village of Great Yeldham, the **Waggon & Horses** is a free house of very wide appeal. As a classic village local, it provides a fine array of cask ales (including the excellent Greene King IPA) to enjoy in a bright, spacious bar with a wealth of black oak beams and an inviting, relaxing ambience generated by proprietor Mike Shiffner and his staff. As a provider of food, it offers good wholesome English cooking served in the bar or in the 32-cover restaurant every lunchtime and evening and all day on Sunday.

As a base for anyone with business in the area or for leisure visitors touring the region, the Waggon & Horses has ten comfortably appointed en suite bedrooms and six more with shared facilities. Outside this distinguished old inn - the oldest part is 16th century - are benches under sunshades, a splendid old farm waggon and ample off-road parking. There are excellent walks and lots of pretty little villages to explore in the area round the inn, and several varied attractions in nearby Castle Hedingham - the eponymous Norman castle, once one of England's strongest fortresses, the Norman Church of St Nicholas, Colne Valley Farm Park and the Colne Valley Railway, a stretch of preserved track on which steam-hauled trains run up to Great Yeldham itself - what a delightful way to arrive at the Waggon & Horses!

Opening Hours: 11-11, Sun 12-10.30

Food: A la carte

Credit Cards: Mastercard, Visa.

Accommodation: 16 rooms (10 en-suite)

Facilities: Car park

Entertainment: None

Internet/Website:
website: www.waggonandhorses.net

180

The White Hart

High Street,
Stebbing,
Nr Great Dunmow,
Essex CM6 3SQ
Tel: 01371 856383

Directions:

Stebbing is situated off
the A120 2 miles east
of Great Dunmow.

Two miles east of Great Dunmow off the Braintree road (A1230), the **White Hart** is tucked quietly away among some lovely little cottages. Built in the 16th century and not greatly changed down the years, this is a really splendid example of a classic English country pub, and in Nick Eldred it has exactly the right man to maintain that old-word charm. After ten years at the helm, Nick has the White Hart just the way he wants it, and that's also just the way his many regular customers want it, as proved by their unfailing loyalty to Nick and the pub.

This is a perfect place to relax in very pleasant, very comfortable surroundings to enjoy a glass or two of well-kept cask ale or to settle down to simple, satisfying, well-presented food served in generous helpings at sensible prices. the food is available from 12 to 2.30 and 6.30 to 9 every day of the week. The bar is bright, cheerful and spotlessly clean, with exposed oak beams, plush red carpets and a huge feature log fire. The A120 is easily reached from the inn, with historic Great Dunmow in one direction and Braintree in the other. Also nearby, at Little Easton, are the Harold Peto-designed gardens of Easton Lodge, while to the north of Stebbing is the pretty village of Great Bardfield with a rural museum, a 14th century church and a restored windmill going by the name of Gibraltar.

Opening Hours: 11-3 & 5-11, Sun 12-3 & 5-10.30

Food: A la carte

Credit Cards: None

Accommodation: None

Facilities: Car park

Entertainment: Quiz nights in winter

Local Places of Interest/Activities: Great Dunmow 2 miles, Thaxted 6 miles.

The White Horse | 181

Southminster Road,
Dengie,
Essex CM0 7LP
Tel/Fax:
  01621 779288

Directions:

Dengie lies about
4 miles north of
Southminster
just off the B1021.

A short drive north from Southminster brings the motorist to the village of Dengie and the 300-year-old **White Horse**, where the Barker family - father Michael, daughter Abigail and others - keep the welcome mat out throughout the long opening hours. This particular White Horse is well ahead of the field in the old-world charm stakes, and the slate-flagged floors, the rustic furniture, the heavily beamed ceiling, the open fire and the wealth of ornamental brassware paint a splendidly traditional scene. This makes a lovely inviting setting for unwinding with a drink or something good to eat. Abigail is the cook, and her home cooking is one of the pub's chief assets.

Straightforward, satisfying fare is served from opening time till 8 in the week and till 5 on Saturday, attracting hungry walkers, cyclists and tourists as well as loyal regulars, and the Sunday roast lunch is guaranteed to be a sell-out. There's always a cheerful, convivial feel here, and things really buzz on a Saturday night, when there's live music. This area of Essex, between the Crouch and the Blackwater, is the most remote in the county, and after a walk on the desolate Dengie Peninsula, with the tang of the sea carried in on the east wind, the good things provided by the White Horse will be even more appreciated. To the south of Dengie, the old market town of Southminster is well worth a visit, and beyond it, Burnham-on-Crouch is the yachting centre of Essex.

Opening Hours: 11-11, Sun 12-10.30

Food: A la carte

Credit Cards: None

Accommodation: None

Facilities: Car park

Entertainment: Live music Saturday

Local Places of Interest/Activities:
Southminster 3 miles, Bradwell 4 miles,
Burnham-on-Crouch 6 miles

182 The White Horse

Pleshey,
Nr Chelmsford,
Essex CM3 1HA
Tel: 01245 237281

Directions:
Pleshey lies off the
A130 about 6 miles
north of Chelmsford.

Food and drink both play prominent roles at the **White Horse**, a classic country inn with a history going back to 1483. The original red-tiled roof takes the eye from the car park, and the interior is quite amazing, with brick and tiled floors, brick or plaster walls, and ancient beams and timbers adding up to a setting that is second to none in terms of character and ambience. The inn is run in fine style by the husband and wife team of Mike and Jan Smail, Mike in the kitchen and Jan front of house. In the splendid restaurant, with linen tablecloths and gleaming crystal, Mike produces a fine choice of dishes that include classics such as steak & kidney pie or roast duck as well as some more esoteric and original offerings. An excellent wine list accompanies the food, and there are cask ales for those who prefer the hop to the grape.

The monthly gourmet nights are occasions to savour, and the inn really bounces on Saturday night, when the monthly jazz session takes place. The function suite, which can seat 60, is an ideal venue for private parties or special occasions. Outside, the White Horse has extensive parking space, a patio and a spacious lawn. Pleshey is surrounded by a mile-long earthen rampart, protecting its castle, very little of which survives. There are good views from the mound, which at a mere 60' is nonetheless one of the highest points in Essex. The village is really delightful, with a number of thatched cottages close to the pub, and the area is an excellent one for walkers and ramblers.

Opening Hours: 11-2.30 & 6-11, Sun 12-3.30

Food: A la carte

Credit Cards: Amex, Mastercard, Visa.

Accommodation: None

Facilities: Car park, function suite

Entertainment: Monthly Jazz Nights on a Saturday

Local Places of Interest/Activities:
Chelmsford 6 miles, High Easter (Aythorpe Post Mill) 2 miles

Internet/Website:
e-mail: thewhitehorse@ukonline.co.uk

The White Horse 183

Ramsden Heath, Nr Billericay,
Essex CM11 1NA
Tel: 01268 710297
Fax: 01277 711227

Directions:
Ramsden Heath is about 2 miles east of
Billericay off the B1007, on a minor road
that runs across to the A130.

Alex Carroll is the hardworking landlord at the **White Horse**, one of the most popular pubs in the area. He previously ran a very successful establishment near Chelmsford before transferring his business interests to this pleasant part of Essex in the countryside east of Billericay. The oldest part of this splendid pub dates back to the 16th century, and quality is the keynote throughout, with thick pile carpets, handsome furnishings and gleaming brass. A single-storey extension houses the 100-seat restaurant, which offers a broad-based menu of traditional cuisine that includes seafood, steaks, pasta, seasonal game and an immensely popular carvery that has built up a large band of followers.

Food is served lunchtime and evening on Monday and all day on other days of the week. Senior citizens can take advantage of a special deal on Thursday lunchtimes. A marquee is available all year round for private parties and special occasions, and also in the grounds is a children's play area with a trampoline to keep the little ones bouncing and happy. In nearby Billericay, the Chantry House and Barleylands Farm Museum are well worth visiting, and even closer to the White Horse are the extensive waters of Hanningfield Reservoir and the extensive acres of Norsey Wood Country Park, an area of ancient woodland managed by the traditional technique of coppicing.

Opening Hours: 11-11, Sun 12-10.30

Food: A la carte & Bar Meals

Credit Cards: All the major cards

Accommodation: None

Facilities: Car park, children's play area with trampoline

Entertainment: Quiz Tuesday

Local Places of Interest/Activities: Billericay 2 miles, Norsey Wood 1 mile

184   The White Lion

6 Church Street,
Sible Hedingham,
Essex CO9 3NS
Tel: 01787 462534

Directions:

Sible Hedingham is 3 miles northeast of Halstead off the A131.

Sible Hedingham is mentioned in the Domesday Book as being the largest parish in England, but visitors should have no difficulty in getting on the trail of the **White Lion**. Built in the 17th century as a small row of cottages, it is a true locals local, with a quaint, no-frills interior and an open log fire to keep things snug. The cask ales, including IPA from Greene King, are kept in tip-top condition by Charles Coote, who runs the White Lion with his wife Michelle. Straightforward bar snacks - sandwiches, soup, hot pies and the like - are served all day, every day, and a function room that can accommodate up to 75 is a popular venue as a place for a party. Families are always welcome at the White Lion, and there's an area where children can romp in safety.

Live music is played on the last Saturday of the month and on Bank Holidays. This is a really delightful, unpretentious place where a 15-minute 'pop-in' could easily last a couple of hours! There's also plenty of interest in the village and the surrounding area, from the village church, where there's a monument to Sir John Hawkwood, a son of Sible Hedingham who fought at the Battle of Crecy, to the mighty Castle Hedingham 2 miles up the B1058. Its impressive stone keep, four storeys high, is one of the tallest in Europe. Also at Castle Hedingham are Colne Valley Farm Park and the Colne Valley Railway and Museum.

Opening Hours: 11-11

Food: Bar snacks

Credit Cards: None

Accommodation: None

Facilities: Car park, children's play area, function room

Entertainment: Live music last Saturday of the month + Bank Holidays

Local Places of Interest/Activities: Halstead 3 miles, Castle Hedingham 2 miles, Gestingthorp 4 miles

Internet/Website:
e-mail:
   michelle@hedinghamwhitelion.fsnet.co.uk

The Wig & Fidgett 185

THE WIG & FIDGETT

Straight Road, Boxted,
Nr Colchester, Essex CO4 5QZ
Tel: 01206 272227

Directions:

Boxted is reached by minor roads off the
A134 or A12 5 miles north of Colchester.

What is surely the only **Wig & Fidgett** in the land is a fine old inn dating from 1667. Truly a hidden gem, the inn is tucked away along little lanes in a part of the country that is made for walkers and lovers of the outdoors. The compact bar-lounge with a small seated dining area is delightfully and unpretentiously rural, and the local customers appreciate the relaxed ambience generated by landlord Keith Griffiths. This is a man who respects his beer and he loves to serve the best. He keeps an ever-changing choice of real ales and is proud to have tripled his sales of ale since becoming the proprietor here at the end of 2001. to go along with the splendid ales is a selection of no-frills, good-value dishes served throughout the inn's opening hours - that is, all day every day.

The Wig has a pool table and a beer garden, with parking spaces at the front. There's a karaoke session once a month. Boxted's church has some Roman bricks in its fabric, and there are other interesting churches in the neighbouring villages, notably Wissington, Stoke-by-Nayland and the stone-spired Church of St Mary in Polstead. A few miles to the east are the major tourist attractions of Constable Country.

Opening Hours: 11-11, Sun 12-10.30

Food: Bar meals

Credit Cards: None

Accommodation: None

Facilities: Car park

Entertainment: Monthly karaoke

Local Places of Interest/Activities: Stratford St Mary 3 miles, Stoke by Nayland 3 miles, Colchester 5 miles,

186   *ALPHABETIC LIST OF INNS*

ALPHABETIC LIST OF INNS

ALPHABETIC LIST OF INNS **189**

ACCOMMODATION

ALL DAY OPENING

CHILDRENS FACILITIES

196   *CREDIT CARDS ACCEPTED*

CREDIT CARDS ACCEPTED

GARDEN, PATIO OR TERRACE   199

200 GARDEN, PATIO OR TERRACE

GARDEN, PATIO OR TERRACE | 201

CHAPTER 4: ESSEX (CONT.)

LIVE ENTERTAINMENT

204 RESTAURANT/DINING AREA

RESTAURANT/DINING AREA 205

206 | *RESTAURANT/DINING AREA*

PLACES OF INTEREST

Hidden Inns Order Form

To order any of our publications just fill in the payment details below and complete the order form *overleaf*. For orders of less than 4 copies please add £1 per book for postage and packing. Orders over 4 copies are P & P free.

Please Complete Either:

I enclose a cheque for £ [　　　　　] made payable to Travel Publishing Ltd

Or:

Card No: [　　　　　　　　　　　　]

Expiry Date: [　　　　]

Signature: [　　　　　　　　　]

NAME: [　　　　　　　　　]

ADDRESS: [　　　　　　　　　]

POSTCODE: [　　　　　　　　]

TEL NO: [　　　　　　　　]

Please either send or telephone your order to:

Travel Publishing Ltd
7a Apollo House
Calleva Park
Aldermaston
Berks, RG7 8TN

Tel : 0118 981 7777
Fax: 0118 982 0077

The Hidden Inns of East Anglia

	PRICE	QUANTITY	VALUE
Hidden Places Regional Titles			
Cambs & Lincolnshire	£7.99	....	....
Chilterns	£8.99	....	....
Cornwall	£8.99	....	....
Derbyshire	£7.99	....	....
Devon	£8.99	....	....
Dorset, Hants & Isle of Wight	£8.99	....	....
East Anglia	£8.99	....	....
Gloucestershire, Wiltshire & Somerset	£7.99	....	....
Heart of England	£7.99	....	....
Hereford, Worcs & Shropshire	£7.99	....	....
Highlands & Islands	£7.99	....	....
Kent	£8.99	....	....
Lake District & Cumbria	£8.99	....	....
Lancashire & Cheshire	£8.99	....	....
Lincolnshire and Nottinghamshire	£8.99	....	....
Northumberland & Durham	£8.99	....	....
Sussex	£8.99	....	....
Thames Valley	£7.99	....	....
Yorkshire	£8.99	....	....
Hidden Places National Titles			
England	£10.99	....	....
Ireland	£10.99	....	....
Scotland	£10.99	....	....
Wales	£10.99	....	....
Hidden Inns Titles			
East Anglia	£5.99	....	....
Heart of England	£5.99	....	....
Lancashire and Cheshire	£5.99	....	....
North of England	£5.99	....	....
South East England	£5.99	....	....
South of England	£5.99	....	....
Southern Scotland	£5.99	....	....
Wales	£5.99	....	....
West Country	£5.99	....	....
WelshBorders	£5.99	....	....
Yorkshire	£5.99	....	....
TOTAL			

*For orders of less than 4 copies please add £1 per book for
postage & packing. Orders over 4 copies P & P free.*

Hidden Inns Reader Reaction

The *Hidden Inns* research team would like to receive reader's comments on any visitor attractions or places reviewed in the book and also recommendations for suitable entries to be included in the next edition. This will help ensure that the *Hidden Inns* series continues to provide its readers with useful information on the more interesting, unusual or unique features of each attraction or place ensuring that their stay in the local area is an enjoyable and stimulating experience.

To provide your comments or recommendations would you please complete the forms below and overleaf as indicated and send to:

The Research Department, Travel Publishing Ltd,

7a Apollo House, Calleva Park, Aldermaston, Reading, RG7 8TN.

Your Name:

Your Address:

Your Telephone Number:

Please tick as appropriate: Comments ☐ Recommendation ☐

Name of *"Hidden Place"*:

Address:

Telephone Number:

Name of Contact:

Hidden Inns Reader Reaction

Comment or Reason for Recommendation:

....

....

....

....

....

....

....

....

....

....

Hidden Inns Reader Reaction

The *Hidden Inns* research team would like to receive reader's comments on any visitor attractions or places reviewed in the book and also recommendations for suitable entries to be included in the next edition. This will help ensure that the *Hidden Inns* series continues to provide its readers with useful information on the more interesting, unusual or unique features of each attraction or place ensuring that their stay in the local area is an enjoyable and stimulating experience.

To provide your comments or recommendations would you please complete the forms below and overleaf as indicated and send to:

The Research Department, Travel Publishing Ltd,
7a Apollo House, Calleva Park, Aldermaston, Reading, RG7 8TN.

Your Name:

Your Address:

Your Telephone Number:

Please tick as appropriate: Comments ☐   Recommendation ☐

Name of *"Hidden Place"*:

Address:

Telephone Number:

Name of Contact:

Hidden Inns Reader Reaction

Comment or Reason for Recommendation:

Hidden Inns Reader Reaction

The *Hidden Inns* research team would like to receive reader's comments on any visitor attractions or places reviewed in the book and also recommendations for suitable entries to be included in the next edition. This will help ensure that the *Hidden Inns* series continues to provide its readers with useful information on the more interesting, unusual or unique features of each attraction or place ensuring that their stay in the local area is an enjoyable and stimulating experience.

To provide your comments or recommendations would you please complete the forms below and overleaf as indicated and send to:

The Research Department, Travel Publishing Ltd,
7a Apollo House, Calleva Park, Aldermaston, Reading, RG7 8TN.

Your Name:

Your Address:

Your Telephone Number:

Please tick as appropriate: Comments ☐   Recommendation ☐

Name of *"Hidden Place"*:

Address:

Telephone Number:

Name of Contact:

Hidden Inns Reader Reaction

Comment or Reason for Recommendation:

....

....

....

....

....

....

....

....

....

....

Hidden Inns Reader Reaction

The *Hidden Inns* research team would like to receive reader's comments on any visitor attractions or places reviewed in the book and also recommendations for suitable entries to be included in the next edition. This will help ensure that the *Hidden Inns* series continues to provide its readers with useful information on the more interesting, unusual or unique features of each attraction or place ensuring that their stay in the local area is an enjoyable and stimulating experience.

To provide your comments or recommendations would you please complete the forms below and overleaf as indicated and send to:

The Research Department, Travel Publishing Ltd,
7a Apollo House, Calleva Park, Aldermaston, Reading, RG7 8TN.

Your Name:

Your Address:

Your Telephone Number:

Please tick as appropriate: Comments ☐ Recommendation ☐

Name of *"Hidden Place"*:

Address:

Telephone Number:

Name of Contact:

Hidden Inns Reader Reaction

Comment or Reason for Recommendation:

....

....

....

....

....

....

....

....

....

....